Deconstructing
Feminist Psychology

Gender and Psychology
Feminist and Critical Perspectives

Series editor: Sue Wilkinson

This international series provides a forum for research focused on gender issues in – and beyond – psychology, with a particular emphasis on feminist and critical analyses. It encourages contributions which explore psychological topics where gender is central; which critically interrogate psychology as a discipline and as a professional base; and which develop feminist interventions in theory and practice. The series objective is to present innovative research on gender in the context of the broader implications for developing both critical psychology and feminism.

Sue Wilkinson teaches social psychology and women's studies at Loughborough University. She is also Editor of *Feminism & Psychology: An International Journal*.

Also in this series

Subjectivity and Method in Psychology
Wendy Hollway

Feminists and Psychological Practice
edited by Erica Burman

Feminist Groupwork
Sandra Butler and Claire Wintram

Motherhood: Meanings, Practices and Ideologies
edited by Ann Phoenix, Anne Woollett and Eva Lloyd

Emotion and Gender: Constructing Meaning from Memory
June Crawford, Susan Kippax, Jenny Onyx, Una Gault and Pam Benton

Women and AIDS: Psychological Perspectives
edited by Corinne Squire

Attitudes towards Rape: Feminist and Social Psychological Perspectives
Colleen A. Ward

Talking Difference: On Gender and Language
Mary Crawford

Feminism and Discourse: Psychological Perspectives
edited by Sue Wilkinson and Celia Kitzinger

Deconstructing Feminist Psychology

edited by

Erica Burman

SAGE Publications
London • Thousand Oaks • New Delhi

First published 1998

SAGE Publications Ltd
6 Bonhill Street
London EC2A 4PU

SAGE Publications Inc.
2455 Teller Road
Thousand Oaks, California 91320

SAGE Publications India Pvt Ltd
32, M-Block Market
Greater Kailash – I
New Delhi 110 048

British Library Cataloguing in Publication data

A catalogue record for this book is available
from the British Library

ISBN 0 8039 7639 9
ISBN 0 8039 7640 2 (pbk)

Library of Congress catalog card number 97–068906

Typeset by Mayhew Typesetting, Rhayader, Powys
Printed in Great Britain by Biddles Ltd, Guildford, Surrey

Contents

Acknowledgements

– To the authors for their enthusiastic response to the proposal for this book, and all their work.
– To Janet Batsleer and Ian Parker for their substantive material and personal support during its preparation.
– To Women's Studies and Discourse Unit students for their reminders of the importance of these issues, especially in helping me remain a 'challenging woman'.
– To Brenda Goldberg for her timely photocopying and disk deftness.
– To the participants at the 1995 Women and Psychology conference at Leeds, UK, for powerfully showing me why we both need, and need to deconstruct, feminist psychology.
– To Anne Woolf for the loan of her kitchen at a crucial time in the drafting of the introduction.

Erica Burman

List of Contributors

Lise Bird is a Senior Lecturer in Education at Victoria University of Wellington in Aotearoa New Zealand. She was trained as a cognitive psychologist in Australia, but moved countries and disciplines as she started to include feminist, cultural studies and post-structural perspectives in her work. She is interested in critical reworkings of 'known' ideas about intelligence, self-esteem and motivation within educational psychology.

Erica Burman teaches psychology and women's studies at the Manchester Metropolitan University, UK. Her work is in the areas of feminist critiques of developmental psychology, subjectivity and discourse. Her previous publications include *Psychological Theory and Feminist Practice* (edited, 1990), *Discourse Analytic Research* (with I. Parker, 1993), *Deconstructing Developmental Psychology* (1994), *Qualitative Methods in Psychology* (with P. Banister, I. Parker, M. Taylor and C. Tindall, 1994), *Challenging Women: Psychology's Exclusions, Feminist Possibilities* (with P. Alldred, C. Bewley, B. Goldberg, C. Heenan, D. Marks, J. Marshall, K. Taylor, R. Ullah and S. Warner, 1996) and *Psychology Discourse Practice: From Regulation to Resistance* (with G. Aitken, P. Alldred, R. Allwood, T. Billington, B. Goldberg, A. Gordó-López, C. Heenan, D. Marks and S. Warner, 1996).

Mary Crawford is Professor of Psychology and Women's Studies at West Chester University of Pennsylvania, USA. She is author, co-author or editor of five books. *Women and Gender: A Feminist Psychology* (with R. Unger, 1992; 2nd edition 1996) and *In Our Own Words: Readings in Women and Gender* (with R. Unger, 1997) are widely adopted texts for teaching the psychology of women and gender. Other works include *Gender and Thought* (with M. Gentry, 1989), *Talking Difference: On Gender and Language* (1995), and *Gender Differences in Human Cognition* (with P. Caplan, J.S. Hyde and J.T. Richardson, 1997). She is currently serving on the editorial boards of the journals *Psychology of Women Quarterly*, *Feminism and Psychology* and *Contemporary Psychology*.

Mary Crawford received her PhD in experimental psychology from the University of Delaware. She is a Fellow of the American Psychological Association and the American Psychological Society.

Heidi J. Figueroa Sarriera is Associate Professor at the Department of Psychology, Faculty of Social Science, Río Piedras Campus, University of Puerto Rico. As a transdisciplinary social psychologist she is involved in research on cultural representations of high-tech designs. She is assistant editor with Steven Mentor and Chris Hables Gray (editor) of *The Cyborg Handbook* (1995). She also co-edited with Madeline Román and María M. López, *Más allá de la bella (in)diferencia: Revisión postfeminista y otras escrituras posibles* (1994).

Lenora Fulani is a practising social therapist at the East Side Center for Social Therapy and is on the faculty of its training center, the East Side Institute for Short Term Psychotherapy, New York. She is a founder and co-executive producer of the All Stars Talent Show Network, the largest and most successful anti-violence program for inner-city youth in the USA. A pioneer of the third-party movement in the USA in 1988, running as an independent candidate for the US Presidency, she became the first woman in American history to be on the presidential ballot in all 50 states. She chairs the Committee for a Unified Independent Party, and in 1995, Fulani was elected to the 31-member General Council of the independent Transnational Radical Party. She is the editor of *The Psychopathology of Everyday Racism and Sexism* (1987), co-author of *Independent Black Leadership in America* (1991), and author of *The Making of a Fringe Candidate, 1992* (1993). Lenora Fulani received her PhD in developmental psychology from the City University of New York.

Frigga Haug is Professor in the Department of Sociology at the University for Economy and Politics, Hamburg, Germany. She has been a visiting scholar at the following universities: Copenhagen, Innsbruck, Sydney, Klagenfurth, Toronto and Durham in North Carolina. Her main field of research is empirical methods in social psychology, work research and women's studies. Her previous posts were in psychology at the Free University of Berlin, and in women's studies at the University of Hamburg. While her editorial and collectively written work is well-known inside and outside Germany, translations of her work into English include *Female Sexualization: A Collective Work of Memory* (1987) and *Beyond Female Masochism: Memory-work and Politics* (1992). Having finished a project on women's fears and anxieties, she is currently researching about women and culture and gender-specific learning processes. She has recently written two mysteries.

Gordana Jovanović is Assistant Professor of General Psychology and Personality Theory at the Department of Psychology, and works as a researcher in Developmental Psychology at the Institute of Psychology, University of Belgrade, Yugoslavia. She earned her MA and PhD degrees at Belgrade University. She was Alexander-von-Humboldt research fellow at the Johann Wolfgang Goethe University in Frankfurt-on-Main (Germany) in 1984, 1985 and 1989. Her scientific publications are on the philosophical foundations of psychology, contemporary social theories, historical psychology, psychoanalytic theory, semiotics, modernity and postmodernity. She is author of *Simbolizovanje i racionalnost* (*Symbolization and Rationality*) (1984), and *Frojd i moderna subjectivnost* (*Freud and Modern Subjectivity*) (1997). She also translates from German. This is her first publication on feminist psychology.

Amanda Kottler is a clinical psychologist and a lecturer at the University of Cape Town. She is currently based at the Child Guidance Clinic, where she convenes and teaches in the first year of the MA (Clinical Psychology) training programme. She is also a psychotherapist in private practice. Over the past ten years, drawing on discourse and conversation analysis, her main research interests and publications have been concerned with the complexity of identity issues (race, gender, sexuality) and definitional problems (sexual and racial harassment/violence). Current research and writing interests include self psychology, intersubjectivity and contemporary relational theory. Her publications include *Culture, Power and Difference* (with A. Levett, I. Parker and E. Burman, 1997).

Ann Levett was an associate professor and a clinical psychologist at the University of Cape Town until 1996. Her main research interests have been in discourse analysis and other qualitative approaches to gender and power-related issues. She is now a psychotherapist. She is co-editor with Amanda Kothler, Erica Burman and Ian Parker of *Culture, Power and Difference* (1997).

Margot Pujal i Llombart gained a PhD on the topic of feminist knowledge, gender and science, and the social construction of women's identities from the Universitat Autonoma de Barcelona, Catalonia, Spain in 1991. She has been teaching social psychology and the psychology of groups in the Unitat de Psicologia Social there since 1989. She also teaches on postgraduate courses on socioconstructionism, critical theory and gender, 'gender as a category to analyse psychosocial reality' and on 'Otherness as a social construction'. Her current research and writing interests are in the areas of subjectivity, power relationships, social change and autobiography.

1

Deconstructing Feminist Psychology

Erica Burman

This book emerges from a context where feminism is starting to have some impact in psychology, within the psychology curriculum and within professional practices. In northern, industrialized societies where psychological concepts and services form a daily part of our inner and outer lives (in the form of personally held precepts about relationships, mental health and well-being, as well as those explicitly regulating our lives via state apparatuses), feminist critiques of the white, middle-class, male, rational problem-solving subject of psychology are currently having some impact. This has been reflected in academic psychology in courses on gender and psychology, and especially 'the psychology of women', and in the statutory sector of health and welfare provision with the funding and organization of specialist services for women, including women's therapy centres.

But despite some success in putting gender issues on psychology's agenda, this book reflects concerns emerging about the forms this attention to gender assumes; the spaces it is accorded, and what this correspondingly excludes. The institutional arenas are constructed so that feminist work can easily be ghettoized, marginalized or otherwise treated as an optional extra, leaving the (non-feminist) body of psychology intact. Further, this construction of feminist psychology in relation to the dominant forms of psychology tends to limit the range and political nuances of the forms of feminism that gain institutional recognition. Familiar exclusions – of non-normative cultural and sexual identities – are reproduced within a model of woman that thereby threatens to become just as homogenizing and coercive as the model of man it claimed to challenge. It is the (actual and potential) reproduction of these exclusions that forms the topic for this book.

However, this book is not, or not only, about 'feminist psychology' and its discontents. Rather, the critiques presented here focus less on the limits of the category 'feminist psychology', but take this as a symptom of a more general problem to consider what its presence allows and disallows. They ask: what work does this arena perform for the discipline of psychology? What does this do for the existing social order, including the gender, cultural and sexual hierarchies psychology informs and maintains? What forms of political engagement and intervention does it promote, both in relation to the rest of psychology and in connection with feminist movements and campaigns elsewhere? Who does it speak for, and to? So in this book 'feminist psychology' is an object of critique in so far as it functions to contain rather than extend feminist interventions in psychology, and to reproduce the conceptual and political difficulties of psychology. That is, the value of the work so far conducted within the rubric of 'feminist psychology' is not in question. Rather, corresponding with the mood of self-reflection within women's studies generally, this book evaluates the extent of that contribution in relation to the shifting parameters of struggle within historically, geographically and politically diverse conditions.

This introductory chapter attempts to elaborate the contexts for varieties of feminist interventions in and around psychology and to explore the range of possible and actual relationships between feminist and deconstructionist critiques of psychology. This includes making the case for deconstruction as a form of feminist critique as well as acknowledging problems with deconstruction for feminist politics. The second half of the chapter outlines the structure of the book and summarizes the main contribution of each chapter. It ends by commenting on features arising from the process as well as substantive content of this book, for feminist politics in general as well as for feminist psychologists in particular.

Psychology of Women and Feminist Psychology

So far I have treated 'feminist psychology' and the 'psychology of women' as if they were equivalent, but this smooths over important areas of debate, or at the very least eclipses historical discontinuities. The psychology of women emerged as a reflection of 1970s Anglo–US feminism (see Matlin, 1993; Squire, 1989; and Unger and Crawford, 1992 for accounts). Its call for a woman-centred psychology (e.g. Baker Miller, 1976) aimed to speak of and for the specificity of women's experiences of psychology – as recipients or practitioners, as feminized objects of psychology's male gaze. But in claiming to speak for/about women, advocates of the psychology of women threatened to perpetuate mainstream psychology and recuperate feminist interventions into psychology's practices, in at least five ways:

1   By extending psychology's gaze into new arenas previously undisclosed to, or unrecognized by, psychology.

2 By colluding with positivism in retaining a commitment to existing methods and tools of investigation, rather than throwing the whole enterprise of scientific psychology (with its ethic of instrumentality, manipulation and control) into question.

3 By colluding with psychology's efforts to exclude and ghettoize attention to gender issues in its creation of a separate area in psychology for women's experiences and positions.

4 In its privileging of gender it is in danger of colluding with malesteam psychology's tendencies towards abstracting and reifying social categories and identities. In doing this it remains allied with, or functions as a variety of, psychology and could thus be read as producing an ahistorical account that treats women's experiences and qualities as inherent or essential, rather than as emerging in relation to definitions of masculinity.

5 Within a set of psychological models which treat categories of identity as separate, stable and additive, and in subordinating other structuring parameters of identity to gender, it is in danger of ignoring how other marginalized positions enter into experiences of gender.

These difficulties have been rehearsed elsewhere (Bohan, 1992; Burman et al., 1996a; Squire, 1989) and reflect more general difficulties in presuming commonality between women (Riley, 1988; Spelman, 1988).

Feminist Psychology

Unlike the (strategically named) 'psychology of women', feminist psychology, with its change of gendered agency from object ('of women') to subject ('feminist'), is an explicitly politicized arena. It is correspondingly less easily relegated to the position of a psychological area of study (although this was once an important tactic, see for example, Wilkinson and Burns, 1990). 'Feminist psychology' names a strategic space between feminism and psychology; it is not a stable topic area, but rather identifies a site of contest (over what counts as knowledge, who defines this, and how it is arrived at). Important work has been done challenging psychology's traditional devaluation or pathologization of qualities culturally associated with femininity (in relation to such diverse topics as methods, motherhood, education and mental health). But for all that feminist psychology manages to ward off the psychology of women's tendencies towards marginalization from the rest of psychology and essentialism of what women are supposed to be, it still tends to leave relatively unexamined the forms of feminism it takes as its reference

point. Squire (1989) shows how the main strands of liberal/
egalitarian, radical/cultural and psychoanalytic feminisms have
found their reflections in the forms feminist psychological interventions have taken. While outside psychology feminists have been
increasingly challenged to address the marginalization of working-
class, black and lesbian perspectives ((charles), 1992; Wilton, 1993),
feminist psychology has yet to address these claims consistently,
although this work is now beginning (e.g. Bhavnani and Phoenix,
1994; Walkerdine, 1996; Wilkinson and Kitzinger, 1993).

Post-feminist Psychology?

Advocates of post-structuralism and especially postmodernism have
suggested that traditional frameworks for envisaging and mobilizing
for social progress and for emancipation are now outmoded and
irrelevant. While directed towards the confinements of Enlighten-
ment thinking, and linked politically with disillusionment in marxism
(over stalinist repression and more recently the break-up of the
former Soviet Union), challenges to modernity also apply to feminism (Flax, 1991; Fraser, 1992; Lovibund, 1989; Soper, 1991). They
acquire still more relevance in helping to ward off aspirations for a
single, unitary feminist psychology. Rather than becoming enlisted
into the pressures towards academic empire-building, these critiques
invite us to attend to the diverse, multiple forms that feminist psychology can take. The untidy, unruly disorder of the proliferation of
feminist psychologies can no longer be contained within the polarities of outside or inside psychology, or crude notions of masculinity
and femininity. Rather than remaining within the monological mode
by setting feminist psychology against the main/malestream, postmodern ideas refuse to allow such easy juxtapositions and highlight
how more wide-ranging conceptual and political transformations
need to take place. Postmodernist and deconstructionist ideas are
therefore drawn upon in this book not to disallow the emancipatory
project of feminism, but to strengthen feminist interventions,
especially in relation to psychology.

Feminism and Deconstruction

Claims of a postmodern condition have found support from some
feminists for the critique of dominant western and male models of
subjectivity that have ignored or devalued the multiple, fragmentary
and contradictory modes that characterize women's experiences (e.g.
Charles and Hughes-Freeland, 1996; Weedon, 1987). Postmodernist
ideas have equally evoked strong feminist hostility, not least for their

appropriation of feminist ideas and their claims to deconstruct subjectivity at the precise political moment when, within northern industrialized countries at least, feminism is beginning to make some headway (Brodribb, 1992; Jackson, 1992; Lovibund, 1989). Further, while postmodernist and feminist approaches are increasingly informed and fuelled by post-colonial critiques, postmodernist approaches threaten to disavow the very recognition of the power hierarchies they highlight by imposing a uniform dispersal of subjectivity on very diversely organized and positioned individuals, movements and peoples. Feminists have not been slow to point out the hidden return of the western male ego within such formulations, and the consequent denial of the power this continues to exert even when assuming a rhetoric of postmodern fragmentation and pluralism. The contributions in this collection speak from an engagement with the politics of deconstruction. As such, the chapters address two different, but not unrelated, feminist arenas: feminist engagements with deconstruction, and feminist psychologists in particular. Later in this chapter I identify specific interventions authors make within these two projects. The point I want to highlight now is that the question of how to retain a sense of feminist agency as well as acknowledging multiplicity figure strongly in this book.

In their differing ways, the contributions in this collection elaborate a critical analysis of the methods, topics, models and cultural–political presumptions that structure such work as would broadly be considered 'feminist psychology'. But what is really thrown into question here is the very distinction between feminist and (supposedly non-feminist?) psychology, and correlatively between feminist psychology and feminist activism. If we approach psychological practices with the feminist suspicion they merit, then how can we intervene without also perpetuating those same practices of exclusion and oppression? Are those of us who would assume (or presume the viability of) the designation 'feminist psychologist' deluding ourselves about the extent of critique and space for contest that we can initiate?

Distributing Feminist Psychology?

On this score it is instructive to consider the complexity and variegation of forms feminist interventions in psychology take in particular contexts, a significant cultural–political matter that my trawl for authors powerfully reiterated. While the descriptor 'feminist psychology' has gained some currency in Anglo–US psychology (and here, by virtue of Anglo legacies and hegemonies, I include also Australia and New Zealand), elsewhere in Europe, in Africa, in

India, in South America there is no such identifiable area of psychology. In so far as I have been able to gain some insight into the topology of (what I, within the limits of my Anglo categorial system, would want to see as) feminist psychological interventions, this arises for (at least) two reasons. First, some feminist critics of psychology conduct their interventions from other disciplines, most notably women's studies, but also sociology, history, philosophy, literature, cultural studies and economics. That is, they gain a critical distance from psychology by operating from a different academic or professional disciplinary base.

Secondly, of the women I approached to write in this book, those women who were prepared to identify as feminist did not necessarily see their work in psychology as feminist, although they did identify this as being concerned with gender. Some women were openly hostile and suspicious of the limits of an arena called 'feminist psychology' as operating to contain or silence their interventions in the main/malestream. Others, within the context of their work, preferred to identify themselves as social psychologists, either strategically so as not to be marginalized by being labelled 'feminist', or because they genuinely considered that their work was not particularly feminist, although they, in their lives outside the academy, were. That is, their identification with psychology was not structured through a feminist critique of its practices. This was true of feminist academics and psychologists from various countries who declined my invitation to write for this book and from whom I had the sense that they did not recognize or identify with the category of feminist psychology. This includes women I contacted in as diverse (from each other and from my own) contexts as Scandanavia and India. In the absence of such contributions, it is only possible to speculate about the limits and silences within the contents of this book.

This range of practices (and its absences) could well reflect different opportunities for feminist work in psychological practices in particular regions, or an acceptance of dominant Anglo–US conceptualizations of psychology. Certainly, there is no reason to assume that just because a feminist, or even a feminist who works in psychology, lives outside psychology's 'centre' or in a post-colonial country that her engagement with psychology is somehow automatically endowed with critique. This would be to romanticize or exoticize the 'periphery' in just the same way as dominant psychologies have ignored or devalued non-western peoples and cultures. If 'we' (those of us who are western-based feminists) set out to export the 'good news' about psychology (feminist or otherwise) worldwide, are we not still reproducing the classic dynamic of colonialism by assuming that 'we' can provide the authoritative critique? But, equally, are we not subscribing to an equivalent orientalist phallacy if we assume that there is some untouched feminist resource of authentic resistance to colonial psychologies ready to be discovered? (See Frankenberg and Mani (1993) for an equivalent discussion of the politics of feminism and 'post-coloniality' outside psychology.)

Rather than assuming either of these invideous positions, our task is to document the particular forms the traffic in ideas between feminism and psychology has taken, and the different consequences their varying arrangements have for progresssive political intervention. This is the project that this book begins. But it by no means finishes this. As indicated earlier, this book is inevitably partial and incomplete. Indeed, to think of this project as final and achievable would, according to current post-structuralist thinking, be to foreclose its radical potential and render it fundamentally ahistorical and abstracted from place and space.

This book addresses a range of very different arenas in which the project and politics of feminist psychology is under contest. All the chapters in this book are situated commentaries in the sense that they necessarily speak from and to particular contexts, and in the process of editorial comment and revision, further contextualization has been provided. Further, some (Chapters 4 and 9) take as their primary topics the specific character of feminist psychology in circulation in a particular cultural–geographical arena. Clearly, these commentaries can only be indicative, since any claims to representation would not only be inadequate but also tokenistic. Nevertheless, they are highly suggestive of the range and character of issues posed for feminist psychology within diverse contexts.

Hence, an extreme formulation of the starting position of this book might be as follows, that there can be no feminist psychology without either distorting feminist commitments beyond all recognition, or else by transforming psychology into a differently constituted arena. So who is this book for? Who do we address in this enterprise of 'deconstructing feminist psychology'? It would seem that, by its title, this book sets out to alienate its most obvious allies – those who would identify themselves as feminist psychologists. But it is important to distinguish between category and position: deconstructing the category 'feminist psychology' does not disallow or discredit the speaking position or identification of 'feminist psychologist'. Indeed, most of the contributors would probably assume some such identification. Rather, what is put under critical scrutiny here is the structure, organization and reification of feminist psychological work into an arena sporting the title 'feminist psychology' or some such associated label.

This book therefore addresses women like ourselves who are engaged as feminists inside and outside psychology – as researchers, practitioners, activists; as feminists who find themselves drawn to, but wary of, psychological concepts and notions (of, for example, sex roles and assertiveness, and the female ethic of relatedness). We apply a feminist suspicion of psychology to the varieties of psychology that feminists have been able, or allowed, to develop. We do this not to criticize or reproach, but to promote reflection on more general political projects and disciplinary demarcations. The purpose of this exercise is therefore to strengthen feminist analyses and interventions in psychology, not to silence them.

Institutional Origins

The chapters in this book invite a space for reflection and debate that reflects a position of relative security and confidence for feminist initiatives in northern (over)developed societies. Those of us living in such circumstances have witnessed an increasing institutionalization of feminist ideas and initiatives that pose new political problems of working in, rather than against, 'the system' (legal, health and mental health, and educational practices, as well as more explicit forms of 'political' representations). In some cases feminists now provide the services rather than critique them, and the political issues we currently face concern how we maintain a critical distance from the dynamic of recuperation into existing oppressive systems that inevitably, as a structural necessity, threaten to engulf our work.

> As this [marginal] material begins to be absorbed into the discipline, the long established but supple, heterogeneous and hierarchical power lines of the institutional 'dissemination of knowledge' continue to determine and overdetermine its conditions of representability. It is at the moment of infiltration or insertion, sufficiently under threat by the custodians of a fantasmic high Western culture, that the greatest caution must be exerised. The price of success must not compromise the enterprise irreparably. (Spivak, 1993: 56)

However, we should pause to recall – and consider the significance of the omission so far – that this is not the case for feminist interventions everywhere. Outside the post-industrial bureaucracies of northern capitalist countries, the issue for feminist perspectives is not necessarily how to ward off the token 'lip service' relegation of attention to gender issues in equal opportunities policies, or the equation of gender with women. As some chapters in this book suggest, for some women the issue is how to frame these issues so that they get put on the agenda in the first place. However, before 'we' (i.e. feminists in northern industrialized contexts) lapse into colonial paternalism over global distributions of feminist consciousness, we would do well to note how the debates in the so-called 'new democracies' (in this book South Africa) or 'transitional societies' (here former Yugoslavia and, in a rather different sense, 'reunited' Germany) are – through varieties of colonial and imperialist legacies that psychology actively participates in (through the dominance of North American research, models, textbooks, journals) – already well aware of these problems, and are generating their own responses. These responses are forged not only in relation to specific conditions of academic–political arenas, but also through a critical relation with developments from (feminist) psychology's 'centre'.

Three kinds of institutional positions in relation to (deconstructing) feminist psychology are reflected in this book. First, those of us in industrialized, overdeveloped societies are experiencing a period of popular backlash to feminist interventions, of reneging on, or transforming beyond all recognition, commitments to implement feminist demands. Secondly, as indicated by Chapters 6, 8 and 9, other feminists are struggling to develop or maintain feminist and feminist psychological spaces within societies in rapid transformation. According to a third position, feminist critiques and interventions have not taken the form of a specific discernable arena of 'feminist psychology'. The issue for those of us at psychology's 'centre' is to find ways of exploring how to link with and support the range of feminist struggles in and around psychology without imposing our own presumptions of what feminist psychology should be, but equally without losing sight of what it does, and could, mean in specific contexts.

Having identified the contexts for varieties of feminist psychology, the rest of this chapter is concerned with the politics of a deconstruction of feminist psychology. The next section explores the possibilities of deconstruction as a mode of feminist critique. This is followed by consideration of the threat posed to feminist work by deconstruction before turning to the forms deconstruction has taken in psychology and feminist psychologists' engagement with these.

Deconstruction as Feminist Critique

Feminists have not been uncritical of the ways deconstruction has been received as a licence for deradicalization, and the turn to the text as prompting either the race for theory (Christian, 1988), escape from the real (Soper, 1991) or capitulation to the lure of the power of the great white masters associated with poststructuralism (Lacan, Foucault and Derrida) (Jackson, 1992). Nevertheless, feminists have been drawn to deconstructionist and discourse approaches to fuel their critiques. Given its bad press, and reactionary uses in some contexts, it is worth noting how deconstruction has been defined by the supposed originator of deconstruction, Jacques Derrida:

> If then it lays claim to any consequence, what is hastily called decon-struction *as such* is never a set of technical procedures, still less a hermeneutic method operating on archives or utterances in the shelter of a given and stable institution; it is also, and at the least, the taking of a position, in work itself, toward the politico-institutional structures that constitute and regulate our practice, our competences, and our performances. (Derrida, 1984/1992: 22–3; original emphasis)

Far from ushering a form of apolitical moral relativism, decon-structionist approaches, and certainly where they meet with feminist work, can fruitfully challenge dominant orthodoxies in knowledge and its production. The binary classifications that have structured and ordered social life in the modern era – of male/female, black/white, man/animal, man/machine – are all now shown to be per-meable, or less than absolute opposites. More than this, they are shown to secure prevailing social arrangements of oppression. In this sense they are not equal polarities but hierarchies that reproduce inequalities. The deconstructionist strategy is not simply to draw attention to these culturally constructed categorizations and relations, but to revalue the traditionally subordinate pole of the binary (e.g. female over male; black over white) and to explore how doing this reveals previously naturalized or conventionalized sets of assumptions.

In many respects this is a project compatible with a feminist commitment to emancipatory and empowerment work. Indeed, work related to this perspective is perhaps better known to some feminists in relation to the work of feminist philosopher of science Sandra Harding, or that of historian of ideas, Donna Haraway, particularly in the context of feminist debates about social science research 'methods'. From these authors we have gained the notions of feminist standpoint, of strong subjectivity, of partial perspectives and situated knowledge (Haraway, 1989, 1991; Harding, 1986, 1993). These critique the purported rationality of western, male subjectivity, to which psychology is heir, and of which – in its continuing commitment to 'science' – it now stands as stark exemplar.

Deconstructing Feminism?

Deconstructionist approaches throw into question the stability of presumed identities, including categories of political identities and including the type of identity politics that characterized Anglo–US feminisms of the 1970s to 1980s. Given that it has claimed to dissolve the central platform of 'sisterhood' on which that feminism was based, it is not surprising that such work has occasioned virulent hostility. Nevertheless, an emerging body of feminist criticism, ranging from, for example, materialist feminists (Bondi, 1993), foucauldian feminists (Fraser, 1992; Ramazanoglu, 1992) to queer theorists (Butler, 1991) has elaborated this creative encounter with deconstructionism so as to challenge the orthodoxies and hierarchies reproduced within the Anglo–US feminism of that period. These accounts take as their starting point that identities are shifting and mutable, that categories of sexual and gendered identities are therefore in flux and that racialized and gendered positions are not additive or separable but intersect in complex and underdetermined ways (see e.g. Charles and Hughes-Freeland, 1996; de Lauretis, 1989; Nicholson and Seidman, 1995; Weedon, 1987).

Far from implying a flight from politics, feminist subscribers to deconstructionist ideas argue that they equip them to engage in political struggle on a more just basis by virtue of being more specifically situated (Ferguson, 1991; Spivak, 1990; Yuval-Davis, 1993). Thus, according to Elam (1994), the political challenge posed by the juxtaposition of feminism and deconstruction is to create a 'groundless solidarity' between women, that is, (in perhaps more familiar feminist language) to create alliances and coalitions that are partial and probably transitory, and that do not make a priori presumptions about commonality of experience or interest between women that subordinates disadvantaged women to implicitly dominant norms. Rather, such commonality as there can be must be forged rather than presumed. Still more important, the basis for alliance or work together need not be sameness: common cause over action rather than commonality of identity is not only enough, but perhaps is the best we can hope for.

In part this style of politics may be an accurate reflection of the drift towards single issue campaigns and the demise of an ostensible unitary 'women's movement' that is evident at least in the UK and the USA. Moreover, far from implying a flight from political engagement and escape from notions of personal responsibility and political commitment, Elam argues that a deconstruction of the integrated separable subject implies greater, rather than diminished, responsibility to others: the responsibility is no less for not being uniquely personal. Rather deconstruction's critique of the autonomous rational subject highlights how a recognition of the fiction of subjective singularity necessarily implies an ethical responsibility to others: 'The singularity is responsible to an Other that exceeds and precedes it; it owes a debt that can never be fully repaid, but must be honored, be recognised, with consistent attentiveness' (Elam, 1994: 110). This usefully moves the locus of political responsibility away from individual motivation, or of personal responsibility mobilized through such notions as guilt. By such means moral–political struggles are invigorated rather than diminished. Deconstructing individuality liberates personal guilt without exonerating the subject from action:

> . . . justice does not involve paying one's debts. Believing that one's debts can be paid is a fundamentally irresponsible belief: the desire to wash one's hands of responsibility to others. Rather, justice involves recognition of the debts that cannot be paid, the debts that set a limit to one's autonomy. To recognise such debts as unpayable is not to write them off either – it is rather to commit oneself to an endless work of reparation without the final solace of redemption. This, for instance, is the debt America owes its native peoples. (Elam, 1994: 111)

Deconstructing Psychology

Perhaps of all the social and human sciences, psychology appears slow to respond to critical innovations in theoretical and political debates. In part this stems from the claims to science that still predominate, in particular over discussions of 'method' which is taken as being neutral and value-free. Outside psychology, in sociology and politics, feminist debates have long made radical interventions in discussions of research processes and practices (Roberts, 1981; Stanley, 1990; Stanley and Wise, 1983, and others). In recent years such analyses of research have been incorporated into discussions about the gendered forms and relations of psychological research (Burman, 1990a; Hollway, 1989; Wilkinson, 1986). But the more recent and contentious developments in social theory and cultural studies appear largely to have passed psychology by. The preoccupations of the new arenas of critical theory (Easthope and McGowan, 1993), of deconstruction, postmodernism, queer theory, cybersubjectivities, gay and lesbian studies and post-colonial studies (for example) largely fail to reach the training manuals and curricula of psychologists. Percolation to such barometers of the dominant culture of psychology as *American Psychologist* all too frequently take the form of discussion of feminist approaches to research (Riger, 1992) or a man writing about identity politics (Sampson, 1993).

Feminism, Deconstruction and Discourse

Feminist psychologists have not been slow to recognize the destabilizing potential of deconstructionist critiques. In the UK the key text ushering in the critique of the rational, unitary male subject of psychology was Henriques, Hollway, Urwin, Venn and Walkerdine (1984), closely followed by critiques of method offered by Wilkinson (1986), Hollway (1989), Bhavnani (1993), Burman and Parker (1993), Henwood and Pidgeon (1995), Griffin, Henwood and Phoenix (forthcoming). Currently, feminist and critical work flourish under the sign of social constructionism and 'discourse', although as elsewhere this is not an internally consistent or continuous set of positions (see e.g. Burman et al., 1996b; Wilkinson and Kitzinger, 1995). Furthermore, also as elsewhere, there are problems with the assumed association between discourse and gender (Burman, 1990b, 1991; Gavey, 1989), just as there are between feminist and qualitative approaches to research (Kelly et al., 1992). Nevertheless, a major feature of the transgressive potential of qualitative approaches arises from the ways the experiences and politics of marginalized researchers not only informs the research process, but can also gain reflection in its product. In this sense, we can understand the claim that 'Discourse analysis is implicit ideology critique, because the position of the researcher is reflexive' (Parker, 1992: 40).

A related problem, reflecting also the marginalizing of feminist psychology and discussions of gender as relevant only to social psychology, is the way discourse work has been relegated to the arena of social psychology. Indeed, some of the key texts have identified themselves in those terms, so that Potter and Wetherell (1987) take as their subtitle 'beyond attitudes and behaviour' and so confine their critique to the arena of social psychology. Similarly Parker *Discourse Dynamics* (1992) bears as subtitle a rather non-specific reference to 'social and individual psychology'. Nevertheless it should be noted that previous published work assuming the discourse of 'deconstructionism' did indeed have far-reaching implications that extended beyond social psychology, not least of which was (paradoxically) Parker and Shotter's (1990) volume of that name. Perhaps as a reflection of publishers' as well as researchers' confidence, more recently the arena has proliferated with manifold varieties that focus on textuality (Curt, 1994), and deconstruction as critique is now explicitly focusing on cognitive and abnormal psychology (Burman et al., 1996b; Middleton and Edwards, 1992; Parker et al., 1995). It is worth noting, though, that the conjunction of discourse work with cognitive or biological approaches is not *necessarily* disruptive or deconstructionist in effect, as attested by the recent emergence of 'discursive psychology' (Edwards and Potter, 1993) as a recognized area of psychology and the Harré and Gillett (1995) volume claiming to combine harmoniously discourse and neuropsychological approaches. As usual, the story of discourse–

psychology relations is rather different when the work is explicitly feminist.
So notwithstanding the specific forms that the political debate over relativism has taken in psychology (see e.g. Burman, 1993; Edwards et al., 1995 versus Gill, 1995), discourse and deconstructionist perspectives have usefully relativized psychology. While these ideas have been elaborated in more detail elsewhere (e.g. Burman, 1991; Burman and Parker 1993), I summarize below their potential specifically in relation to the project of (deconstructing) feminist psychology.

1   *Challenging truth claims*: discourse and deconstructionist ideas challenge psychology's truth claims by treating these as fictions, stories or only partial truths alongside other possible accounts.
2   *Partial perspectives*: in emphasizing historical or contextual particularity, they force psychology to move from, or at least to acknowledge, the culture, gender and context-free character of its claims, and, beyond this, allow exploration of what such abstraction hides. Thus:
3   *Hidden investments*: they expose the ideological functions of claims to neutrality, according to which objectivity can be seen as a reflection of western (male) dominated rationality, with claims of detachment masking its ethic of manipulation and instrumentality, and collusion with dominant political agendas.
4   *Anti-essentialism*: instead of claiming to fathom the inner qualities or hidden depths of people's minds, discourse and deconstructionist work highlights the textually mediated character of representations of experience (Banister et al., 1994; Burman and Parker, 1993). Here it departs markedly from the more humanist psychological endeavours; rather than aiming to recover previously undisclosed meanings, discourse research attends to the construction of such reports as accounts produced in relationships. The importance for feminist work lies in this shift from giving voice to the victim, to listening to speaking subjects who actively claim this position and do not passively wait to be granted the opportunity.
5   *Fragmenting identity*: deconstruction not only decentres the stability of male-identified psychology, but also instills a reflexive vigilence towards its feminist varieties.
6   *Speaking bodies*: the focus on specificity prompts not only attention to the material production of psychology's theories and practices, but also scrutiny of which bodies do the speaking, whom they address (or constitute as their audience), and for whom they claim to speak.

In line with the call to attend to the local (Haraway, 1991), we could perhaps say that, irrespective of their political ambiguities elsewhere, deconstruction and postmodern ideas can usefully inform critical and feminist interventions in psychology: 'So tactically and paradoxically, the move towards the postmodern in social [and all the rest of] psychology should be supported because it is right to defend a modern understanding of the world and modern political projects' (Parker, 1992: 80).

Deconstructing Feminisms in Psychology

Moving now to review these themes as they appear in this book, a number of key strands of feminist deconstructionist critiques are reflected in the chapters. Almost all the contributors highlight the oppressive ways in which categories of identity (feminist and non-feminist) have been used to compartmentalize and obscure aspects of women's identities. Similarly, they treat experience as not only a key resource for feminist politics, but also as a socially constructed text. The traditional opposition between theory and practice is challenged by all the chapters, since they highlight how psychological theories are intimately tied to specific historical and cultural practices, and illustrate this by reference to the variety of arenas in which feminist psychology is played out: education, mental health, policy, popular psychology and academic practice. As both Pujal (Chapter 2) and Fulani (Chapter 7) argue, the work of deconstruction means that not only can we come to understand how the prevailing discursive arrangements have come about, but we can also focus on their processes, including the processes of their reproduction, as well as their effects. By such means a deconstruction of feminist psychology is not subject to the charge of offering 'mere' critique. Indeed, the chapters in this book in different ways all provide examples of practical intervention that ward off the charge of nihilism and lack of commitment so often associated with deconstructionist and postmodern accounts.

The particular focus for the chapters in Part One: Towards a Deconstruction of Feminist Psychology is on the forms of feminism that gain institutional recognition and support in psychology. In Chapter 2 Margot Pujal i Llombart discusses the ways feminist politics can become eroded within the practice of academic and empirical psychology. She argues that this arises through continuities between psychology and feminism in terms of their discursive functions in warranting practice. The false division between 'theory' and 'praxis' in psychology works to naturalize psychology's active and historical complicity in naturalizing power relations. Equally, feminists challenging psychological practices run the risk of failing to acknowledge the ways they reproduce or collude with psychology, in particular through a subscription to a relatively homogeneous and essentialized notion of gender. But there is a second false distribution of theory and praxis whereby psychology is seen to contain the theory and feminism the practice. This works not only to reify psychology as an entity amenable to correction by feminist interventions, but also abstracts feminist practice from its multiple political and theoretical bases. Hence this chapter usefully highlights how a self-defined feminist psychology can work perversely to undermine its avowed project, and cautions against treating this arena as something more than the institutional language game or strategy of intervention than it is.

Having set up this general critical framework Heidi Figueroa Sarriera in Chapter 3 takes issue with the model of social roles associated with G.H. Mead. This has been a powerful resource for both feminist psychologists and feminists in general. She argues that it includes elements that connect it both to modernist and postmodernist frameworks. While apparently useful to theorize the variety of social positions we occupy, this model still retains a commitment to a precultural, fundamentally asocial self that exists outside social relations of power, privilege and oppression. The popularity of this framework beyond psychology, especially for feminists (in the guise of socialization theory or even popular notions of 'conditioning') facilitates a reductionist approach to social programmes and interventions that allow apparently positive measures aiming to support women to focus only on individual change, and that work to leave the prevailing structure of power relations intact. Notwithstanding the contemporary relevance and attraction of postmodern analyses, Figueroa Sarriera highlights how these share important continuities with traditional modern approaches to women's positions that potentially work to shore up women's oppression further. As well as highlighting intellectual and political limitations, this chapter therefore offers an important resource for feminists in indicating not only how psychological (and sociological) frameworks inform public policy, but also how these theoretical approaches are present in a colonial context where post-colonial debates have special relevance.

We move next from psychology's 'periphery' of colonial outpost to its 'centre', North America, heartland of the rational individualism and autonomy so beloved of malestream psychology and the target of feminist critiques. In the USA, with its mass market of self-help books and professional trainers, the demarcation between academic and popular psychology (as with high and low culture in postmodernism) is blurred. In Chapter 4, Mary Crawford offers a deconstructive critique of assertiveness training (AT) as a case study of the intersections between popular practice and academic research industry. Developing the critique of role theory elaborated in Chapter 3, Crawford analyses how, notwithstanding their supposedly empowering effects for women, assertiveness training programmes reproduce profoundly class and culture-ridden stereotypes about sex differences that are portrayed as essential. They thus naturalize culturally dominant assumptions about male agency and female passivity, and imply a model of relationships and social functioning based on self-interest. Moreover, the reliance in training practices on formulaic techniques not only violate natural language patterns and create socially deviant speech acts (that would likely undermine their success in practice), they also fail to theorize the inequalities arising from social class, ethnicity, power and status which determine speech style and privileges. Thus enacted by the AT movement is a complex exemplar of the relationships between psychology and the culture in which it is embedded, and to which it now offers scientized explanations of women's subordination, including a new set of pejorative labels for women.

Chapter 5 shifts the discussion from feminist misconceptions about the value of appropriating mainstream models to an analysis of feminist psychological practices. Taking the literature on gender and educational achievement as a case study, Lise Bird offers a concise history of feminist engagements with empirical psychology. She charts how a feminist commitment to empirical psychological techniques of investigation, alongside pressures to produce significant and demonstrable results, has fostered the demise of a focus on gendered positions in education. The early successes of feminist research in using the paradigm of 'learned helplessness' to identify girls' 'fears of success' or the role of teacher expectations – all work that is widely known and discussed in broader feminist circles – came to a halt when it appeared that the 'effect' had 'washed out'. As a consequence research shifted from the study of sex/gender differences to an equally reductionist focus on problem factors in the responses of a putatively androgenous subject. Reflecting on her own research practice as well as commenting on others, Bird describes this diversion from a feminist agenda and collusion with the limitations of empiricist psychology as 'sidestepping and sandbagging'. She moves on to engage critically with the more post-structuralist-inspired analyses of feminist educationalist practice (such as those offered by Davies and Walkerdine), further deconstructing their deconstructions by playing with practices of reading and writing research encounters, so highlighting how they can still allow occlusions of marginalized, racialized and sexual identities.

Deconstruction and Reconstruction

Contrary to popular assumption, a deconstruction of psychology is not a fancier way of talking about its destruction; nor is it equivalent to calling for a reconstruction of an improved variety (market forces notwithstanding). An interesting tension that runs through this book is that between the rigorously anti-essentialist styles of deconstruction and its more humanist varieties. Given feminism's commitment to a political project of social change, requiring subjects capable of action and organization, it is perhaps no surprise that reconstruction as well as deconstruction figure in the accounts (although as editor I admit that the prevalence of this theme was unexpected). The chapters in this second part of the book all explicitly call for a reconstruction as well as deconstruction of psychology, or rather they see the two as integrally related. This may seem a retrograde move, a humanist failure of nerve at the anti-essentialist rigours of deconstruction. Or the idiom of deconstruction may recall the brief flurry of critical psychology books of the 1970s (e.g. Armistead, 1974; Gillham, 1978) that now read as hopelessly over-optimistic about the scope for change. But far from either a narrowly reformist or idealist–utopian rendering of 'reconstruction', these chapters take this as the next necessary step for feminist psychology to advance out of the clutches of both psychology and a depoliticized deconstruction.

In Chapter 6 Frigga Haug takes as her focus the way analyses of 'the everyday' have been used to inform discussion of women's positions, focusing initially on the adequacy of the widely used concepts of the double burden, oppression and subordination. While acknowledging the importance of the debates over the politics of deconstruction, she therefore prefers to start from a concern with the resources feminists have drawn upon to warrant the study of women's worlds. As such, the commitment to empirical study of and for women has long been a feature of feminist work, and relies upon notions of a specifically feminist epistemology of research which she discusses as both laying claim to scientific generalizability but still remaining connected to political demands for women's emancipation. Haug starts by evaluating the contributions of marxist, gramscian and phenomenological perspectives for feminist work, highlighting how these either ignore the specificity of women's positions or still fail to include the experiences of the women whose daily lives they theorize. From this discussion of criteria for the adequacy of feminist 'methods', she turns to the work of three important feminist theorists, Dorothy Smith, Carol Gilligan and her own, to explore what they offer for feminist psychological analyses. The juxtaposition of these works not only highlights the theoretical differences at issue, but also indicates something of the cultural specificities of their domains of application. In deconstructive spirit, tensions and contrasts are identified between approaches without privileging one particular account. In terms of the project of de/reconstruction, Haug argues that while experience is always only accessible via account, it is this which also gives it its transformative power. She offers an account of how her approach to memory-work provides a way into the analysis of the everyday by eliciting stories of resistance that foster the emergence of new political agencies.

Taking as her reference points a commitment both to a relational psychology (as formulated by Gergen) and to radical therapeutic practice associated with the work of Fred Newman as well as the intellectual critique of language games, Lenora Fulani in Chapter 7 revisits the now familiar feminist arena of controversy over the work of Carol Gilligan and her (early) analyses of a feminine ethic of care (Gilligan, 1982). This work is treated as a specific example of a more general set of questions about feminist morality as they arise in teaching and research practices. Speaking from her position as a black feminist activist, Fulani argues that, important and transformative though this work was initially, its current circulation fails to challenge the dominant psychology because it offers neither a radical critique of science (including psychology), nor of morality. Because of its commitment to modern psychological methods she suggests it remains descriptive, cognitive and instrumentalist, rather than focused on activism. As such, for all its continuing popularity, it restricts current forms of feminist psychology because it fails to engage with genuine questions of morality and reinstates a notion of research as morally neutral and male-biased.

Gilligan figures also in the next chapter in Gordana Jovanović's call for a communicative psychology. More general in scope than the previous two chapters, this explores the structure of subjectivity presupposed and perpetuated by mainstream psychology, and the reasons why feminists both challenge but ultimately (she claims) still need some relation with this. Writing from the 'transitional society' of former Yugoslavia, the categories of woman and psychology are, like everything else, in flux. Jovanović takes a strong position, arguing against the formulation of a specific feminist psychology as antithetical to the broader project of changing women's positions. She thus claims to decentre deconstruction, by destabilizing feminist psychology's deconstructions of psychology and arguing instead for the need for a return to grand theory. Drawing approvingly on developments in 'new paradigm' and 'sociogenetic' psychology, she elaborates her arguments in relation to the topics of politics, nationalism, empathy, the public and the private, female sociality and emotions. She argues that just as it is necessary to recognize a particular standpoint (such as feminist psychology), so it is also important to recognize its relationship with psychology – both to make *and* to comprehend its interventions. Indeed, the particular standpoint can only be accessed, she argues, via more general, global frameworks which render feminist psychology as a separatist project ultimately futile.

As is evident from these contributions, not all the authors in this book would choose to identify themselves with deconstruction outside a psychology context. Rather, they perceive themselves as conducting work of an equivalent critical and disruptive significance. Moreover, interventions that are deconstructionist in effect within psychology may be far from a deconstructionist position elsewhere. In Part Two of this book, perhaps even more than in Part One, we see the connections with wider political affiliations that prompt the drive towards reconstruction.

The final contribution, Chapter 9, by Ann Levett and Amanda Kottler traces the tentative emergence of feminist psychology in 'the new' (post-apartheid) South Africa. Here the discursive arena presents quite a different set of challenges for feminist psychology. Reversing the subordination of 'race' to gender characteristic of feminisms elsewhere (Kottler, 1996), they discuss the difficulties of creating a space to articulate gender inequalities in the context of the overwhelming state and institutional oppression of black people through the apartheid regime. They show how in a South African context the discussion of 'difference' that has become so fashionable in women's studies, and tends to code for discussion of power relations, is tainted with historical and actual practices of racial segregation, oppression and brutality. Moreover, psychologists have played an important role in both supporting and dismantling the apartheid regime, and because of this is a deeply politicized and divided discipline (de la Rey, 1997). This is very different from psychological practice in most industrialized countries, where the claims to social efficacy are largely rhetorical, or certainly more indirect. The authors discuss their positions as progressive middle-class, white South African women, and their work as feminist psychologists in a context where issues of psychology's 'relevance' and 'appropriateness', as well as intellectual isolation from radicals observing the academic boycott, make connections and specificities of feminist psychological intervention compelling and urgent topics.

In its attention to specific events, organizations, conferences, this chapter may appear more anecdotal than others, but this is because the authors describe a history of institutional engagement as feminists and as psychologists, that as yet has been undocumented. While perhaps seeming far from the usual academic concerns of deconstruction, the issues of representation and interpretation that are so central to these debates are here confronted very directly: who speaks for whom and on what basis? The challenge here is two-way: not only is it a matter of identifying and instigating feminist initiatives, but also of considering what feminism, and specifically feminist psychology, has to offer black and white women in a southern country. Psychology, as an expression of the modern project of development presents both problems and promises to South Africa. The authors correspondingly suggest that feminists need to engage with, and within, this discipline that – for better or worse – will play a significant part in its future. However, what a feminist psychology might be in the context of such differences of privilege as well as culture between women remains at best unclear, and is perhaps an impossible project.

Translations

This book therefore spans a range of cultural, geographical and political contexts, and part of its rationale is to illustrate the different character and agenda for feminist psychology in these diverse arenas – if indeed the category has any meaning at all. The authors are all well known writers in their fields, and have written these pieces specifically for this volume. Nevertheless, the process of production of this book reproduces many of its key themes and tensions, including the postmodern attention to new technologies – since much (and in some cases all) of the editorial commentaries and development of working relationship between authors and editor took place via email and fax.

Further, while this book is an English language volume, half its substantive chapters were first written in other languages (e.g. Spanish and German). As editor, I requested authors to supply their drafts in English – a clear piece of cultural imperialism – and I am grateful to them for arranging for (and funding) translation, or for writing in a second language. Nevertheless, even when rendered into English, anomalies and estrangements of meaning remained, and the authors and I (in some cases also with their translators) have engaged in lengthy correspondences over specificity of claims and nuances of wording. I want to record here my gratitude for the extensive revisions they were willing to make, as well as recording how the editorial tasks posed for me far exceeded my own expectations.

But more than mere intellectual labour, we (the authors and I) were forced to address in a very concrete way the conceptual issues about interpretation and (non)transparency of language that form part of the problematic of deconstruction. Correspondingly, I cannot claim, nor would I want to claim, that the contributions in this volume sit easily with each other linguistically or conceptually: that is, they may not 'read' for the native English speaker with equivalent ease. I have understood my role as editor as one of promoting clarity of presentation of ideas, without erasing differences. These include discontinuities of reference points of literature, political affiliations that may be 'foreign' to some (English-speaking) readers, or even familiar ideas drawn upon in unconventional ways, and which were perhaps read in translation by the author. While not presuming that a text addresses its readers in the same way, since we are all multiply positioned in relation to it, there are clear discontinuities in this book wrought by reading the 'same' text either in translation or across major differences of geographical, political and cultural contexts (such as South Africa), ranging from substantive ideas to even apparently small matters of style.

To take a small example, in editing Chapter 2, I questioned Margot Pujal i Llombart's use of the generalized 'we' which in English-speaking feminist texts has come to be associated with a malestream, colonizing voice that fails to admit its specificity. She, however, responded by claiming that she saw her use of 'we' as not only facilitating the (reader's) identification with the text, but also as limiting its individualism. It seemed to me that it was not my place to impose stylistic–argumentative features embedded in the cultural–politics of one language on to work formulated in another. Moreover, in the guise of a query over style we were embarking on a broader discussion of the sexual/gender politics of categories of interpellation. Hence, rather than sloppy editing, the discontinuities of phraseology that remain in these chapters stand as a reminder, as traces of the difference that rendering into English cannot, and perhaps should not, efface. I leave them not only as an indication of lack and loss, of what we cannot quite grasp of those cultural contexts that are intimated here, but also as intervention. In his essay 'The Task of the Translator', that foreshadows many of the themes of contemporary discussions of postmodernism and deconstruction, Walter Benjamin highlights the transformative function of translation – as changing the language into which the text is translated as well as that of its original formulation: 'Translation is so far removed from being the sterile equation of two dead languages that of all literary forms it is the one charged with the special mission of watching over the maturing process of the original language and the birth pangs of its own' (Benjamin, 1955/1970: 74). But even as translation cannot erase differences, so we should not get so seduced by postmodernist-speak that we fail to remember how differences can be ideologically engineered via broader political interventions in language. The recent separation of Serbo-Croatian into Serbian and Croatian stands as a powerful reminder of this, as Gordana Jovanović pointed out to me in discussion of her work in Chapter 8.

Connections and Intersections: Feminisms under Scrutiny

One of the most significant instigators and effects of deconstructing feminism(s) has been the challenge of theorizing the intersections between varieties of cultural–political and gender identities. Lesbian, black, 'Third world' and post-colonial critics have demonstrated the poverty and limits of western feminist agendas – at the level of theory (privileging gender identifications over racialized and cultural positions) and campaign objectives ((charles), 1992; hooks, 1990; Tang Nain, 1991). Examples of the cultural presumptions of 1970s western feminism are, firstly, that the promotion of women's reproductive choices was initially understood as exclusively a matter of access to abortion, whereas women of the south and black and minority women of the north, and lesbian and disabled women everywhere, were and are fighting for the right to have and keep their children. A second problem is the way calls for women's safety away from the threat of male violence on the streets collude with racism towards black men and build directly on the legacies of lynching (Carby, 1982; Davis, 1972).

Clearly, if used uncritically, the term 'post-colonial' can harbour its own neo-colonial continuities and obscure specificities of locations and positionings, and this is part of the paradoxically homogenizing dynamic of the current move towards globalizing postmodern identities. Outside psychology, majoritized and minoritized women are exploring the ways forms of femininity, including feminism, have been structured according to racialized, classed and racist practices (Chaudhuri and Strobel, 1992; McClintock, 1995; Ware, 1992). Similar critiques have been developed in relation to research processes (e.g. Afshar and Maynard, 1994). These debates are now being taken up in psychology (Bhavnani and Phoenix, 1994; Mama, 1995; Walkerdine, 1996), while postmodern critiques of psychology are also being used to turn the critical gaze on to psychology's eurocentrism and to invite attention to the other psychologies emerging away from Europe (Kottler and Levett, 1996; Levett et al., 1997).

While the primary address in this book is to the putative arena of feminist psychology, the critiques offered nevertheless have important consequences for feminist strategies generally. Indeed, various forms of feminism are challenged by these chapters. Crawford (Chapter 4) highlights the continuities between popular psychology and feminism (also including feminist therapy) as promoting US social norms of individualism, autonomy and valuation of explicit negotiation. Pujal i Llombart (Chapter 2) does a similar job with academic feminism's collusions. Various chapters (3, 4 and 5) critique role theory as a common resource for both feminism and psychology. Similarly, Chapters 7 and 8 ward off the romanticizations of women's natures and identities. In particular, Chapter 7 offers a critique of the current notion of standpoint, preferring instead the more perspectival formulation of vantage point. Feminist representations of memory, including personal history, come in for feminist scrutiny in Chapter 2, and, via the notion of memory-work, in Chapter 6. Finally, the strategies of 'sidestepping and sandbagging' that Bird identifies with feminist psychologists in Chapter 5 are by no means exclusive to this discipline.

This book therefore joins with the emerging body of feminist literature that calls for a deconstruction of 'imperial feminism' (Amos and Parmar, 1984) and demands that we think through, not simply connections between 'race' and gender, but how these identifications and positions intimately structure each other, in different ways, in different contexts. The lesson of Chapter 9 is not simply that the project of feminist psychology requires redefinition in the context of what was, until recently, a context of racial segregation. Rather, the challenge to feminist psychology is to take on board what this means for the feminist psychologies we promote 'at home' as well as 'away'. On this score Chapter 4 shows how psychology, including feminist psychology, continues to ignore oppressed minoritized gendered identities at its 'centre'.

Further, the heterosexism of feminist psychology, as reproduced also within the presumed heterosexual model of Everywoman 'the psychology of women' elaborates in relation to the psychology of men, is critiqued throughout the book. While perhaps less 'visible' than some of the other cultural and geographical issues addressed in this book, the chapters challenge not only the model of subjectivity elaborated within its models; in the drive towards specificity and differences their call to attend to the diversity of women's experiences and lifestyles is very much driven by lesbian critiques of psychology and the academy (Wilkinson and Kitzinger, 1993;

Wilton, 1993). Attending to the power relations between women, and not presuming commonalities (of interest or experience) highlights the limits of feminist psychology. In this book the heterosexism of feminist analyses is demonstrated in the challenges to traditional ways of reading girls' and education literature (Chapter 5), in the presumption of cross-gender family arrangements (Chapters 3, 7, 8 and 9), and in the intertwining of gendered and heterosexist notions within the attribution of women's caring natures (Chapters 2, 7 and 8).

In the end, the paradoxical political venture of deconstructing feminist psychology formulated here is about facilitating more useful ways not only of *thinking* about women's positions in and in relation to psychology's practices, but also of *acting* on them. While forms of political intervention are necessarily structured according to the local situations to which they apply, surrendering 'feminist psychology' as a specific arena of expertise could prompt feminists in psychology to organize with those outside the discipline, and to work across traditional professional boundaries in order to counter psychology's injustices to all women. Equally, using what 'inside' knowledge we have to critique the discipline, including our own participation in it, may be one of the most useful resources we can bring to those struggles. In such ways feminist psychologies and their deconstructions function in a relation of dynamic and reciprocal tension, as exemplified also by this book. If deconstruction has taught us anything, it is that how texts function is as much (if not more) a matter of reading as of writing. The issues of location and interpretation − of discontinuities, differences and the possibilities of alliances between feminists and (feminist) psychologies − that have structured the preparation of this book are posed anew now that this passes from us, its authors, to you its readers.

References

Afshar, H. and Maynard, M. (eds) (1994) *The Dynamics of Race and Gender*. Sussex: Taylor and Francis.

Amos, V. and Parmar, P. (1984) 'Challenging imperial feminism', *Feminist Review*, 17: 3–19.

Armistead, N. (ed.) (1974) *Reconstructing Social Psychology*. Harmondsworth: Penguin.

Baker Miller, J. (1976) *Toward a Theory of Women's Psychological Development*. Harmondsworth: Penguin.

Banister, P., Burman, E., Parker, I., Taylor, M. and Tindall, C. (1994) *Qualitative Methods in Psychology: A Research Guide*. Buckingham: Open University Press.

Benjamin, W. (1955/1970) *Illuminations*. London: Cape.

Bhavnani, K.K. (1993) 'Tracing the contours: feminist research and feminist objectivity', *Women's Studies International Forum*, 16(2): 95–104.

Bhavnani, K.K. and Phoenix, A. (eds) (1994) *Shifting Identities, Shifting Racisms: A Feminism & Psychology Reader*. London: Sage.

Bohan, J. (ed.) (1992) *Seldom Seen, Rarely Heard: Women's Place in Psychology*. Boulder, CO: Westview Press.

Bondi, L. (1993) 'Locating identity politics', in M. Keith and S. Pale (eds), *Place and the Politics of Identity*. London: Routledge. pp. 95–118.

Brodribb, S. (1992) *Nothing Mat(t)ers: A Feminist Critique of Postmodernism*. Melbourne: Spinifex.

Burman, E. (ed.) (1990a) *Feminists and Psychological Practice*. London: Sage.

Burman, E. (1990b) 'Differing with deconstruction: a feminist critique', in I. Parker and J. Shotter (eds), *Deconstructing Social Psychology*. London: Routledge. pp. 208–20.

Burman, E. (1991) 'What discourse is not', *Philosophical Psychology*, 4(3): 325–42.

Burman, E. (1993) 'Beyond discursive relativism: power and subjectivity in developmental psychology', in H. Tam, L. Mos, W. Thorngate and B. Kaplan (eds), *Recent Trends in Theoretical Psychology* (vol. 111). New York: Springer Verlag. pp. 433–40.

Burman, E. and Parker, I. (eds) (1993) *Discourse Analytic Research: Repertoires and Readings of Texts in Action*. London: Routledge.

Burman, E., Alldred, P., Bewley, C., Goldberg, B., Heenan, C., Marks, D., Taylor, K., Ullah, R. and Warner, S. (1996a) *Challenging Women: Psychology's Exclusions, Feminist Possibilities*. Buckingham: Open University Press.

Burman, E., Aitken, G., Alldred, P., Allwood, R., Billington, T., Goldberg, B., Gordo Lopez, A., Heenan, C., Marks, D. and Warner, S. (1996b) *Psychology Discourse Practice: From Regulation to Resistance*. London: Taylor and Francis.

Butler, J. (1991) *Gender Trouble: Feminism and the Subversion of Identity*. New York: Routledge.

Carby, H. (1982) 'White woman listen! Black feminism and the boundaries of sisterhood', in Centre for Contemporary Cultural Studies (CCCS), *The Empire Strikes Back: Race and Racism in 70s Britain*. Basingstoke: Hutchinson. pp. 211–33.

(charles), H. (1992) 'Whiteness – the relevance of politically colouring the "non"', in H. Hinds, A. Phoenix and J. Stacey (eds), *Working Out*. London: Taylor and Francis. pp. 29–37.

Charles, N. and Hughes-Freeland, F. (eds) (1996) *Practising Feminism: Identity, Difference, Power*. London: Routledge.

Chaudhuri, N. and Strobel, M. (eds) (1992) *Western Women and Imperialism: Complicity and Resistance*. Bloomington, IN: Indiana University Press.

Christian, B. (1988) 'The race for theory', *Feminist Studies*, 14: 167–79.

Curt, B. (1994) *Textuality and Tectonics*. Buckingham: Open University Press.

Davis, A. (1972) *Women, Race and Class*. London: The Women's Press.

de la Rey, C. (1997) 'On politics, activism and discourse analysis in South Africa', in A. Levett, A. Kottler, E. Burman and I. Parker (eds), *Culture, Power and Difference: Discourse Analysis in South Africa*. London: Zed Press. pp. 189–97.

de Lauretis, T. (1989) *Technologies of Gender: Essays on Theory, Film and Fiction*. Basingstoke: Macmillan.

Derrida, J. (1984/1992) *Mochlos: Or, the Conflict of the Faculties*, in R. Rand (ed.), *Logomachio*. Lincoln, NE: University of Nebraska Press.

Easthope, A. and McGowan, K. (eds) (1993) *A Critical and Cultural Studies Reader.* Buckingham: Open University Press.

Edwards, D. and Potter, J. (1993) *Discursive Psychology.* London: Sage.

Edwards, D., Ashmore, M. and Potter, J. (1995) 'Death and furniture: the rhetoric, politics and theology of bottom line arguments against relativism', *History of the Human Sciences,* 8: 25–49.

Elam, D. (1994) *Feminism and Deconstruction: Ms en Abyme.* London: Routledge.

Ferguson, K. (1991) 'Interpretation and genealogy in feminism', *Signs: Journal of Women in Culture and Society,* 16(2): 322–39.

Flax, J. (1991) *Thinking Fragments: Psychoanalysis, Feminism and Postmodernism in the Contemporary West.* Berkeley, CA: University of California Press.

Frankenberg, R. and Mani, L. (1993) 'Crosscurrents, crosstalk: race, "postcoloniality" and the politics of location', *Cultural Studies,* 7(2): 293–311.

Fraser, N. (1992) 'The uses and abuses of French discourse theories for feminist politics', *Theory, Culture and Society,* 9: 51–71.

Gavey, N. (1989) 'Feminism, post-structuralism and discourse analysis: contributions to feminist psychology', *Psychology of Women Quarterly,* 13: 459–75.

Gill, R. (1995) 'Relativism, reflexivity and politics: interrogating discourse analysis from a feminist perspective', in S. Wilkinson and C. Kitzinger (eds), *Feminism and Discourse.* London: Sage. pp. 165–86.

Gillham, B. (ed.) (1978) *Reconstructing Educational Psychology.* London: Macmillan.

Gilligan, C. (1982) *In a Different Voice.* Harvard, MA: Harvard University Press.

Griffin, C., Henwood, K. and Phoenix, A. (eds) (forthcoming) *Standpoints and Differences: Essays in the Practice of Feminist Psychology.* London: Sage.

Haraway, D. (1989) *Primate Visions.* London: Verso.

Haraway, D. (1991) *Simians, Cyborgs and Women.* London: Verso.

Harding, S. (ed.) (1986) *Feminism and Methodology.* Milton Keynes: Open University Press.

Harding, S. (1993) *Whose Power? Whose Knowledge?.* Buckingham: Open University Press.

Harré, R. and Gillett, G. (1995) *The Discursive Mind.* London: Sage.

Henriques, J., Hollway, W., Urwin, C., Venn, C. and Walkerdine, V. (1984) *Changing the Subject: Psychology, Social Regulation and Subjectivity.* London: Methuen.

Henwood, K. and Pidgeon, N. (1995) 'Remaking the link: qualitative methods and feminist standpoint theory', *Feminism & Psychology,* 5(1): 7–30.

Hollway, W. (1989) *Subjectivity and Method in Psychology.* London: Sage.

hooks, bell (1990) *Yearning: Race, Gender and Cultural Politics.* London: Turnaround.

Jackson, S. (1992) 'The amazing deconstructing woman', *Trouble and Strife,* 25: 25–31.

Kelly, L., Regan, L. and Burton, S. (1992) 'Defending the indefensible? Quantitative methods and feminist research', in H. Hinds, A. Phoenix and J. Stacey (eds), *Working Out.* London: Taylor and Francis. pp. 149–60.

Kottler, A. (1996) 'Voices in the winds of change', *Feminism & Psychology,* 6(1): 61–68.

Kottler, A. and Levett, A. (eds) (1996) Special Issue on 'Postmodernism', *South African Journal of Psychology,* 26(3): 123–202.

Levett, A., Kottler, A., Burman, E. and Parker, I. (eds) (1997) *Culture, Power and Difference: Discourse Analysis in South Africa.* London: Zed Press.

28   Deconstructing Feminist Psychology

Lovibund, S. (1989) 'Feminism and postmodernism', *New Left Review*, 78: 5–28.

Mama, A. (1995) *Beyond the Masks*. London: Routledge.

Matlin, M. (1993) *The Psychology of Women* (2nd edn). Orlando, FL: Harcourt, Brace Jovanovich.

McClintock, A. (1995) *Imperial Leather: Race, Gender and Sexuality in the Colonial Contest*. London: Routledge.

Middleton, D. and Edwards, D. (eds) (1992) *Collective Remembering*. London: Sage.

Nicholson, L. and Seidman, S. (eds) (1995) *Social Postmodernism: Beyond Identity Politics*. Cambridge: Cambridge University Press.

Parker, I. (1992) *Discourse Dynamics: Critical Analysis for Social and Individual Psychology*. London: Routledge.

Parker, I. and Shotter, J. (eds) (1990) *Deconstructing Social Psychology*. London: Routledge.

Parker, I., Georgaca, E., Harper, D., McLaughlin, T. and Stowell Smith, M. (1995) *Deconstructing Psychopathology*. London: Sage.

Potter, J. and Wetherell, M. (1987) *Discourse and Social Psychology*. London: Sage.

Ramazanoglu, C. (ed.) (1992) *Up Against Foucault*. London: Routledge.

Riger, S. (1992) 'Epistemological debates, feminist voices: science, social values and the study of women', *American Psychologist*, 47(6): 730–40.

Riley, D. (1988) *'Am I that Name?': Feminism and the Category of Woman in History*. London: Macmillan.

Roberts, H. (ed.) (1981) *Doing Feminist Research*. London: Routledge and Kegan Paul.

Sampson, E. (1993) 'Identity politics: challenges to psychology's understanding', *American Psychologist*, 48(12): 1219–30.

Soper, K. (1991) 'Posmodernism and its discontents', *Feminist Review*, 37: 1–22.

Spelman, E. (1988) *Inessential Woman*. London: The Women's Press.

Spivak, G.C. (1990) 'The intervention interview', in S. Harasym (ed.), *The Post-Colonial Critic*. London: Routledge.

Spivak, G.C. (1993) *Outside in the Teaching Machine*. London: Routledge.

Squire, C. (1989) *Significant Differences: Feminism in Psychology*. London: Routledge.

Stanley, L. (ed.) (1990) *Feminist Praxis*. London: Routledge.

Stanley, L. and Wise, S. (1983) *Breaking Out: Feminist Consciousness and Feminist Research*. London: Routledge and Kegan Paul.

Tang Nain, G. (1991) 'Black women, sexism and racism: black or antiracist feminism?', *Feminist Review*, 37: 1–22.

Unger, R. and Crawford, M. (1992) *Women and Gender: A Feminist Psychology*. New York: McGraw-Hill.

Ware, V. (1992) *Beyond the Pale: White Women, Racism and History*. London: Verso.

Walkerdine, V. (ed.) (1996) *Feminism and Psychology* (special issues on social class), 6(3): 355–456.

Weedon, C. (1987) *Feminist Practice and Post-structuralist Theory*. Oxford: Blackwell.

Wilkinson, S. (ed.) (1986) *Feminist Social Psychology*. Milton Keynes: Open University Press.

Wilkinson, S. and Burns, J. (1990) 'Women organising in psychology', in E. Burman (ed.), *Feminists and Psychological Practice*. London: Sage. pp. 140–62.

Wilkinson, S. and Kitzinger, C. (eds) (1993) *Heterosexuality: A* Feminism & Psychology *Reader*. London: Sage.

Wilkinson, S. and Kitzinger, C. (eds) (1995) *Feminism and Discourse*. London: Sage.

Wilton, T. (1993) 'Queer subjects: lesbians, heterosexual women and the academy', in M. Kennedy, C. Lubelska and V. Walsh (eds), *Making Connections: Women's Studies, Women's Movements and Women's Lives*. London: Taylor and Francis. pp. 167–79.

Yuval-Davis, N. (1993) 'Beyond difference: women and coalition politics', in M. Kennedy, C. Lubelska and V. Walsh (eds), *Making Connections: Women's Studies, Women's Movements, Women's Lives*. London: Taylor and Francis. pp. 3–10.

Part 1

TOWARDS A DECONSTRUCTION OF FEMINIST PSYCHOLOGY

2

Feminist Psychology or the History of a Non-Feminist Practice

Margot Pujal i Llombart

If the existence of feminist psychology is to be useful, it could only be justified by a **real** capacity for social critique and by the exercise of action capable of transforming existing power relations between men and women, that is to say, between people in general. This implied doubt as to the need for an area of knowledge called feminist psychology stems from the reality of the 'individualism' which largely predominates in psychology and from the 'particularism' associated with some feminist positions. These are two highly contradictory characteristics with regard to the basic objective and social change which feminist practice pursues, whether it be in academic or other contexts.

However, leaving aside this first impression, we shall address the specific question of what is called feminist psychology. As such, the category of feminist psychology within the academic sphere in the Spanish state does not exist. In relation to it, some very small but scarcely consolidated groups have emerged, whose work has been scorned and which occupy highly marginalized positions. What is more, within the social and human sciences, it has been other disciplines (history, sociology, anthropology, philosophy, geography, etc.) rather than psychology which have sought to bring the question of women out into the open. These disciplines have not worked, however, so much in terms of feminism (although the importance of feminist sources have been recognized at the outset), but have preferred to use the category 'gender studies' or 'women's studies'. Also, their central task so far has been to reveal the invisibility and the disregard shown to the role and functions of women in society on the part of studies in social sciences. In the Spanish state, then, the presence of psychology in these forums has been negligible, and, at all events, it has rather been social psychology that has displayed a greater awareness of this question.

Though it may be based on an impression rather than an exahustive analysis, it should be said, however, that there is at the moment in our country a more 'favourable' or more precisely 'falsely tolerant' general climate in certain sectors of the academic world, which are willing to accept and/or import the feminist psychology emanating from the USA or the UK. We might say that feminist psychology is acquiring a value of use: always, though, on condition that it does not distort too much the other psychology and that it keeps to one side, something that totally betrays its starting point. In this way, a trivialization and segregation of this work arises, to the point that it is turned into a 'subscience', by women and for women, with very little capacity to transform and which serves rather as a form of indoctrination or identification.

It is this context which has led us in this chapter to address feminist psychology and to propose a series of epistemological discussions in relation to the practice of 'gender studies', made through different disciplines, rather than making feminist psychology a specific focal point; maybe because the latter is lagging behind and is the one facing strongest resistance, but also because we believe that these discussions span the different social sciences for the simple reason that all of them have drunk from the waters of positivism and the representationist model for a long time, and share the problem of androcentrism as well as the reductionism of specialization.

Much of the work done on gender and on the role of women within history, sociology, philosophy, anthropology, etc. has attempted to correct this androcentric bias by introducing and making visible women and everything that surrounds them, by means of the reconstruction of parts of knowledge, albeit using in many cases old epistemological instruments, positivism and representationism: instruments which in themselves generate effects of domination and exclusion, especially if indiscriminate use is made of them, even though they displace the point of focus and action. The aim of this chapter, then, is to show how feminist knowledge has inherited, in many cases, these assumptions of mainstream science and the *perverse effects* which derive from this use, and also to point to some ideas in relation to its transformation, so that academic feminist practice might be more effective.

The false dichotomies between 'theory and practice' and between 'theory and politics' will be the twin central axes along which we shall try to approach the different critiques of the dominant epistemology and its effects. The first part will centre on the question of how psychology, by virtue of the fact that it defines itself as theoretical in its academic setting, ignores the practical/political effects (or power efffects) which its discourse has, in the sense of *excluding* and/or at the same time *inventing* (by the abnormality that it implies) that which has adopted the label 'feminine' or 'referring to women'. Unmasking this language game was the 'leitmotiv' of the emergence of feminist knowledge.

In the second part of the chapter, an attempt will be made to analyse how certain feminist discourses in their self-definition as political action (or practice), in the social sphere, forget their theoretical bases, which have ended many times in a *naturalization*, *essentialism* and *universalization* of the category 'woman'. Feminist psychology, or feminist knowledge in general, which is the result of an attempt at correcting psychology and social knowledge on the part of feminism and which means an *approximation between two types of discourse* of very different origins, has turned on many occasions into a *hybrid, the theoretical foundations and the power and political effects of which prove to be rather confused*. However, in order to consider this confusion and to try to clarify the task which feminist academic practice is really carrying out, going beyond its explicit discourse and also taking into account its power effects or practical effects, we deem it necessary at the same time to deal with both epistemological and practical questions. This is because, in the final analysis, they are inextricable, and more so if we concentrate on the academic context, as is our case.

It is because of all this that we need to analyse how an important part of feminist knowledge, in the course of its emergence and evolution, has gradually inherited certain epistemological assumptions, which, in Ibáñez's terms (1994) might be qualified as myths. These, taken together and applied to gender studies, would constitute a *syndrome that would hinder a truly feminist academic practice*. We are referring to the following assumptions:

- the myth of valid knowledge as a correct and reliable representation of reality;
- the myth of the object as a constitutive element of the world;
- the myth of reality as an entity independent of us;
- the myth of truth as a decision-making criterion.

The most important thing, however, in relation to these myths is how, through some feminist discourses, they have been building a collective history with regard to women that, in some cases, has had the effect of establishing/constructing *closed and particularist realities*, with their resulting power and normative effects. To approach them, it is intended here to make an analysis/deconstruction of the notions of experience and evidence in relation to the collective history of women, taking as the main theoretical–methodological tool the analysis of the processes of dialogic ethics and of social memory .

Perhaps the need for an area of knowledge called feminist psychology can be seen as symptomatic of the fact that something is not quite right. However, if the following reflections help to shed a little light on the internal contradiction arising from a particular feminist rhetoric becoming an academic practice which seeks to be effective in the assumption and transformation of specific power relations, in particular those linked to the question of gender, we will declare ourselves satisfied.

The History of a 'Fallacious Separation' between Theory and Practice

The emergence of feminist psychology: an exercise of reflexivity within mainstream psychology

As a theoretical, scientific discipline and through the 'language game' (in Wittgenstein's, 1953, terms) of science, mainstream psychology has tried to 'portray' the various forms of subjective life by forgetting a great many non-subjective processes (cultural, historical, institutional, power, etc.), which act as the enabling conditions and discursive practices that generate such subjectivity. This work has long made the discipline an instrument of domination which has acted by legitimizing certain dominant social relations and making them seem natural, as is the case of the relationship between men and women, which are presented as reified subjectivities with independent existences. Through these epistemological suppositions, psychology has contributed to the establishment of power relationships hidden behind the 'innocent' game of identities and differences. However, the difference always has an ideological meaning:

> a difference is always thought of within a particular relationship, one with a fixed point, a centre which orders its surroundings and which is used to measure all things; a point of reference, . . . an origin of the definition. (Guillaumin, 1992: 97)

However, with the radical 'hermeneutical turn' of recent years caused by feminist and non-feminist critical theories (Hekman, 1990; Ibáñez, 1994; Latour, 1987; Nicholson, 1990; Rorty, 1979; Rose, 1989) in their attack on representationalist knowledge, psychology (whether it be feminist or not) has been dramatically made to assume the responsibility of facing up to the *non-existence of independent knowledge* and the fact that knowledge in itself is *an act of participation in the social world*, as some studies of sociology of science have shown. Psychology has also had to give way to the evidence that the social position from which we narrate the world is reflected in the very social situation we hope to realize, 'the place from which we speak determines what we say and why we say it' (Zavala, 1993: 177).

In turn, we have experienced how this psychosocial reality becomes dependent on the way we explain it and the language we use. Our discursive practices are political actions which invert society owing to the fact that some discourses, such as that of mainstream psychology, translate 'truth effects' into power effects (Foucault, 1976; Ibáñez, 1989; Pujal, 1992; Rose, 1989; Sampson, 1993). This is why we have reached the point of wondering, in the terms of Evelyn Fox Keller (1994), which types of self, subjects, positions are attracted, identified and reflected by the knowledge produced, by the reality painted in dependent form; how the questions which direct our means of producing knowledge reflect and build different types of subjectivity and social feeling. At the same time, we wonder how these subjectivities are expressed in the products of this adventure which, on many occasions, attempts to mask the self in an act of irresponsibility disguised as objectivity. We are referring here to the positivist distinction between subject and object.

Feminist theories and criticisms (de Lauretis, 1987; Harding, 1991; Hekman, 1990; Nicholson, 1990; Wilkinson, 1986) from the political or academic world have made an important contribution in destabilizing the positivist criteria which supported the social sciences as a whole. This has consequently impacted on psychology which is strongly linked to the social sciences, despite the positivist aim to separate them through a certain atomization of its objects of study. The contemporary figure of author or authoress (whether or not she be feminist), immersed in the object under study, has made it possible to reunite psychology with other social sciences.

The fact is that feminist critical contributions have played a crucial role in the process of unmasking the objectivist fallacy, and have revealed the social dimension which is present in the production of psychological knowledge driven into oblivion by the positivist project. They have participated in unmasking the effects of power, domination and exclusion derived from representationalist knowledge, which is understood to be the axis of the referential discourse aspiring to reflect objectively social and psychological formation.

Feminist criticism has added to the general criticisms made of the classical model of production of knowledge. These have led to the key claim that behind scientific practice there are always social and ideological presuppositions which are what really direct the history of knowledge, by making a new complaint about the regulatory presence of a masculine ideology in most scientific practices (de Lauretis, 1987; Hekman, 1990; Nicholson, 1990). This ideology both directs specific ways of observing, investigating and choosing the object of study as well as the way to relate to the object.

According to emerging feminist criticism, it has been through the system of disymmetrical thought, which is characteristic of modernism, that gender ideology has operated and regulated the social relationships. This system makes systematic use of hierarchies and divisions between social categories such as: public/private, subject/object, mind/body, culture/nature, objective/subjective, masculine/feminine. Apart from this, as a result of the truth regime which accompanies scientific knowledge in our society, these asymmetrical categories have also profoundly impregnated the knowledge of common sense, and have produced an idea of human experience to be perfectly divided in two, mutually exclusive, worlds: the masculine world and the feminine world. In this way, feminism criticism has demonstrated how gender relationships are inserted into the social nature of scientific subjectivity, which has created itself as inter-subjectivity in order to confer implicitly upon itself normative power, or the power to define the world and nature.

If gender relationships are not alien to the subjectivity of modern science, or more than this, if such subjectivity moves gender frameworks through the theories on human beings which it defines as being general or universal, there is no other way to alter effectively these effects of domination, produced when everything is replaced by a part, than to begin with the reconstruction of the scientific subjectivity which gives legitimacy to it. In this sense, it has been necessary to reveal the will to power of the modern scientific project, rejected and expressed at the same time, as it is responsible for having allowed and reinforced the exclusion of women as subjects and historical objects many times, by an androcentric construction, as we will see later. To explain this kind of exclusion, we find inspiration in Foucault when he says that if one is not a subject of history, neither can one be its object.

Having come this far, feminist criticism has shown that most theories about human beings that have been construed as general are no more than fiction which, at a certain time and by virtue of a series of fortuitous circumstances and particular interests, became a controlling, dominating subjectivity, which we call masculine gender. Based on these criticisms, which began to appear in the 1960s, the predominant masculine interpretation of 'mainstream psychology' became clearer. It is from these criticisms, with the explicit intention of correcting the effects of domination which have come forth from this way of constructing psychological theories, that what is known as 'feminist psychology' has emerged. But the development of this arena of knowledge has not been as expected.

Tools for an exercise in reflexivity within feminist knowledge
However, in terms of social memory, if we consider the question of feminist knowledge today, we are forced to take a different approach from the one that we would have taken if we were in the 1970s or 1980s. Today, we have had the experience of seeing and participating in the gender studies of the academic world, as well as seeing how some women have acceded to the means of production in the public light (e.g. in politics, academics, business, art). In fact, we are able to project an image of this recent experience by saying that we are witnessing the power of a certain *exquisite feminism*. This is why we will try to see to what extent, how and through which processes a discourse of resistance to domination has become or works as a discourse of power.

Actually, this feminist understanding cannot be impervious to the critical review which it has itself allowed if it does not wish to initiate new practices of domination. The connections established between knowledge, power and subject in the field of critical theory must also affect feminist psychology in an exercise of reflexivity.

In this sense, the attribution of effects generating social realities to discursive psychology (Harré and Stearns, 1995) cannot be isolated from the simultaneous psychosocial restraint of the same social reality. In fact, the place or social position from which the discourse is put to work is not a 'psychosocial' vacuum, thus it may betray the social place from which one wishes to speak. The very principle of inter-textuality makes it impossible to resist power exercised from other places if resistance is not exercised simultaneously to the place these others have built for us in psychological terms.

The distinction that Michel Foucault (1994) makes between power relationships and those of domination is very useful for a reflexive exercise in feminist psychology. The former enables the practice of freedom in a bidirectional manner, such as the exercise of negotiation; on the other hand, the latter alludes to the situation by which the power relationships have become static and fixed and only leave room for the practice of freedom in one single direction. In this sense it may be admitted that 'liberation' supposes the political and historical conditions which allow the practice of freedom, but which, at the same time, open an area of new power relationships which will have to be controlled by means of new practices of freedom.

Central to this way of considering the inter-relationships between discourse and psychosocial reality is the assumption of a non-deterministic paradigm, which takes us back to the problem of power relationships and the practices of resistance as well as to the concept of freedom. The last contributions of Michel Foucault centre directly on this concept and connect it to both the ethical and political dimensions, to what the author refers to as the 'ethical problem of the practice of freedom' (Foucault, 1994). In this way, ethics are conceptualized as the 'reflexive side of freedom' which leads us to problematize the liberal notion of freedom and reconceptualize it as:

> a way of controlling and unleashing power . . . a good sovereign is precisely the one who exercises power as is due, that is, by exercising his power at the same time over itself. It is exactly the exercise of power over itself that will regulate power over others. (Foucault, 1994: 118)

This idea offers a strong criticism to the dominant concept of western freedom. More than this, it also destabilizes some of the understandings from which feminist knowledge and also psychological knowledge are developed. Key instances of this are the ideas of the external nature of domination with respect to resistance, and the dichotomy of domination against subordination, treated as self-sufficient conditions, in terms of structure, and in determining whether or not what is being said is legitimate. And so the rhetoric of victimization has gained enough force to sustain a certain feminist order with effects of domination and self-complacency. These effects arise from the fact that the explicit gender position from which one is speaking is seen as more relevant than what is actually said and done through discourse. They lead to what we could call the naturalization of feminism which could provide us with rather undesirable situations and new power relationships. To break with the static, atomized image of the psychosocial reality which springs from this rhetoric, we therefore propose that the positions of victim and victimizer should be rewritten as exchangeable, and as a product of actual relationship in context.

In order to rewrite this, however, we must also first consider the problem of the theory of subject, which has been inherited from the representationalist conception of knowledge, in the sense that negotiation is necessary for the very exercise of freedom. It is desirable to replace the logic of a single and autonomous identity with that of a dialogic and emergent self, from which one considers that interiority is produced through the relationships with others. In fact, the concept of dialogic relationship drawn up by Mijail Bajtin is very useful to us in this task:

the subject speaking is not a fixed entity, a fragmented subject, nor is it a subconscious exteriorization of 'alter ego' but rather 'another equitable awareness placed next to mine, in relation to which only my own awareness may exist' . . . the epistemological metaphors of Bajtin – polyphony and the practice of dialogue – are an aid to understanding the placement of ideas, methods and styles, not only in social and political contexts but also with our sight on the future thinking of new creations. The way is laid open for the unstable process of meaning and subject and thus to bringing out everything that is open, everything mobile and all that is relative against what is finished, concluded and static. (Zavala, 1993: 177)

One criticism of the notion of identity from dialogic covers both majority and normative identities as well as minority identities. Otherness, understood as difference, is dependent on a centred norm. It is therefore fallacious to set about deconstructing the difference without effecting the deconstruction of norms. In many cases, feminist psychological discourse (such as Hyde, 1991) has fallen precisely into this fallacy as it has become more generalized and institutionalized: having copied the identity model in its attempt to give femininity its own, independent and natural existence, women were then unable to escape gender alienation.

In this sense, and with respect to power effects connected with the 'language-game' of identity and difference in our western societies, it is destabilizing to replace the notion of identity (majority and/or minority) with the notion of 'ethics as a reflexive practice of freedom' which would bring about resistance. Such resistance would be based on the deconstruction of the self through certain practices of freedom which do not only rely upon the production of knowledge of the self and the restraint caused by this.

It is in the light of these theoretical concerns that we will try to evaluate the effects of power, control and domestication that arise from the feminist knowledge which traverses the area of feminist psychology and, of course, comes to light in the everyday life of women. We refer to a dimension which we consider basic to any understanding of social dynamics, the social memory applied to the discursive construction of social change with respect to the role that feminist practices can play in it.

The History of a 'Fallacious Approximation' between Theory and Practice

Deconstructing the category of gender within feminist discourse
It seems that the same historical system of dichotomic and asymmetrical thought which has brought the categories of Nature and

Culture against each other up to the present continues to modulate most discursive practices dealing with the sex/gender system. In fact, asymmetrical thought not only affects the different forms of conservative and patriarchal discourses but is also present in most feminist discourses, which is also the case in feminist psychology. Clearly, the language-game established with this asymmetry in the two orders of discourse (conservative and critical) is radically different, but its social effects may be compared in terms of the power effects driven by means of the 'truth rhetoric' – whether it be the truth related to the different, unequal Nature of the sexes of patriarchal rhetoric, or the truth of the History of Women's Liberation and sex equality of feminist rhetoric.

The link which, in fact, allows us to compare the two rhetorics refers to a whole group of socio-historical processes which have brought out 'women' as a collective subject and object. These processes have produced and regulated, in sociological and psychological terms, the sex and gender categories which have long served specific projects of domestication, humbling and control (separation of the means of production from reproduction, of the political from social and relational aspects). Moreover, the seduction which leads one to think that social reality is not previously fixed and that it is possible to create change effects by projecting our sight on it, tells us absolutely nothing about the ethical and political dimensions of the changes sought. This dimension can only be perceived in the actual socio-historical context in which the discursive feminist practice appears, and it is in relation to the different social actors in the context that we are able to identify it.

In fact, the act of expelling the ontological determinism from our critical discursive magma does not, as people sometimes wish to believe, automatically give rise to the abandonment of other determinisms, such as the historical one, either through pure self-complacency or because of an excess of enthusiasm. Therefore, in a deterministic, naturalist paradigm, the relationship which is established between discourse and psychological reality is that of representation and correspondence. The socio-historical dimension is absent given that we are moving within a system of dichotomous and asymmetric thought which brings truth and error face to face, by virtue of their degree of subjectivity/social contagion. However, the historical aspect is present in the framework of a social, deterministic paradigm, but only as a 'history which constructs the past to legitimate the present' (Vázquez, 1995: 4) and not as a social memory process which politically regulates the experience of the present or as a process of differentiation, reflexivity and resistance to the present by virtue of significant past referents. In this sense, the action of remembering may be considered a potentially subversive act (Sebastiani, 1991). Within the logic of historical essentialism and social determinism, the past is construed to legitimize the present and constitutes the product of a rigorous psychosocial subjection to the established present, legitimized in a particular social context. In this sense, the feminist rhetoric underlying psychology gives rise to the building of gender as an historical past which legitimizes the feminist order of the present, staged by two different, independent psychologies which correspond to men and women as universal categories (Hyde, 1991; Sau, 1992). It seems paradoxical therefore, that once the socio-historical dimension of the category of woman has been recognized (Harding, 1991), discourses continue to be organized round this category in an essentialist way which demonstrate the following:

> that, having assumed gender as a cultural register (one of domination) instead of another space we call 'sex' it is as if there were no other chance to answer than to consider the existence of a surplus, an 'irreducible' element 'inherent' to women's bodies which makes us different from men and which, as a result, is constituted as liberation. (Correa et al., 1994: 40)

In fact, the feminist rhetoric which invades most of feminist psychology, academic and not academic, shows that

> once the false awareness of women, a product of their subordination to the patriarchal order, is broken, the feminine subject, or true feminist subject, flourishes. This is how an articulate movement should express itself, as a Great resistance in which differences are reconciled (women into Woman). (Correa et al., 1994: 43–4)

The feminine element is suggested as absent from the past and the established order of incorporating it legitimately and victoriously in the present comes about through participating in a binary, universalist, futurist and teleological project: sex equality. In other words, the seeking to be another is made natural and is constituted in a new authoritarian, psychological value.

According to this psychology directed towards what is called 'sex equality', the right way to proceed is to present the truth about the sexes in the light of new, improved theories, which configure new technologies of gender. This is how legitimacy is given to the production of new knowledge, sometimes on woman in the singular, in different areas (psychological, narrative, political, artistic, management, etc.) around the axis of what is feminine, which in turn creates 'its own layers of feminine ranking and thus becomes another discourse of women's regulation' (Figueroa Sarriera et al., 1994: 23). Actually, this feminist psychology participates deeply in the historical legacy of identity logic and assumes the presence of an autonomous, undivided, unified, universal subject:

> the theoretization of gender has gravitated around the relationship between the universal categories of 'person' and gender . . . in this way we accept the existence of a personal identity which is configured in the first instance and which, a moment later is befallen by sexual identity or gender . . . in this sense the differences and diversity between women were thought of according to their intersections with other categories such as class, race, nation. (Correa et al., 1994: 41–3)

This subjection to the present created by identity logic can be explained by means of the substitution and conversion of a certain collective memory in objective history, destined to normalize, legitimize and regulate the current social order, which, in the light of a previously established project, is considered the best mechanism for attaining it (Vázquez, 1995). The consequences of these discursive practices are as follows: first, the psychological and social aspects are blurred and fixed; secondly, the different, 'true' psychological memories often elaborated, founded on processes of disidentification, are silenced; and, thirdly, a certain natural goodness is attributed to the psychosocial change.

In this sense, through this historical teleologism of feminist rhetoric, the relationship between discourse and reality continues to be one of representation and correspondence with effects of psycho-social subjection, but which are stronger in women than those generated by the naturalist paradigm. In fact, the representation of the psychological present is valued more positively in the sense that it has assumed the effort of combating all the social obstacles (as is the case of gender) which appear through historical (patriarchal) proceedings and which have disturbed the established natural course in history of progress towards sex equality or the emancipation of Women. Therefore, the female forgers of this feminist History are constituted as true heroines of humanity, which implicitly raises them to a position superior to other mortals, among which there are women who do not identify themselves with this discourse.

On the consequences for the public and private lives of women
of feminist constructions of gender as a category
Feminism as an objectivization of history of women in general, of which the final consequence is its scientific correlate in psychology, is detrimental to the idea of the past as a social experience and social memory (see also Haug, this volume), acting as a possible condition of resistance and reflexivity with respect to the present, and as a guide to the future. This alternative notion of experience as a social

memory introduces a dimension of reflexivity which problematizes the idea of experience as immediacy or origin of knowledge. It necessitates setting out a policy in personal experience which is important for political action towards the 'outside world'. If we try to integrate the idea of experience with that of social memory, it is because social memory is not only implicit in discursive practices but is also present in the body and remains there through its movements, although under another name.

The imaginary aspect of the body, emotions and everything linked to 'what is neither rational nor discursive' has been very important in feminist rhetoric and has given legitimacy to the concept of experience as immediacy. However, beyond the culture/nature distinction, the body cannot be interpreted as possessing some kind of 'essence', but rather as representing a particular recipient of social subjection in which we must intervene in order to weaken the different forms of domination:

> Body is the bearer of individual memory. It has registered the gesture, the word, the 'mother' tongue, the glance, and trust. It has responded with its ability to smile, to cry, to enjoy. It has experienced support or help-lessness. It has suffered fright, mistrust, overprotection, rigidity. It has recorded both the hint of primary attachments and the social bonds built up from the family, the school, the 'others', with both the present and the missing persons. These relationships have imprinted this body with shocks, mistreatment, suspicions, cruelty, or through smiles, with tenderness, warmth, caresses. (Lira, 1995: 10)

As Elisabeth Lira indicates, this social memory registered in the body must be resituated in social and political contexts if we wish to transform it to be able to intervene in the established present: in order to forget, it is necessary to remember. This re-meaning also supposes a distancing from the discursive and corporal subjection to the present favoured by the objectivized history constructed for feminism.

In short, the ethical and political dimension of discursive actions is defined by the way the different social actors experience, narrate and negotiate the meaning of the local present from their social memories and not through the objectivist narrations which exist a priori, drawn up from the present. We thus accept the 'implosion' of the gender category by 'considering that the technologies of gender produce discursive fields, multiple discourses which produce the subject 'woman' in a variety of different ways not excluding antagonistic, transverse discourses which contradict each other' (Correa et al., 1994: 41–3).

The experience of the present may be subject to a rewriting of the past and projection in the future (Vázquez, 1995). However, at the same time social memory (meaningful past) modulates the very experience of the present and its projection into the future. Thus the socio-historical processes which produce the social reality deal with a paradoxical relationship between discursive practice and psychosocial reality, in the sense that the discourses of feminist psychology, drawn up for social change, can open the door to new forms of domination by repeating the same story in another way. On the one hand, the psychosocial experience of the present, as it is immediate though subject to objectivized History, acts both as producer and rigidifier of everything psychosocial. On the other hand, it is through discursive practices which distance us from the present by virtue of meaningful past referents (social memory), and possible experiences of disidentification with the objectivized present, that true social change is possible.

According to this account, the project of feminist psychology would therefore be registered in a movement of domination through the exercise of production and sclerotization of everything psychosocial, with specific consequences both in daily private life through psychological discourse on maternity, affection and sexuality, and in public through the projection of the psychological aptitudes of professional women. This, for instance, is the case of assertiveness which, is attributed as lacking in women dominated by the patriarchal order (see Crawford, this volume). This is a process of inclusion and exclusion created from the new identity of women.

For example, with respect to 'professional' work and the participation of women in this area, María Milagros López describes the evolution of feminist rhetoric, which obviously has its correlative form in psychological science through the projection of different psychological aptitudes in new women, 'the appropriation of a discourse which was not actually directed at us, but which then came to define the ethics of domestic work and which finally is embraced without distances' (López, 1994: 133). This, as Madeleine Román (1994) has indicated, has led to a comparison between paid work and value, and has become the 'moral judge of the value of people and, furthermore, of their capacity as social subjects and agents' (Correa et al., 1994: 37).

In fact, this narrative on work turned into an enormous discursive flood:

> to transform the restlessness of women into a search for jobs was to find a great store of feelings and moralities, maybe the largest that feminists have found at any time in the 19th and 20th centuries. It even moved conservatives out of the language of feelings into the language of employment and work. However, the result was also a simplification of the claims of women and a dilution of matters to help the situation, to see

the restrictions as leisure, to associate purpose with work, liberty with the obligations of a paid job. This suggests how easily the rhetoric of the ethics of work bogs down distinctions and, by blurring meanings, becomes a common point of tyranny. (Rodgers, 1978: 209)

Moreover, the exquisite postures derived from this moralization of work have many consequences: as Nydza Correa (Correa et al., 1994) indicates, they result in the impeding of alliances with women, who are constituted as receivers of welfare state benefits, or with the women who continue to live in an even more traditional context, which gives rise to further relationships of domination. In these cases, the very key to reading feminism as linear progress towards sex equality, brings about the attribution of a 'non-feminist' present to women who live in another way, which is delegitimized because it is identified with the past 'which has not been overcome' and is considered as alienating gender. It is this process that opens the door to new power relationships in the area of feminist knowledge.

In this sense, it is clearly desirable to produce alternative discourses of isolated units and contexts emerging in specific situations which do not have the creation of identities as a purpose. To do this we need to disrupt the dichotomies which fix, regulate and produce everything psychosocial through objectivizations of history, by making use of discursive practices based neither on knowledge (as the power of Reason), nor on Emotion (as the power of the body). Rather, we need to integrate them and give them new meaning in the light of the different social memories.

In conclusion, identity as a common point always has a tyrannical dimension in the sense that it subjects the present and marginalizes and silences acts of disidentification. It therefore makes it impossible for social actors in a certain context to negotiate meanings and change the social order. However, it is an arduous task to undo the path trodden by historical identities, as forgers of world representations (either conservative or critical) and also reified in individual bodies and minds. It would mean renaming them as such to remember, both in general and individually, how they emerged, through a costly exercise in social memory. This reminder, which, to a certain extent and paradoxically, would mean 'forgetting' the present, is the condition for enabling a resistance exercised without domination to open cracks in, and for, everything social with different views of the future. Putting into practice these processes of social memory, understood as forms of resistance, allows us to deconstruct thoroughly fixed theories of identity in such a way as to articulate the project of deconstruction with the reconstruction of a form of femininity liberated from the operations of gender and sexism. But the most important consequence is that it enables us at the same time to put into effect a real feminist practice that does not undermine or annul itself. Such awaits the arena of feminist psychology.

References

Correa, N., Figueroa Sarriera, H.J., M.M. López and Román, M. (1994) '"Las mujeres son, son, son": implosión y recomposición de la categoría', in H. Figueroa Sarriera, M.M. López and M. Román (eds), *Más allá de la bella (in)diferencia: revisión post-feminista y otras escrituras posibles*. Río Piedras, Puerto Rico: Publicaciones Puertoriqueñas. pp. 34–50.

de Lauretis, Teresa (1987) 'The technology of gender', in T. de Lauretis (ed.), *Technologies of Gender*. Bloomington, IN: Indiana University Press. pp. 1–30.

Figueroa Sarriera, Heidi, López, Maria Milagro and Román, Madeleine (eds) (1994) *Más allá de la bella (in)diferencia: revisión post-feminista y otras escrituras posibles*. Río Piedras, Puerto Rico: Publicaciones Puertoriqueñas.

Foucault, Michel (1976) *Historia de la sexualidad*. Vol. I. Madrid: Siglo XXI.

Foucault, Michel (1994) *Hermeneutica del sujeto*. Madrid: La Piqueta.

Fox Keller, Evelyn (1985) *Reflection on Gender and Science*. London: Yale University Press.

Fox Keller, Evelyn (1994) 'La paradoja de la subjetividad científica', in D. Schnitman (ed.), *Nuevos paradigmas, cultura y subjetividad*. Barcelona: Paidós. pp. 143–73.

Guillaumin, Colette (1992) *Sexe, race et pratique du pouvoir: l'idée de nature*. Paris: Côté-femmes.

Harding, Sandra (1991) *Whose Science? Whose Knowledge?* Milton Keynes: Open University Press.

Harré, Rom and Stearns, Peter (1995) *Discursive Psychology in Practice*. London: Sage.

Hekman, Susan (1990) *Gender and Knowledge: Elements of a Post-modern Feminism*. Cambridge: Polity Press.

Hyde, J. Sh. (1991) *Psicología femenina: la otra mitad de la experiencia humana*. Madrid: Morata.

Ibáñez, Tomás (1989) 'La psicología social como dispositivo deconstruccionista', in T. Ibáñez (ed.), *El conocimiento de la realidad social*. Barcelona: Sendai. pp. 109–34.

Ibáñez, Tomás (1994) *Psicología social construccionista*. Mexico. Universidad de Guadalajara.

Latour, Bruno (1987) *Science in Action*. Milton Keynes: Open University Press.

Lira, Elisabeth (1995) 'Remembering: passing back through the heart', unpublished manuscript.

López, María Milagros (1994) 'Feminisimo, dependencia y estado benefactor: relaciones de desasosiego en la sociedad post-trabajo', in H. Figueroa Sarriera, M.M. López and M. Román (eds), *Más allá de la bella (in)diferencia: revisión post-feminista y otras escrituras posibles*. Rio Piedras, Puerto Rico: Publicaciones Puertoriqueñas. pp. 124–39.

Nicholson, L. (1990) *Feminism/Postmodernism*. London: Routledge.

Pujal, Margot (1992) 'Poder, saber, naturaleza – la triangulación "masculina" de la mujer y su deconstrucción: análisis de una invención psicosocial'. PhD dissertation, Barcelona: Publicacions Universitat Autonoma de Barcelona.

Pujal, Margot (1994) 'La marca del género en la encrucijada entre subjetividad e intersubjetividad', *Iztapalaga: revista de ciencias sociales y humanidades*, Año 14, No. 35: Mexico: UAM. pp. 131–42.

Pujal, Margot and Vázquez, Félix (1992) 'La política difusa: "el nombre de la mujer" discurso objetivo o construcción del discurso', *Boletín de Psicología*, No. 34: pp. 124–43.

Rodgers, D. (1978) *The Work Ethic in Early Industrial America, 1850–1920*. Chicago: University of Chicago Press.

Román, Madeleine (1994) '"Préndeme fuego si quieres que te olvide. . ." del delito pasional a lo pasional del delito', in H. Figueroa Sarriera, M.M. López and M. Román (eds), *Más allá de la bella (in)diferencia: revisión post-feminista y otras escrituras posibles*. Río Piedras, Puerto Rico: Publicaciones Puertorriqueñas. pp. 152–63.

Rorty, Richard (1979) *Philosophy and the Mirror of Nature*. Princeton, NJ: Princeton University Press.

Rose, Nicholas (1989) *Governing the Soul: Technologies of Human Subjectivity*. London: Routledge.

Sampson, Edward (1993) *Celebrating the Other: A Dialogic Account of Human Nature*. London: Harvester Wheatsheaf.

Sau, Victoria (1992) *Otras lecciones de psicologia*. Bilbao: Maite Canal.

Sebastiani, Chiara (1991) 'L'atto sovversivo del ricordare: Memoria, tradizione, ideologia', in P. Jedlowski and M. Rampazi (eds), *Il senso del pasato: per una sociaologia della memoria*. Milan: Franco Angeli. pp. 43–9.

Vázquez, Félix (1995) 'Memoria colectiva y gobernabilidad: la transición política desde un gobierno autoritario'. Unpublished manuscript.

Wilkinson, Sue (ed.) (1986) *Feminist Social Psychology: Developing Theory and Practice*. Milton Keynes: Open University Press.

Wittgenstein, L. (1953) *Investigaciones filosóficas*. Barcelona: Editorial Crítica.

Zavala, Iris M. (1993) 'Una poética del imaginario social', *Anthropos*, No. 145: 36–40.

3

Rethinking Role Theory and its Aftermath

Heidi J. Figueroa Sarriera

The assumptions of Role Theory (RT) have guided research agendas across the social sciences, particularly within sociology, social psychology, anthropology and feminist studies. Since the 1960s, the paradigm associated with the notion of 'sex roles' in feminist studies has been the key reference point for any research that was to be considered 'politically correct feminism' within academic circles and the militant-feminist political scene. This chapter will dispute the usefulness of this paradigm by developing the following argument: that the epistemological basis and political implications of RT represent both a continuity and a discontinuity with respect to the project of modernity. Notwithstanding how RT has been subject to criticism, it is important to discuss the particular tensions produced for RT within the problematic of modernity/postmodernity because it gives us a more dynamic – and sometimes paradoxical – image of a theory in its epistemological and political domains. However, in an attempt to settle this score, I suggest that the basic presumptions of Role Theory – viewed within the contemporary postmodern context – have clearly reached their limits as social psychological analytical tools.

With this in mind and using the conceptualizations of G.H. Mead as an exemplar of Role Theory, I will explore what these presumptions are, take up some of the epistemological and political implications of the construction of the category 'role', and, more specifically, consider how this category has been incorporated into feminist research as 'sex roles'. Throughout this account I will seek to establish a dialogue of sorts between certain ideas associated with the debate on postmodernity and some of the modernist assumptions of the feminist psychological research agenda.

Discerning Role Theory

G.H. Mead's work has figured prominently in the development of feminist work on gender through his general account of social roles.

Developing his formulations early in the twentieth century, he is considered the originator of RT. This theory has been helpful, for example, in providing an alternative theoretical base from which one might question the reduction of the concept 'personality' to a mere set of traits which has been dominant for so long in psychosocial research. Mead, on the other hand, was also interested in explaining the self-conscious formation of individuality. According to him, this formation occurs through the adoption of the roles assumed by different people that surround the child during the process of her or his development. Eventually, the system or subsystem of social relations that corresponds to her or him are ultimately and completely internalized in accordance with a socially determined position. Social roles are defined, then, as a set of activities, qualities and types of behaviour associated with specific social positions. These positions exist independent of the individual and are part and parcel of the socio-cultural structure. Thus the child does not internalize society in an abstract sense, but reproduces within her or himself historically determined, concrete social structures. For Mead, this 'introjection' of roles is inherent to the spawning of self-consciousness, to the person itself. The presence of the self, although already outlined by social relations, only becomes possible by way of the 'fixation' of the person to the social structure, through her or his adoption of different social roles.

For Mead, it is the mediation of language that makes the presence of the person possible. He believes that a distinguishing characteristic of the person resides in the ability of the organism's psyche to perceive itself as an object in relation to itself. In terms of Hegel's paradigm, the 'self' only becomes possible in relation to an 'other'. The key mechanism through which this becomes viable is linked to the adoption of roles that are always imbricated in language. Through the adoption of a 'generalized other' a self-conscious individual is formed and situated within a given social context.

Mead, however, indulges in a fetishised representation of language, conceiving this in univocal and coherent terms. The 'other', also conceived of in these terms, serves as the key source of possible social roles. The failure to consider the fact that this 'other', as well as language, is actually configured by a multiplicity of voices that are not always in harmony or coherent, facilitates the introduction of the category 'person' from a perspective thoroughly circumscribed by modernist parameters. It should come as no surprise then that Gino Geramani, in his Introduction to the Spanish language version of Mead's *The Spirit, Person, and Society* (1965), makes special note of the strong influence that Mead's theory has had in the development of social psychology, particularly in the experimental studies of the psychology of the 'self' of Sherif and Cantril.

The mediation of language in the development process of the child is presented as organized into two stages: the 'playing stage' and the 'sport stage'. In the sport stage, the child adopts the role of the 'other', which can be that of a person or an animal that has by one way or another entered her or his life. The child 'is one thing at one moment and another at another moment, what she or he is at a given moment does not determine what they will be in the following moment' (Mead, 1965: 175). On the other hand, the sport stage implies a greater degree of stability and organization. In this stage, a 'conversion' process occurs. The 'others', who are required in order to carry out a shared activity, are internalized by the person so that the organized activity can be carried out and the determination of the success of the performance of the role can be measured in relation to the realization of the overall activity.

In contrast to this scheme, but extending the metaphors of RT, the so-called postmodern self would seem to resemble the child in the playing stage, on account of its indeterminacy, its connections to a protean multiplicity of contingent social actions, much more so than it would the organized child of the sport stage. The organized child implies stability and presupposes a teleological premise; that of a successful performance of social roles that can be measured in degrees of efficiency and productivity within a given social system. It is not in the least bit surprising, then, that so many studies in social psychology have incorporated a concept of 'roles' that relies on quantitative methods manifested in attitude and opinion scales which rest upon an inconspicuous productivist premise of consistency and efficiency.[1] Included here are those of a feminist persuasion, such as instruments like the Sex Role Stereotype Questionnaire (SRSQ), the Sex Role Inventory of Sandra Bem (BSRI), and the Attitudes Towards Women Scale (AWS). (For a critical examination of the utilization of measurement in the research on attitudes, see Martín-Baró, 1985; and Potter and Wetherell, 1987, among others.)

However, one can argue particularly in post-industrial societies that, given the destablilization of the 'fixation' process of the person to social structures and the crises of the concept of identity, the 'child' of Mead bears a striking resemblance to the postmodern 'adult'. If this is so, it would be equally plausible to propose that his theories prefigured, at least in the context of the social sciences, what is now referred to as the postmodern condition. For Mead, the 'self' does not appear as a mere container of essentialist traits (such as those associated with the personality, or with the notion of reason), but is perceived to be constituted by intersubjective relations that are played out within specific socio-historic contexts. The process of the constitution of the subject actually occurs on the outskirts of the general social framework.

But the interest of Mead in conserving the individuality of the person through the problematic category of the 'self' – conceived of as an agent of historical change – also preserved some clearly modernist assumptions with respect to the creativity and the promotion of the transformation of the social environment. In contrast to this, under the postmodern condition, the subject is constituted within a permanent process of displacement (Lyotard, 1989); it is not conceived of as an agent of history, nor as the bearer of a given identity (whether this be as a worker, student, man or woman, etc.) due to its fixation to a given set of social structures. The postmodern subject is not the centred subject of the 'knowing self', but assumes nebulous contours which render the principles of prediction, characteristic of the positivist logic guided by the imperatives of social engineering, completely inoperative.[2]

Both aspects – situating identity formation within social contexts and the image of the 'self' as an agent of historical change – are seductive appeals of RT in feminist research. Nevertheless, as we will see, the application of RT in specific social contexts can sometimes function as a technology of power that supports official policies, and represents and constrains women's political actions in acceptable ways.

In the next section I move on to analyse how RT has been used to explore gender difference, and its functions and implications for feminist social psychological research.

Gender Role Research in Question

The introduction of a recently published book on the development of gender roles includes a section that merits particular attention. I reproduce this extract as the basis for subsequent analysis:

> Some years ago I was interviewing nine-year-old students about stories as part of a project on children's writing. I had just finished one interview and was making some quick notes when the next child came into the office. I looked up, and an odd thing happened: I could not tell whether the child was a boy or a girl. The usual cues were not there: The child's hair was trimmed in a sort of pudding-bowl style, not really long but not definitely short either. The child was dressed in a gender neutral outfit of jeans, sneakers, and a loose t-shirt, like most of the children at the school. The name on the interview permission slip was 'Cory', which did not clarify matters much as it could be either a boy's or girl's name. Still puzzled, I began the interview and found myself becoming increasingly

frustrated at not knowing Cory's sex. I quickly realized how many unconscious assumptions I usually made about boys and girls; for example, that a girl would probably like a particular story about a horse and be willing to answer a few extra questions about it, or that a boy would probably start to get restless after a certain point and I would have to work a bit harder to keep his attention. After the interview, I went out to watch the class on the playground at recess. Sometimes Cory played with the boys, other times with the girls, and when the class was called to come inside, Cory stood in line between a girl and a boy; no clues there. There seemed to be no way to tell from Cory's behavior whether Cory was a boy or girl, and to this day I don't know the answer. (Beal, 1994: 3)

What is of particular interest here is that this author, after this introduction, hastily points out the case of Cory (which in fact appears in the book under the subtitle: 'The Cory Incident') as precisely 'that incident', something unusual and unquieting, since each child had displayed that they had learned from an early age the roles associated with their gender. She immediately proceeds to define gender roles:

By *gender roles* we mean the behaviors that are expected of males and females within a particular society, including dress and appearance, work and leisure activities, obligations within the family, skills, and social behavior. Part of the process for young children is to learn to be male or female, to master the behaviors that are expected for their sex, just as they learn to speak a particular language. (Beal, 1994: 4; original emphasis)

Although later she points out that these roles are more flexible than they appear to be, this is seen as due to the distinct ways that different cultures may define feminine and masculine gender roles. Consequently, the indeterminate nature of the 'Cory incident' does not lead the author towards an exploration of the contemporary forms in which the boundaries of gender roles are becoming much more elusive and fluid, and even less so towards an understanding of the a priori adjudication of these roles.

One could point out, and rightfully so, that the author is not necessarily inscribed within a *feminist* perspective. However, the a priori acceptance and adjudication of sex roles and stereotypes is representative of an old tradition in feminist social psychological research, as Condor (1986) has shown. Condor, in her methodological analysis of the research on sex roles and stereotypes in the feminist psychosocial literature, has argued that to the degree an author assumes beforehand certain premises with respect to what constitutes being 'traditional' (for example, it is often implied that being 'traditional' is the opposite of being 'feminist'), she or he is alluding to processes of objectification. This methodological critique also suggests that many of the scales used have been constructed from a feminist perspective whose political agenda revolves mainly around issues pertaining to equal rights, so that they often adopt masculine standards.

I suggest that Beal implicitly establishes semantic equivalencies between 'feminism' and what one might call 'first-wave feminism' whose key area of struggle was the equal rights project. Consequently, the premises which serve as the basis on which to interpret and mediate the data of the research express a tendency which would situate them within a social engineering perspective, particularly as this relates to the insertion of women within the realm of waged labour. The following assertion by Condor would tend to support this notion: more generally, opinion statements which supposedly reflect traditional orientations tend to focus on the inability of women to perform male roles, or to hold powerful positions outside the home. For example, 13 of the 18 'traditional' items in Brogan and Kutner's (1976) SRO scale are concerned with 'career', as are 11 of the 17 items on Mason and Bumpass's (1975) SRI scale (Condor, 1986: 104).

In so far as the objective of feminist research has been to discern the ways in which sex roles in particular societies have perpetuated the subordination of women, this research has produced a re-articulation of social engineering discourse. In other words, too often feminist research has been inscribed within an equal rights project that presses for the incorporation of women to the social world on the same terms as men. This research is oriented towards the identification of those factors that contribute to prejudicial views against women and that hinder women's incorporation on equal terms, with respect to men, to diverse social areas: the domestic realm, or those of labour, politics, public life, and so on.

One can note various presumptions that, irrespective of their intentions, locate the overall perspective of these analyses firmly within an agenda complicit with that of social psycholological research in general, an agenda which can hardly lay claim to feminist priorities. In the first place, this research is characterized by a commitment to technocracy in order to assure the optimal functioning of the system rather than careful reflection upon undermining the assumptions on which the present social order exists. Secondly, these presumptions are also characterized by a reproduction of modes of thought expressed in terms of dichotomies meant to articulate spaces of asymmetrical power relations. They do not destabilize the social assumptions upon which such asymmetries are mounted, such as those that produce categories like 'masculine' versus 'feminine'.

Psychologizing/Naturalizing the Social Order

The psychology, as well as the sociology, of sexual difference has produced the following dichotomies. The first is the 'individual/society' binary (Hollway, 1989). It derives from the premise that the subject (understood as an individual, meaning, as an autonomous being in relation to its context, a self-contained entity) is a coherently constituted entity that enters into a series of exchanges with its environment. In this way, the environment, according to the interactionist perspectives, can transform the patterns of behaviour of the individual. For example, let us examine the following questions: How does the 'dual shift' day affect women? How does marriage affect the possibility of success in a woman's professional life? Or, as a classic text on women and sex roles asks:

1   What are the effects of sexism or prejudicial attitudes upon women and men today? How do these limit options for both sexes?
2   What is the reason for differences between women and men? Do these differences have a biological basis or are they based solely upon the values and teachings of our culture?
3   What are the psychological effects of traditional sex roles upon women and men? How are these sex roles changing? What will be the effects of these changes on the lives of women and men?
4   What factors serve to maintain traditional sex roles? Will these factors show changes? (Frieze et al., 1978: 1)

These questions, in great measure, assume that the social is constituted by social roles, which are in turn assumed to be coherent and unitary, and that the tensions arise when these roles confront the psyche of the individual. For example, when a women is inscribed in several roles simultaneously the question is seen to be about how this multiplicity of roles will have a psychological impact on her. In other words, how will the adoption of a particular role (of a wife, let us say) enter into conflict with another (that of a manager of a bank, for instance)? The roles are reduced to socially determined categories – given a certain social ordering – and they transform the lives of women and the possibility of their integration to this order. Here, there is no intervention that would call into question the aforementioned social order and the social assumptions upon which the said order rests. In this sense, to the degree that such assumptions are guided by the task of producing egalitarian sex roles within the existing social order, they clearly reflect the hegemonic paradigm of modern psychosocial research. By way of contrast, like Bauman's (1989) proposals for sociology, a postmodern psychology seeks to destablilize the aspirations that would contribute to a project of social engineering and emphasize a critical analysis of social discourses that claim to define what counts as 'reality'. Such a project would analyse how these discourses instil what Foucault (1985) called 'regimes of truth' which serve to cancel out or render invisible alternative interpretations of reality.

It is not surprising to note, then, the popularity of the analyses of sex roles that form part of the 'theoretical' justification of different projects of psychosocial intervention which do not reflect upon how such practices constitute part of the framework of the strategic plans of the state developed either behind the backs, or at the expense, of women. (This occurs whether women are the interventionists or the intervened, since as Riley (1988) points out, after the nineteenth century, women emerged as a sociological and psychological category given their proximity to the order of 'the social' in a dual sense: as agents of the social – intervening at different levels – and as the objects of social reforms.)

In Puerto Rico the area of feminist psychology does not exist as such, but we have a strong strand of (psychological and other) research that adopts feminist positions; CERES – Centro de Estudios, Recursos y Servicios de la Mujer – is one such attempt. Most of this work uses the category of role to explain women's 'conditions', especially as related to sexuality and mental health problems. Burgos and Díaz (1990) – in a paper published by CERES – dealing with sexuality and Puerto Rican culture concluded that more research must be carried out about women's sexuality in order to clarify women's roles and participation in our society. These authors claim that the high statistical rate of anxiety in women living in the metropolitan area could be related to sexual insatisfaction. For these authors Puerto Rican culture and sexuality are linked to our colonial situation (Spanish colonialism and from 1898 to the present, US colonialism). But in doing so, they reproduced pathologizing discourse of the colonial biopolitical power.

> Puertorican people have lived almost five centuries of colonialism. This colonial situation has implied a lack of decisional power which is reflected in the imposition of norms, habits, laws and living styles; low self-steem and dependence in men and women in all life areas, sexuality included. (Author's translation of Burgos and Díaz, 1990: 4)

Further, it is interesting to notice that in other research subscribed by one of the above authors the same mental health statistics were used to link anxiety with housewives' roles. 'In fact, mental health statistics in Metropolitan Area external clinics show that anxiety disorders are the major problem within women and that the majority of these women are housewives' (author's translation of Burgos and Colberg, 1990: 21). Most of this kind of research ends with suggestions to professionals serving the female population, or with general ideas about workshops on employment, sexual harassment or domestic violence laws and/or common sense techniques of self-steem and stress management.

The Galateo Project was developed in Puerto Rico by a Puerto Rican females research group and follows the above illustrated strand. In Bravo et al.'s (1994) account, the project was made up of women who were female-heads-of-households of the public housing complex known as Galateo in Río Grande, Puerto Rico, who demonstrated an interest in achieving a certain level of schooling in order to link themselves to the world of waged labour. With respect to this project the authors make the following assertions:

> This project is proof of how the government responds through one of its agencies, the Right to Work Administration, to the development of all sectors of society and exemplifies its faithful achievement of the guarantee of constitutional rights for all. (Author's translation of Bravo et al., 1994: 75)

Further on they state:

> This project has responded to the need that the Puerto Rican welfare system has in developing alternative programs of integrated social services for women and their families which guarantee an adequate response to the necessities of the residents of the poor communities of Puerto Rico. (Author's translation of Bravo et al., 1994: 78)

But, what is the Puerto Rican welfare system? Who defines it and from the perspective of what social space? It is not a question of denying the possibility that projects such as these could provide a space through which to discern certain problems that affect the lives of women in a given community. Rather, it is a matter of denouncing the lack of critical reflection on the part of those agents on how such practices are 'happily' inserted within state-sponsored social designs for social engineering. Michel Foucault has shown that bio-politics constitute effects of power upon the body which determine the boundaries between the 'normal' and the 'pathological', defining and redefining the production of a disciplinary regime of the body within the broader social fabric. Drawing on these ideas, the functionalist approach which has characterized the incorporation of RT into feminist research has contributed further to the conceptual failure to question the political dimensions of community intervention.

Secondly, in recent years, there has been a proliferation of research on so-called minority communities in the USA (Hispanic, Asian,

African-American, and others). Much of this research rests on the premise that there exists a clearly established and differentiated idea of what constitutes feminine gender roles. In some cases, there have been attempts to exploit these 'understandings' of gender roles in order to obtain specific objectives. For example, in a research project geared towards the prevention of the spread of AIDS, developed by the Cultureline Corporation, titled *Hispanics and HIV: Strategies and Tactics for Education/Prevention*, it is suggested that the attitudes associated with 'marianismo' among Hispanic women should be exploited in order to design campaigns of prevention. 'Marianismo' refers to a type of women's gender role that values her role as a mother and protector of her home and family (alluding to the Virgin Mary). The research recommends that equivalences be drawn between the advocacy of safe sex and what it means to be a good mother in Hispanic communities.

It would certainly be difficult to say that such a view rests on feminist assumptions. What is quite clear, however, is how the idea of gender roles forms part of a discursive strategy of knowledge-power that, in this last case, relocates women as the pivotal point within the family or the domestic sphere while functioning primarily to insert feminist discourse (and its agents) within hegemonic social engineering. This process reached its heyday with the institutionalization of feminist discourse in governmental politics in the 1970s through special offices, commissions and programmes that work to regulate women, as well as feminist politics, within the structures of state, law and order.

Gender Roles as Limiting Conditions

The discipline of psychology has proven itself to be most obstinate with respect to reflecting on its own political dimensions, and reluctant to engage in feminist debates in a manner that would make these central to the discipline (Ibáñez, 1993; Squire, 1989). It comes as no surprise at all that the internal mechanisms of the discipline, reacting in response to the political pressures of feminist debates, have dealt with these issues by circumscribing their development within specific spaces of discussion where gender relations are viewed almost exclusively from the perspective of the conflict between gender roles. On an epistemological and methodological plane the discipline is quick to provide the categorical assumptions which facilitate simple translations of these debates within positivist and neo-positivist parameters. On a political plane, it provides the conceptual framework that permits a re-articulation and recycling of conspicuous technologies of power to be effected over groups of women, while it simultaneously assures the administrative and governmental capacities of the state.

Secondly, research takes as its starting assumption that masculine and feminine gender roles exist (again, in accordance with dichotomous thinking), that they are a given in social life, that they work in opposition to one another, and that the feminine roles are subordinated to masculine ones. What do we really stand to gain with this approach? The research is geared towards understanding the impact of these roles on the lives of women and towards a more equitable distribution of these roles, particularly as they relate to the domestic-familial sphere.

I propose, on the other hand, a type of justice which partakes of a very particular interpretation of what 'social equity' is. What is lost in assuming this approach? On one hand, we become limited in our capacity to approximate ourselves to the contradictory ways in which these supposed roles are constructed in contemporary societies; on the other, we lose sight of the contradictory relations that women (and men) encounter with these roles.

In the postmodern era, the centre of social life is no longer production but in fact revolves around consumption. This has brought with it the commodification of so-called domestic chores as can be noted in the proliferation of 'fast-food' restaurants, laundries, home-delivery of food, childcare services, and a marked tendency to enrol children in educational institutions at a very early age (many 'pre-school' institutions accept children from the ages of 1–4 years old). This last tendency is clearly visible in Puerto Rico, not only among the economically disadvantaged, made possible through social programmes like Head Start, but among the more affluent sectors of society as well, through the plethora of Montessori, Piagetian and other private schools which are characterized by odd philosophical mixtures concentrated in the metropolitan area and on its outskirts. The resultant emerging life-forms seem to suggest a malleability of so-called social roles that are ever more distant from a stable and fixed matrix of a shared social understanding of what these roles might be (indeed, one could go so far as to question if such a matrix ever existed).

In the third place, it is assumed explicitly and at times implicitly, that there is a distinction between sex and gender (see also Chapters 2 and 4). The first category is viewed as a given, as a product of nature; it is, plainly put, what is anatomically and biologically observable, reduced to the presence of either a vagina or a penis. The second, that is, gender, is considered a social construct which is nonetheless ultimately based on that which is viewed as natural, on one's sex. This sex/gender dichotomy has been called into question by recent feminist debates that have shown how a heterosexual normativity has been reproduced within feminist discourse (see e.g. Butler, 1992). This happens to the degree that one accepts sexual differentiation as something that is naturally given, since this privileges reproductive functions as a regulative axis of the construction of sexual difference. In turn, such assumptions inevitably lead to an identification with, and reproduction of, heterosexuality (the penis–vagina union type of sexual relation) as the privileged norm for sexuality, instead of challenging or destablilizing such assumptions which clearly imply the reinforcement of daily oppression for a considerable sector of women and men with other sexual preferences.

Beyond Unitary Binaries

We could, in fact, assume a more radical position and state that feminist discourses about sex roles which are predicated on the supposed distinction between sex and gender (which is, incidentally, a modification of the nature/culture dichotomy) have become, if not resolutely then at least tendentiously, irrelevant. This would certainly seem to be the case within the context of a postmodern condition characterized by dubious bio-technical 'advances' in reproduction that have widened the breach between sexual activity and reproductive activity. Notwithstanding the hyperbolic fantasies of the world of cinema and science fiction, the eventual separation of these activities has become increasingly viable. Presently, reproduction without the mediation of sexual activity between a couple is plainly feasible. In fact, the only sexual practice that stubbornly remains has been reduced to the solitary masturbatory practice of a nameless ejaculator whose only comfort are the cold, sanitized walls of a clinic restroom, where reproductive problems are nicely tended to. Adele Clarke (1995) shows how this separation already forms part of the graphic and discursive representations of medical and bio-technical tests. Thus sexuality becomes an extremely fluid notion which requires, perhaps, new axes of control, like, for instance, a text of contamination, an epidemic, a fatal virus (see also Figueroa Sarriera, 1994).

I will end by expressing my commitment to a re-articulation of research practices that assume a postmodern sensibility, and advocate a new research agenda framed in what one might call postmodern feminist social psychology. Smart (1993) proposes a practice geared towards research and critique that challenges the regimes of truth associated with multiple power relations mobilized and deployed by sociology. Similarly, we can challenge not only the regimes of truth associated with the asymmetries of inter- and intrasubjective masculine/feminine distinctions, but a much broader array of relations of power. To do this in psychology, it would be necessary to rid ourselves of our modernist baggage: in particular, the commitment to social technologies that order and rule social life and the positivist assumption that the social fact – as an object of study – has an existence which is absolutely external to the discursive practices which produce it (like psychology, for instance).

In order to return to Mead's primary intuition of the simultaneous social and indeterminate dimensions of the constitution of the person, I suggest the following precautions. First, that we should move away from the insistence on the discovery of coherent and univocal versions of gender difference. This would shift our emphasis towards discerning the multiplicity of axes around which social meanings related to supposed gender roles are constructed. Secondly, such a move would highlight how social meanings are not only plural, but even contradictory, and that these only become partially fixed within the precarious contingency of a specific social moment. Thirdly, within this exercise a postmodern psychology would imply, among other things, a commitment to question, challenge and destabilize social institutions – such as gender roles and psychology – and all discursive practices whose aim is the production of asymmetrical relations of power by way of the construction of identities that facilitate greater social control and governability.

Notes

I would like to thank my friend Miguel Gómez for his valuable work in the English translation of this chapter.

1 For Lyotard, Goffman's work, as in, for instance, *The Presentation of the Person in Everyday Life*, (1971), is oriented towards the antagonistic aspects of language where 'to speak is to fight' and where the '"self"' does not amount to much, but is not isolated, it is, rather, trapped in a tightly woven tapestry of social relations which are currently more complex and mobile than ever before' (Lyotard, 1989: 27 and 39).

2 In other accounts, this subject develops within a new sensibility devoted to a 'lust for life', that would seem to be vindicated by popular Puerto Rican sayings like 'sarna con gusto no pica, y si pica no mortifica' [roughly translated as, If the pain is too pleasing it doesn't hurt, and if it merely hurts it surely is not going to kill you] and 'a mí me matan pero yo gozo' [I know that this could kill me, but at least I'll die enjoying it], and also in what Maffesoli (1984) has called 'contemporary Dionysian practices'. Some examples of these practices would be popular festivals, sexual communities of all types, popular gatherings, bohemian life-styles and other spaces of social contention. Maffesoli denominates these tendencies towards gregariousness, which arises as a practice in contention with the individualism of the project of modernity, as 'new tribal socialities'.

60 Deconstructing Feminist Psychology

References

Bauman, Z. (1989) 'Sociological responses to postmodernity', *Thesis Eleven*, No. 23.

Beal, C.R. (1994) *Boys and Girls: The Development of Gender Roles.* New York: McGraw-Hill.

Bravo, M., Colberg, E.M., Martínez, L.M., Martínez, M.S. and Seijo, L.R. (1994) *Genero y mujeres puertoriquenas.* Centro de Investigaciones Sociales, Universidad de Puerto Rico, Recinto de Río Piedras.

Brogan, D. and Kutner, N. (1976) 'Measuring sex roles orientation: a normative approach', *Journal of Marriage and the Family*, 38: 31–40.

Burgos, Nilsa M. and Colberg, Eileen (1990) *Madres soltelras con jefatura de familia: características en el hogar y en el trabajo.* Centro de Investigaciones Sociales, Universidad de Puerto Rico, Recinto de Río Piedras.

Burgos, Nilsa M. and Díaz, Yolanda I. (1990) *La sexualidad: análisis exploratorio en la cultura puertorriqueña.* CERES, Centro de Investigaciones Sociales, Universidad de Puerto Rico, Recinto de Río Piedras.

Butler, J. (1992) *Gender Trouble: Feminism and the Subversion of Identity.* New York/London: Routledge.

Clarke, A. (1995) 'Modernity, post-modernity and reproductive processes (1890–1993), or mommy, where do cyborgs come from anyway?', in Chris Hables Gray, Heidi J. Figueroa Sarriera and Steven Mentor (eds), *The Cyborg Handbook.* New York/London: Routledge. pp. 139–55.

Condor, S. (1986) 'Sex role beliefs and "traditional" women: feminist and intergroup perspectives', in Sue Wilkinson (ed.), *Feminist Social Psychology: Developing Theory and Practice.* Philadelphia: Open University Press. pp. 97–118.

Figueroa Sarriera, H. (1994) 'El cuerpo de la mujer como frontera de negociación: la construcción del cuerpo femenino en el discurso biomédico sobre mujeres VIH+', in Heidi J. Figueroa Sarriera, María M. López and Madeline Román (eds), *Más allá de la bella (in)diferencia: Revisión posfeminista y otras escrituras posibles.* Río Piedras, Puerto Rico: Publicaciones Puertorriqueñas. pp. 189–208.

Foucault, M. (1985) *La arqueología del saber.* Mexico: Siglo XXI.

Frieze, I.H., Parsons, J.E., Ruble, D.N. and Zellman, G.L. (1978) *Women and Sex Roles. A Social Psychological Perspective.* New York/London: W.W. Norton.

Hollway, W. (1989) *Subjectivity and Method in Psychology: Gender, Meaning and Science.* London: Sage.

Ibáñez, T. (1993) 'La dimensión política en la psicología social', *Revista Latinoamericana de Psicología*, 25(1): 19–34.

Lyotard, F. (1989) *La condición posmoderna.* Madrid: Ediciones Cátedra, SA.

Maffesoli, M. (1984) 'La rebelión del cuerpo', *El País.*

Martín-Baró, I. (1985) *Acción e ideología: psicología social desde centroamérica.* San Salvador: UCA Editores.

Mason, K. and Bumpass, L. (1975) 'U.S. women's sex role ideology, 1970', *American Journal of Sociology*, 80: 1212–9.

Mead, G.H. (1965) *Espíritu, persona y sociedad.* Buenos Aires: Editorial Paidós.

Potter, J. and Wetherell, M. (1987) *Discourse and Social Psychology.* London: Sage.

Riley, D. (1988) *'Am I that Name?' Feminism and the Category of 'Women' in History.* London: Macmillan.

Smart, B. (1993) *Postmodernity.* New York/London: Routledge.

Squire, C. (1989) *Significant Differences – Feminism in Psychology.* London/New York: Routledge.

4

The Reciprocity of Psychology and Popular Culture

Mary Crawford

Within contemporary academic psychology in the USA, few would argue that feminist perspectives are actively suppressed, or even marginalized in any ordinary sense of the word. Indeed, it is remarkable how thoroughly institutionalized the 'psychology of women' has become in the three decades since the field began to emerge (Unger and Crawford, 1996). Several journals published by respectable academic presses reach a wide circulation. Just over half of US colleges and university psychology departments offer courses on women and gender, including 172 graduate programmes. Textbooks and anthologies of readings for these courses have proliferated; at least one is now in its fifth edition, and dozens are in print. Feminist organizations have flourished for nearly three decades. The Association for Women in Psychology (AWP), a large and active group, dates from 1969, and Division 35 (Psychology of Women) of the American Psychological Association, founded in 1973, is one of the largest divisions of the APA with over 6,000 members.

What accounts for this extraordinary assimilation into the discipline? Following the distinction made by Erica Burman in her introduction to this volume, I propose that, for the most part, what has been assimilated is the *psychology of women*, not *feminist psychology*. The leading US journals are tellingly titled *Psychology of Women Quarterly* and *Sex Roles*. Of the textbooks currently available for course adoption, only one uses the word 'feminist' in its title; the others stake their territory as *The Psychology of Women* (Matlin, 1993); *Women's Minds, Women's Bodies* (Rollins, 1996); *Women's Lives* (Lott, 1994), or *Half the Human Experience* (Hyde, 1996).

The psychology of women is a feminist empiricist project (see Harding, 1986): its goal is to remediate psychology's omissions and distortions with respect to women by replacing 'bad science' with 'good science' – that is, scrubbing scientific practices of sexism. The passion and commitment of feminist empiricists should not be minimized. Starting in the late 1960s, they challenged psychology to take notice of women – as professionals, clients, students, and as a focus of research. They voiced this challenge in language psychology could understand, and within the context of a liberal appeal to fairness and equality. They have been rewarded with a certain degree of success and professional acceptance. By focusing on women as objects of research and on previously neglected topics, feminist empiricism has generated a substantial – and politically useful – body of knowledge on important issues such as sexual harassment, domestic violence, mediated images of women, eating disorders, work and achievement, and the social context of mothering.

More ambiguously, the feminist empiricist critique of sexism in research methods has produced elaborate guidelines for 'non-sexist' research and reliance on ever more abstracted quantitative methods such as meta-analysis. 'Gender', a concept enlisted by feminists to open the way towards theorizing cultural discourses of difference and deficiency, has been assimilated as a variable, producing a burgeoning crop of sex-difference research. In the process, it has lost its theoretical meaning, becoming a mere synonym for biological sex (Crawford, 1995). A certain paradoxical quality infuses feminist empiricist psychology: though its origin was in feminist outrage over sexist methods and theories, its projects reaffirm the epistemology on which these methods and theories were based (Harding, 1986; Marecek, forthcoming).

The version of feminist psychology that has become so successfully assimilated in the USA, is, in short, a thoroughly unthreatening enterprise. The relationship between feminism and psychology seems less a marriage than a furtive, clandestine affair, with psychology defining the limits of the relationship and keeping feminism firmly in its place. In public, the two maintain friendly and platonic relations, minimizing the potential danger of an unregulated liaison (Marecek, 1997).

In a 1993 issue of *Feminism & Psychology*, Naomi Weisstein's classic 'deconstruction' of pre-feminist psychology, 'Kinder, Kuche, Kirche as Scientific Law: Psychology Constructs the Female' is reprinted along with commentaries (Kitzinger, 1993). Weisstein's audacious challenge to psychology's neglect of social context, and the more than two decades of research and theorizing that have followed it, have, according to several commentators, failed to disrupt psychology-as-usual:

> Much of psychology (is) still mired in essentialist views about the differences between women and men. (Unger, 1993: 214)

> There has been no slackening in attempts to establish purely biological accounts of sex differences. (Prince and Hartnett, 1993: 220)

Psychology may be so predisposed as a discipline to individualize and decontextualize the phenomena it studies (including gender, sexuality, race and class) that it necessarily depoliticizes these phenomena and thereby functions both as a collaborator in the social reproduction of the status quo and as an obstacle to social change. (Bem, 1993: 231)

Yet current social conditions in the USA threaten even a circumscribed and politically innocuous affair between feminism and psychology (Marecek, 1997). North American mainstream psychology is experiencing a resurgence of political and social conservatism, supported by biological fundamentalism. Thus, recent research has focused on the presumed hereditary basis of crime, mental illness, same-sex sexual orientation, and other 'pathologies'. The new field of evolutionary psychology, which has offered biologically determinist accounts of gendered phenomena such as rape, mother–infant attachment, and male infidelity, is frankly political in its implications, yet claims the objectivity of pure science. In the applied arena, the US health-care crisis has re-medicalized the mental health professions, leading to more use of short-term interventions and drug therapies, and disrupting the hierarchy of fees and prestige in which clinical psychologists were formerly more valued than most other mental health workers.

Jeanne Marecek (1997: 137) argues that in response to these social forces, 'academic psychologists, in a rhetorical move seemingly intended to distance themselves from applied workers and to secure their prestige, have firmly re-inscribed their identity as scientists'. The American Psychological Society, formed to represent academic psychologists (and not practitioners) has grown rapidly. Its major journal is titled *Psychological Science*, and its rhetoric, as well as its lobbying at the federal government level for research funding, reflect the longing of psychology for the cultural prestige of the physical sciences.

Can an assimilated feminist psychology resist the further pull of the discipline in these hard times? Probably not. From the perspective of mainstream psychology, its niche is narrow, its topics specialized, and its concerns trivial: in a recent survey of APA members, Division 35 (Psychology of Women) was rated in the bottom third of the organization's divisions in terms of interest, and the bottom quartile in terms of importance to the field (Harari and Peters, 1987). Thus, its position may be more marginal than its institutionalization would suggest. Those who study women, gender and women's issues within academic psychology may be forgiven if they appear to believe that repudiating the trappings of the scientific establishment, or even questioning them, would be potentially disastrous at this moment in history.

Perhaps in response to these social realities, there are renewed calls for psychologists to distinguish the 'science' of gender (*sic*) from the 'politics' of gender, and to repudiate all political stances in a return to objectivity (Eagly, 1995). There is a spirited defence of decontextualized research on sex differences (see Kitzinger, 1994, for perspectives on the sex difference debate). And, voiced from within feminist psychology, there is an increasingly articulated need to ally with mainstream psychology. The current editorial policy of the Division 35 journal *Psychology of Women Quarterly* describes it as 'a research journal with an empirical, scientific tradition' whose goal is to 'provide a voice for a side of feminist psychology that we want to preserve in this age of Postmodernism' (Russo, 1995, cited in Marecek, 1997).

Though many authors have discussed the strengths and weaknesses of US feminist psychology, most have written as though it stands outside the rest of US culture. But a peculiar (and perhaps unique) characteristic of North American psychology is its dispersal throughout the culture, in versions mediated by mass communications. To begin with, the great majority of middle-class people are introduced to psychology and inculcated with its characteristic methods and perspectives in educational settings; it is one of the most popular courses of study in colleges and universities nationwide. Outside the academy, an enormous industry of self-help literature – books, video and audio cassettes, workshops and seminars – provides advice on improving one's personal relationships, influencing others and achieving career success. As Erica Burman suggests in her introduction, our task in this volume is to document the particular forms the traffic in ideas between feminism and psychology has taken, and their political consequences. The popularization of psychology is one form of this traffic that has been little analysed or understood. Yet it *must* be considered when assessing the potential for progressive political intervention.

Burman argues that the psychology of women (as opposed to feminist psychology) perpetuates psychology-as-usual and defuses feminist interventions into psychology's practices in several predictable ways. It extends psychology's gaze to previously unremarked areas. It colludes with positivism by re-inscribing existing methods and techniques. It ghettoizes gender and issues of concern to women. It reifies social categories, treating them as mere variables, and fostering essentialism. It ignores multiple subjectivities and identities by privileging gender.

In this chapter I will take the assertiveness training movement as a case study, I will look critically at each of these consequences of a psychology of women, and I will offer instantiations of Burman's claims. The assertiveness training movement is an unlikely amalgam of seemingly incompatible components: feminist impulses for social change, channelled into a psychology of woman-as-problem; behaviourist interventions into social interactions; decontextualized empiricist research; feminist therapy; and the 'pop psych' juggernaut. It is fascinating precisely because of these unlikely alliances, and it reveals much about each of the allies. My critique is grounded in feminist psychology, that 'explicitly politicized arena' which asks questions about who defines knowledge, how (whatever counts as) a fact is arrived at, and what the consequences are for women. I will ask what 'work' the AT movement has performed for psychology, and I will explore the limited space for feminist agendas within the movement and within therapeutic interventions more generally.

The Assertiveness Training Movement: An Overview

Starting in the early 1970s, books and articles began to appear which claimed that lack of assertiveness causes problems for people and offered techniques for becoming more assertive. At about the same time, management and consulting firms began to offer assertiveness workshops. During the ensuing 25 years, the assertiveness training movement in the USA assumed monumental proportions.

Research by behaviourist and cognitive-behavioural psychologists formed the background for the movement. Indeed, assertion seems to have been something of a scholarly and therapeutic fad before it became a popular one. Reviews of the research literature on assertion enumerate hundreds of studies (Brown and Brown, 1980; Galassi and Galassi, 1978; Heimberg et al., 1977). Numerous handbooks for clinicians discuss how to implement assertiveness training with people in therapy. One bibliography catalogued 892 journal articles, 664 dissertations, 34 educational films and 82 (mostly mass-market) books, for a total of 1,672 works devoted to becoming more assertive published from 1973 to 1983 alone (Ruben, 1985). The immense cultural production of didactic and educational materials on assertive speech has continued into the 1990s (Rakos, 1991; Wilson and Gallois, 1993). Today, the principles and practice of assertive speech are widely taught to the general public under the rubric of 'leadership' or 'management skills' training.

Women were marked early on as especially in need of assertiveness training. Many of the earliest US mass-market books were aimed specifically at women buyers – *Woman, Assert Yourself*; *The New Assertive Woman*. Some of these became best-sellers and/or were printed in more than one edition (see Bloom et al., 1975, 1980; Butler, 1976, 1981). The AT movement emerged somewhat later in Britain, fuelled by Anne Dickson's *A Woman in Your Own Right*

(1982), which has since been through 17 reprintings. The notion that there is something wrong with women's ways of talking is accepted as a commonplace of communication, as evidenced by the educational video described in a sales brochure sent to my university office in 1995:

> Men, Women, and Language
>
> This video examines origins of gender differences in the use of language. It describes the female tendency to use weakening language such as non-specific adjectives and tag questions, and explores developmental differences and sex-role differentiation. It distinguishes between male and female body language, looking at the use of personal space.

Why do women have these troublesome 'female tendencies' in their talk, and why do they need assertiveness training? Without exception, popular psychology books have blamed gender socialization. For example, *Self-Assertion for Women* noted that 'The acceptance of traditional femininity clearly interferes with female assertiveness' (Butler, 1976: 6). However, authors rarely offered research evidence that women as a group have trouble asserting themselves, other than perhaps a paper-and-pencil inventory given to college students. Rather, they drew heavily on stereotypes of female passivity. Women are said to carry 'early messages' in their heads

> as we tremble before employers, indirectly cajole our husbands, get hysterical with our parents, or inhibit competitive behavior. The concept of assertiveness for women is integrally linked to sex role socialization. And if women's sex role training teaches them anything, it is to be passive and dependent. . . . It is largely through following out the nurturant, docile 'programming' of the female role – denying their own needs and devoting themselves to winning others' love and approval – that women in particular seem to wind up with such severe deficits in assertive behavior. (Wolfe and Fodor, 1978: 141)

In another popular psychology account, women are described as prone to a 'compassion trap' (i.e. too attentive to the needs of others). A quiz is provided for women to assess their weakness on this dimension. Hypothetical situations are provided: a friend arrives for a meeting an hour late, the children refuse to come in from play when dinner is ready. Responses are shown in each case for 'Doris Doormat', 'Iris Indirect', 'Agatha Aggressive', and the ideal, 'April Assertive' (Phelps and Austin, 1975).

As this example shows, assertiveness was conceptualized as the ideal 'happy medium' of speech style. Demanding what one wants is *aggressive*. Failing to ask for what one wants is *passive*. Using indirect tactics is *manipulative*. All these styles are bad, and the self-help books are replete with anecdotes about how they cause problems. According to these books, speech can easily be classified into a few 'types'; only the assertive type is effective, and every woman should learn to speak it.

A gender-role socialization model could potentially be applied symmetrically: if women need assertiveness training to counter socialized passivity, men need it to counter socialized aggressiveness and insensitivity. However, the male half of the model received little attention. The focus on gender socialization in actuality meant a focus on women. The following example, from a model workshop for social workers, shows how therapists were instructed to present assertiveness:

> Women in our society have traditionally been trained to be submissive and self-effacing. As a result of this 'training in helplessness,' many women are unable to speak up for what they feel and need. Assertiveness training can help these women act more assertively and can help aggressive persons tone down the alienating aggressive behavior patterns they learned while growing up. (Callahan, 1980: 13–14)

Note that the client population is divided into 'women', named three times, and 'persons', sex unspecified, named once. Assertiveness training became a virtual panacea for women's social position, recommended for every problem from super-mother syndrome to agoraphobia. In a 1993 debate on 'date rape' on Cable News Network's *Larry King Live*, author Camille Paglia argued that middle-class college students need AT to counter their socialized passivity and prevent men from raping them:

> [I]t's middle-class girls who are being raised to be nice and who are afraid to say 'No' and afraid to make their feelings known and are sort of going – just want a boyfriend, want status on campus. . . . So I think that we have to focus in on the kind of white, middle-class niceness issue here – OK? – that is putting our young women in danger when they arrive on campus. They need assertiveness training, they really do, in ways that – the old rules protected them – in ways that have broken down now.

Paglia seems to have followed the lead of psychologists in assuming that middle-class women are deficient in communication skills and that psychology has the answer to that deficiency. The deficiency is a relic of the past, of our misguided 'conditioning'. The implication, and the promise, is that if we do get help and are trained to speak up for ourselves, good things will happen: we will be respected and admired by others, we will get our own way more often, we will have greater personal and social power. We can even prevent sexual assault.

How to Speak Assertively: The Linguistic World of Assertiveness Training

What were the features of assertive speech as defined by psychologists? How exactly does an assertive person talk, and how can a woman know when she has acheived the assertive ideal in her speech? In order to teach the specific ways of talking defined by trainers as assertive, talk was typically divided into categories such as 'refusals, requests, and expressions' (Booraem and Flowers, 1978). Clients were then trained in specific ways of speaking for doing each of these. The training could include coaching in non-verbal behaviours such as eye contact, distance from other persons and body posture (Booraem and Flowers, 1978; Serber, 1977). The rules for non-verbal communication could be quite prescriptive. In one text, women are told that 'Men typically use less body language than women. Watch their body language and see how they do it' (Manning and Haddock, 1989, cited in Cameron, 1995: 184). The verbal techniques used in AT are composed of prescriptions and rules for constructing one's speech (Gervasio, 1987). These are *linguistic*, not *social* rules: they specify how to frame one's own speech to ensure that one's own needs are expressed, not how to foster mutually satisfying interactions with others. And, like the injunction to 'use less body language', they are often presented without a clear rationale.

Rules specify that speech should be direct. Requests should be in the form of straightforward questions, never indirect references or hints. Refusals should be given without excuses, justifications or apologies. Speakers should focus on their own feelings, desires and beliefs. To best express their feelings, they should use 'feeling verbs' and 'I–me' sentence structure – that is, they should construct sentences in which the speaker is the subject and the topic is the speaker's feelings ('I feel sad and angry when you call me stupid'). They should never say 'I'm sorry'.

A few examples from a trainers' manual illustrate some of the rules and the confidence with which they were promulgated.

On refusing to justify one's behaviour:

> In assertiveness training clients are coached to refuse without excuses and only give reasons if they want to. Even reasons are not required. Clients are also coached to resist 'why' questions since such questions usually encourage providing excuses.

On asking for what one wants:

> Assertiveness training teaches the client to ask with high frequency in order to get more of what she or he wants.

On the usefulness of I–me statements in terminating a relationship:

> The asserter is coached to say, 'The relationship is not working for me and I'm going to move on', etc. The asserter is further coached to respond in the following ways if the partner-recipient defends or asks what she or he can do: 'It's not what you can do; the relationship isn't working for me', 'I can't answer why; it's simply not working for me', 'It's better for me if I move on', etc. (Booraem and Flowers, 1978: 32–42)

In situations where coached requests, refusals and expressions of positive or negative feelings are not enough, clients are taught to use specific 'defensive' and 'offensive' techniques such as the following:

> *The Broken Record*: To be used when one's assertion is responded to with criticism or a topic shift. Do not respond to anything off the point you intend to make. Keep saying, 'But the point is . . .
> *Clipping*: To be used when one is being verbally attacked but the issue is unclear. Answer, but do not add information; instead, wait for the other person to make the issue clear. For example, If A usually makes coffee, and does not, and someone says 'The coffee is not made', A is to reply 'That's right'.
> *The Reinforcement Sandwich*: Present a positive expression of feelings along with a negative one. For example, 'I don't like what you just said and want you to know that because I want to feel comfortable with you.'
> *Fogging*: To be used when the asserter feels that he or she is being subjected to criticism that is manipulative rather than constructive. Acknowledge that there may be some truth in the criticism – but do not explain, offer apologies, or promise to change any aspect of your behavior. A professor, in response to a student's complaints about an exam, for example, might say, 'You could be right, multiple choice exams probably are inherently unfair', but offer no further encouragement to discuss or negotiate a grade change. (Booraem and Flowers, 1978)

There was a consensus among practitioners of assertion training that training in communication skills involves not only direct coaching in speech practices, but also intervention in the emotional and cognitive 'underpinnings' of speech. Thus, Alberti (1977) states that the key elements of assertiveness training are skills training, anxiety reduction and cognitive restructuring. As part of the cognitive restructuring, clients were often told that their beliefs about assertion were irrational. For example, if a client expressed the opinion that she might lose her job if she directly refused an employer's request, she might be labelled as 'catastrophizing'. A therapeutic technique for dealing with catastrophizing was to exaggerate the client's supposedly irrational fears to the point of absurdity. 'Yes, you could lose your job, and then your apartment, and you'd be homeless and you'd starve.'

Deconstructing Assertiveness

The history of the AT movement has been described elsewhere (Crawford, 1995; Rakos, 1991; Wilson and Gallois, 1993), and I will not discuss it at length here. Its origins were a curious mixture of 1970s feminism and behaviourist psychology. Early writers often likened AT to consciousness-raising, or saw it as a logical sequel to raised feminist awareness. Despite its connections to the Women's Liberation Movement, the AT movement soon came to rely on the explanatory rhetoric of social learning theory and the techniques of behaviour modification. Because they viewed behaviour modification techniques as value-neutral (Erwin, 1978) and language as just another behaviour (Skinner, 1957), most theorists and researchers did not question the desirability of assertive speech or critically evaluate the implicit philosophy of language and the social order underlying it. Using the best tools at their disposal, they simply invented assertiveness, and began teaching this invented behaviour.

The values and assumptions about 'healthy' and 'adaptive' inter-personal behaviour that underlay the research literature on assertiveness remained implicit and unexamined. An individualistic ethic made assertion seem everyone's right. A naive belief in stereo-typical sex differences guided therapy for women. The assertiveness construct disguised an implicit male norm that constructed women's speech as deficient and problematical. Finally, the movement failed to theorize how inequalities arising from social class, ethnicity, power and status help determine speech style and speech privileges. I will briefly discuss each of these points before turning to an examination of the relationships among popular culture, therapy and psychological theory.

Individualism versus interdependence
The AT movement is firmly grounded in North American ideals of independence and individualism (Rakos, 1991). Individual feelings and goals are valued above the maintenance and process of relation-ships. Assertive techniques frequently encourage speakers to dispense with reasons or justifications for their feelings or behaviours, imply-ing that individuals should be the sole judges of their actions. Individualism is encoded in the language of assertion techniques, as clients are directed to use 'I–me' language.

The individualism of the assertive philosophy may reflect the influence of the human potential movement. From this perspective, learning specific conversational techniques in order that one's own opinions and decisions should prevail is a route to self-actualization. In a larger sense, it reflects the dominant view of the self in western culture, which is sustained by powerful ideological and structural forces (Lykes, 1985).

Feminist theorists have articulated alternatives to the notion of the autonomous self, such as self-in-relation (Miller, 1984), the self defined in terms of caring and responsibility (Gilligan, 1982), and fluidity in self-development (Kaplan and Surrey, 1984). Perhaps the most sophisticated of these alternative notions of the self is that of social individuality (Lykes, 1985), which reflects the social constructionist perspective that the self is a function of prevailing discourses. There is evidence that people who have experienced social relations of powerlessness and those who have engaged in collective social action have a notion of the self grounded in social individuality in contrast to one grounded in individual autonomy:

> individuals from majority groups (e.g., white upper class males) whose material conditions and social relations are most likely to be consonant with individualism would be more likely to have a notion of the self as autonomous individualism. Persons in less powerful groups (e.g., women, people of color, working class people) are more likely to perceive contradictions between the assumptions of autonomous individualism and their social experiences. These individuals may also experience group solidarity or some sense of the 'givenness' of 'being-in-relation', for their survival as a group may seem possible only in relationship. (Lykes, 1985: 364)

In the assertiveness training movement, the ethic of human interdependence and connectedness was muted by the emphasis on individual rights, and autonomy was held up as the model of mental health. Clients in therapy, as well as consumers attending assertiveness workshops and reading self-help books, were urged to give up an ethic of interdependence under the guise of cognitive restructuring and relinquish a sense of self grounded in social individuality towards the illusory goal of improved mental health.

Until quite recently, no one seems to have asked the targets of assertiveness training about their own definitions of assertiveness. What do women mean when they describe themselves as 'assertive' or 'passive'? Not surprisingly, the meanings of these terms are different for women of different ethnic and cultural backgrounds. Whether these differences are visible in research results depends on the methods used to assess them. In one study, white women and women of colour (African-American, Asian-American and Latina women) responded similarly when asked to rate their agreement with the phrases 'I am assertive' and 'I am passive'. However, when they were asked about the meanings of the words *assertive* and *passive*, results showed that they were responding to quite different constructs. For white women, *assertive* was defined as standing up for oneself – a definition perhaps influenced by the rhetoric of the AT movement – while for women of colour, assertiveness implied speaking one's mind openly, a refusal of self-censorship. For white women, *passive* was most often defined as 'laid-back' or 'easy-going', while for women of colour it implied not saying what one really thinks. For women of colour, *assertive* and *passive* were opposites on the dimension of speaking one's mind, while for white women the two terms seemed unrelated (Landrine et al., 1992).

The tensions among different definitions of assertion is exposed when definitions generated from the professional literature, the popular self-help literature, and middle-class women and men are compared (Wilson and Gallois, 1993). The professional literature obscures the importance of dominance as an element of interpersonal relationships by describing assertiveness in terms of 'self-expression' but not in terms of exercising influence. Professional and popular definitions alike – except for those generated by middle-class men – engage the conflict between concern for oneself and concern for others. While the professional literature is silent on issues of power, dominance, aggression and coercion, these dimensions were emphasized by men – and not women – in their own meanings of 'assertive'.

Clearly, assertion has different meanings depending on the social positions of those defining it. Assertion is defined differently by professionals and ordinary women and men, and the gender-related differences are strongly related to the different social rules for women's and men's behaviour. The meaning of assertion is culturally and historically situated, braided with the individual's social class, power, privilege and gender.

The social construction of a sex difference
Advice to women on how to become more assertive is predicated on the assumption that women are in fact less able to speak effectively on their own behalf than men. This assumption fits neatly into a discourse of opposition in which masculinity and femininity are eternally polarized. Thus, the paradox of using AT to transform women into players of 'new roles' while AT itself is grounded in a masculine/feminine dichotomy (Cameron, 1995). It is interesting to look back at the empiricist rhetoric of the movement and see how sex differences have been produced and justified within it.

From a behavioural perspective, we might ask: Is there a sex difference in assertive skills? While there were many studies describing assertiveness training in all-women groups (which presupposes a difference), there were very few that sought to determine whether women actually behave differently from men in the situations for which assertiveness training was designed. In other words, despite adopting a framework that encouraged them to look for sex differences in a variety of behaviours, most investigators did not in fact look at women and men in mundane interaction.

Even from a simplistic sex difference perspective, it would seem that researchers would have recognized the necessity of conducting field studies and naturalistic observations. Yet there are virtually no studies of behaviour in the sorts of situations that appear on assertiveness inventories. The few that do exist suggest that sex differences are not prevalent. Harris (1974), for example, in a study of frustration and aggression, observed the behaviour of people when someone cut into a queue in front of them. Females and males were equally likely to express displeasure to the offender.

In an interesting series of studies, Moriarty (1975) had confederates act out inappropriate behaviour in increasingly blatant ways. In his first study, college students taking a verbal ability test in a laboratory were paired with a confederate who subjected them to 17 minutes of loud rock music unless they objected. Eighty per cent of the students made no comment at all. Some made indirect nonverbal protests such as cupping their ears, putting down their pencils, or turning to look at the offender. According to Moriarty, most students later rationalized their behaviour, as in the following post-experiment exchange:

Experimenter: Did you tell him to turn it off?
Student: No, it didn't bother me that much.
E: Might it have affected your score?
S: Considerably.
E: Why didn't you tell him to turn it off?
S: I thought about it, but I'm not that kind of person. (Moriarty, 1975: 45–46)

Reasoning that perhaps people would be more assertive in a more consequential situation, Moriarty next told students that the person who scored lower in each pair of students would then be assigned to an electric shock condition. Again, participants were subjected to the accomplice's loud rock music during the test. Again, 80 per cent of students silently endured the situation. As in the first study, they denied being bothered by the music, or said they did not want to cause trouble.

Moving to a more direct confrontation between victim and violator, Moriarty then conducted an experiment in which students taking a test were confronted by a confederate who said, 'Excuse me. I was here a few minutes ago and I left my ring on the table. Did you find it?' Of course, all participants replied that they had not seen the ring. The accomplice persisted in asking whether they had seen the ring and finally asked participants to empty their pockets. Although participants offered verbal resistance ('Are you serious?') every one complied.

A striking feature of this series of studies is that, in common with most psychological studies that draw their samples from white, US, male college students (Sears, 1986), *all the participants were male.* Within the empiricist framework adopted by AT proponents, this work strongly suggests that the notion of an assertive norm (which only women fail to meet) is spurious. As the accomplices' out-of-bounds behaviour became increasingly blatant, the great majority of people failed to assert themselves in the manner that assertiveness trainers would recommend. Instead, they relied on indirect, non-verbal means of protest, and *post hoc* rationalizations that the situation really didn't matter very much.

Studies such as these were rarely conducted within the AT movement. Rather, paper-and-pencil assertiveness inventories were developed to measure self-described assertion. AT advocates tended to rely on these self-reports, which confirmed their beliefs about differences. Even within the difference framework there is no empirical basis, direct or indirect, for assuming a generalized communication deficiency in girls and women. Women as a group are not less competent communicators than men as a group.

Yet the social construction of difference continues. In a recent clinical handbook for professionals (Fodor, 1992), the socialization model is recapitulated under the heading *Male–Female Differences and Assertiveness.* The evidence cited for sex differences consists of two self-help books for women and three empirical studies that used only women participants. The assertiveness construct encoded a male norm that constructed women's speech as deficient and problematical. I have already shown how assertiveness training manuals drew on female stereotypes (e.g. 'Doris Doormat'). These stereotypes have changed surprisingly little over the past 30 years (for a review, see Unger and Crawford, 1996).

Assertion versus passivity is a central and stable dimension of gender stereotypes. Because the prototype of an assertive person is virtually synonymous with the prototype of masculinity, change efforts directed at women were inevitably towards helping women (at least those who could afford therapy and educational workshops) attain stereotypically masculine behaviour. Assertiveness training was prescribed for women with the implicit promise of helping them compete on equal terms with men by adjusting their speech patterns to be more like men's. Rooted in stereotypes that reflect a discourse of difference, the assertiveness-training-for-women bandwagon went forward, led by psychologists, despite very little evidence *from within their own empiricist framework* that the stereotypes reflect clinically or interpersonally important differences.

Social acts without social contexts
The fiction that social relations of power and status contribute little to assertiveness is maintained in many ways in the research literature. In contrast to the hundreds of studies assessing and training assertive skills and traits, there are very few that explore the effectiveness of AT in everyday situations or the effect of assertive speech on recipients. Nor do many studies examine the social reactions of others towards a speaker who uses formulaic assertive techniques. Given the behaviourist rhetoric of the professional literature, the lack of outcome research is both conspicuous and puzzling.

There were plenty of outcome studies in which a group of clients (usually all women) were pre-tested on paper-and-pencil measures of self-esteem, depression, or assertiveness, then attended training sessions for several weeks, then were post-tested on the same measures. These usually showed self-rated improvement. But the movement was promising more than just feeling better about oneself. The social learning perspective underlying assertiveness training clearly predicted that when a woman changed her speech style she could expect 'reinforcing' social responses that would affect her ways of talking in the future. Moreover, self-help manuals promised positive social consequences, from getting one's own way to increased respect. Yet there were virtually no studies on the social consequences of assertive speech. How do people react when they are the recipients of textbook assertive behaviour? When one is on the receiving end of the 'broken record' or 'I–me' language, does one respect and admire the speaker, or experience frustration, anger, or feelings of having been manipulated? What do recipients think about the person who uses an assertive formula?

In an analogue study aimed at the AT community and published in a behaviour modification journal (Crawford, 1988), I demonstrated that assertive behaviour was evaluated differently depending on the sex of the assertive model and the sex and age of the research participant. Assertive women models received the lowest likability ratings of all from older male participants and the highest from older female participants. However, the sex of the assertive model made no difference when competence was being judged.

These results strongly suggested that the meaning of assertion is at least partly in the eye of the recipient. Assertive women were perceived as competent, but less likable, a distinction not made for assertive men. The results also suggested that assertion in real-life settings such as the workplace, where women are highly likely to be interacting with older men in power, may have important costs. It is possible, then, that non-assertion may sometimes be a positive and adaptive strategy for women.

Although there are many studies of interaction that are congruent with my results (reviewed in Crawford, 1995), they are rarely, if ever, cited in the assertiveness training literature. These studies have to do with conversational dominance and assertion as gender-role violations for women. In general, they show that when women behave less assertively than men, their behaviour may well be an adaptive choice rather than a deficiency. As we have seen, there is no convincing evidence that women do not know how to speak assertively. 'Unassertive' speech, rather than being a (female) deficiency in social skills, may reflect a sensitivity to the social impact of one's behaviour. Tentative and indirect speech may be a pragmatic choice for women. It is more persuasive, at least when the recipient is male, less likely to lead to negative attributions about personality traits and likability, and less likely to provoke verbal attack.

Theorizing power and status
With its attention to documenting and remediating women's personal problems of ineffective speech, the assertiveness training movement helped obscure the understanding that women may appear less able to assert themselves because of differences in power, status and social roles. Women are disproportionately represented in low-power, low-status situations and roles. Speakers thus situated are unlikely to be direct and forceful. It is inherent in a low-status role that in it one is

> . . . nestled . . . precisely inside the most contradictory moments of social arrangements. Indeed, it is often women's work to be stuffed inside such spots and to testify that *no contradiction* exists. . . . *Nothing* shatters our coherent social existences. Wives are not supposed to give away the secret of male dependence although they have plenty of evidence; secretaries are not supposed to tell about male incompetence or the incoherence they make presentable; lesbian women are not supposed to 'flaunt' their sexualities . . . ; mistresses are not supposed to tell about the contradictions inside heterosexuality, monogamy, and the promises of marriage; prostitutes are not supposed to tell about the contradictions of intimacy and sexuality; daughters are not to speak of incest; and maids or domestics are not supposed to talk about the contradictions of the world of paid work and family life. . . . Women of all colors and classes are nestled inside these contradictory spots in which the pressures and structures of the economy rub against the pressures and structures of racism, sexism, and heterosexism. Women are sworn to both invisibility and secrecy. (Fine and Gordon, 1989: 162; emphasis in original)

Women's task has been to 'sit inside moments of social contradiction and . . . keep our mouths shut' (Fine and Gordon, 1989: 169). The realities of belonging to a group with little social power – whether women, people of colour, gay and lesbian people, or any other marginalized group – and the double bind of assertiveness for members of these groups are rarely acknowledged in the assertion training literature.

This failure to theorize power is a feature of the empirical research literature on assertiveness from its start, both in its definitions (Wilson and Gallois, 1993) and its methods and procedures (Crawford, 1995; Gervasio and Crawford, 1989). Representation of status and power differentials is entirely absent from the stimuli used in evaluating assertive behaviour. Stimulus materials typically describe the recipient of assertion as a 'friend', 'co-worker' or 'stranger'. In the limited interactional worlds of assertion experiments, models virtually never assert to an authority figure, someone who possesses greater economic or social power, or a partner in a long-term intimate relationship. There is an almost complete lack of attention to 'race', class and status in stimuli. There are no published studies with Asian-American or Hispanic women or men as models, although one might expect that speech norms may be different in diverse communities. Behaviours defined by white psychologists as assertive might not be relevant to other groups. Direct eye contact, refusing to comply with a request, and a firm voice tone might be considered disrespectful within Asian-American or African-American cultures (Cheek, 1976). AT ignores the carefully constructed rituals of *personalismo* (personal, friendly, repeated contact with helpers, salespeople, doctors, etc.) in Hispanic cultures as well (Comas-Díaz, 1985). Interactions of ethnicity and gender are obscured in the white, middle-class world of assertion research. There is evidence that white and black women who are friends agree that the black woman is usually the more assertive of the two (McCullough, forthcoming) and that expected levels of assertion for women differ in black and white social groups (Stanback, 1985). Indeed, as I noted earlier, the very definition of what 'being assertive' means may differ (Landrine et al., 1992).

Assertiveness research is situated in a mythical world of social equality, a world scrubbed of everyday racism and sexism. In the real world, however, roles, and the language that characterizes them, are often related to gender, status and power. If a particular kind of speech is expected as part of a low-status social role, failure to produce this kind of speech will lead to social sanctions. The woman who does not mark her gender through her speech (or who performs a speech style marked masculine) faces costs that have rarely been acknowledged by the psychologists who led the AT bandwagon.

Thus there are many contradictions of prescription and outcome that percolate through the AT literature. I will describe just two examples here:

• One of the most frequently reported 'failures' among clinical clients is that after assertiveness training their relationships seem to be worse rather than better. Assertiveness training may lead to a power struggle with a resistant partner. Moreover, the evidence on factors that affect the likelihood of physical battering is mixed: '[G]iven the contradictory findings on triggers for husbands' abusive behaviors, there is a high risk that if we train such women to be more assertive, we may be subjecting them to further abuse. . .' (Fodor and Epstein, 1983: 151).

• In a review of the outcome literature, the researchers advise clinicians that women should be trained to be assertive initially only with 'men who possess more liberal attitudes toward women's roles in society', because more conservative men may react negatively (Delamater and McNamara, 1986: 153).

The contradictions between the optimism of the AT prescriptions and pessimism about the likely outcomes are not *caused* by the AT movement; they represent classic double binds for women that are very much part of contemporary western culture. The problem is not that these contradictions exist, but that the conceptualization of assertive speech by psychologists has left so little room for them to be addressed.

Assertiveness Training and Feminist Therapy

Assertiveness training was developed originally as a therapeutic technique. Many of its earliest proponents claimed that its origins were in the women's movement and that it constituted a feminist therapy: 'Spurred on by various social liberation doctrines, in particular the women's movement, assertiveness training has supplied useful technology for behavior change and a natural sequel to consciousness-raising rhetoric and group meetings' (Shoemaker and Satterfield, 1977: 49–50). Is AT a viable and legitimate mode of feminist therapy? Or is it merely a way of diverting women's attention from social structural issues and the need for collective action, an inevitably ineffective individual 'solution' to structural power imbalances? As Fodor (1985: 258) asked, 'Is assertiveness training yet another "treatment" that is directed at the victim of social injustice, placing the burden for social change on the backs of individual women?'

For the most part, feminist therapists have not rejected assertion training. Some have accepted its clinical value relatively uncritically. Many of the self-help manuals, continuing education courses, and corporate workshops were (and are) conducted by women, most self-described feminists. Others have recognized the conceptual weaknesses of the assertiveness construct. In writings aimed at behaviour therapists and assertion trainers as well as at their feminist clinical colleagues, they have questioned some of the implicit and explicit assumptions of the movement: that women as a group have a skills deficit that requires intervention; that effective language behaviour can be prescribed and taught easily; and that if women become more assertive they will reap positive social consequences (Fodor, 1985; Fodor and Epstein, 1983; Stere, 1985; Wilson and Gallois, 1993).

One of the earliest feminist critics of the movement was Nancy Henley, who argued that it paid insufficient attention to social context and structures. Henley (1980) addressed clinicians and assertion trainers directly with the charge that, within the assertiveness training movement, both the blame and the responsibility for a solution are placed on the individual when women experience troubles in making others understand and respect their talk.

As the research and clinical literature on assertiveness expanded, feminists began to enumerate its limitations. In a volume aimed at behaviour therapists, Fodor and Epstein (1983) pointed out that there was an overemphasis in the literature on the success of assertiveness training and a 'pointed neglect of the issue of dropouts and failures' (Fodor and Epstein, 1983: 137). Like Henley, they took assertion trainers to task for ignoring issues of power and authority in women's lives.

Feminist clinicians have called for two kinds of changes to ensure that assertiveness training is good feminist practice. Stere (1985) argued that most of the clinical pitfalls of assertiveness training groups for women arise from overemphasis on the expert status of the leader. She illustrates several ways in which leaders reinforce their expert status, thereby neglecting the strengths and resources of clients, and offers alternative methods. Her examples include:

1   *Defining assertiveness and evaluating responses.* When the therapist uses prescribed definitions of 'appropriate' assertive behaviour and evaluates clients' attempts, women may become preoccupied with making a 'correct' response. Instead, the therapist should acknowledge that, given the complexities of human interaction, there is no general 'right' way to speak. Group members should be treated as a valuable resource for suggestions on how to respond in a variety of situations.

2   *Implying that assertiveness leads only to positive social consequences.* By failing to discuss the limitations of individual change, the therapist encourages women to blame themselves if their attempts to 'speak up' are unheard. Instead, the therapist should discuss and acknowledge gender inequities, including the fact that 'people generally are not oriented towards taking the needs and interest of women seriously' (Stere, 1985: 53).

3   *Handing out lists of 'irrational beliefs'.* The emphasis on cognitive restructuring in assertiveness training has led many therapists and group leaders to challenge apparently self-limiting beliefs in clients by labelling them irrational. However, women have a long history of being told by the psychiatric establishment that their beliefs and experiences are irrational; thus this technique risks perpetuating one of the most common ways that women's thoughts are invalidated. In addition, 'irrational' beliefs (such as 'If I assert myself, people won't like me') are shown by research to be quite rational. She suggests that groups of women should be encouraged to examine beliefs and values without the use of the label irrational.

4   *Rehearsing leader-contrived role plays.* Practising contrived situations has little value because the everyday assertion dilemmas of women are usually quite different from those depicted in training exercises. Instead, group members should contribute actual situations from their own experience for role-play and analysis by the group.

Some feminist critics have advocated a shift to a societal focus that addresses social structural inequities (Henley, 1980). Fodor (1985) notes that

> Going beyond individual work, toward creating an environment receptive to strong, assertive women, we need to take our methodology into a broader, more difficult area and address power issues and male domination. . . . [W]e need to go beyond work with individual women and their personal assertiveness issues and begin to use assertiveness techniques to challenge male patriarchal structure. (Fodor, 1985: 261–2)

She suggests, among other strategies, group-work that encourages women to explore the assertive strengths they already possess and to develop woman-defined assertive behaviour.

At least some recent work using the assertiveness construct seems to reflect a more sophisticated and nuanced approach than earlier 'bandwagon' research on self-referred, non-clinical populations of middle-class white women. For example, Fodor (1992), in a volume on social skills training for adolescents, deals extensively with ethical and socio-cultural aspects of assertiveness training and reports work with diverse ethnic groups including Asian Americans, African-Americans and Latinos. She includes class diversity by reporting work with disadvantaged high-risk groups and middle-class suburban substance abusers. Significant, non-trivial issues and situations are addressed, such as using assertiveness training as a tool for advocacy by helping young mothers assert their educational needs to school authorities. Throughout the volume there is an awareness that concepts such as 'social competence' are inherently value-laden and that 'social skills training' in adolescents has sometimes been used in attempts to change behaviours considered problematic by the agents of society rather than by the young people themselves.

A recent effort to reframe AT that is notable for its methodological and conceptual sophistication (Wilson and Gallois, 1993) began by exploring the tensions and contradictions among professional, self-help, and lay definitions of assertiveness. The researchers then elicited knowledge of the social rules governing assertive speech, with special attention to how those rules differ for women and men. Finally, they developed a model for AT that incorporates issues of power, status and dominance. Within it, clients are encouraged to assess realistically the impact of various possible changes in the ways they relate to others by taking into account what is likely to be 'safe' for a person of their age, status and sex, and to consider the costs and benefits of choosing to break social rules. The approach is an attempt to address the gender and power politics of assertion in a pragmatic fashion:

> A choice that everyone, including clients in assertion training, must make is whether they want to live within their present power structure or to attempt to change it. . . . In the latter case, people must recognise that they are operating as agents of social change, with the attendant risks of unexpected reactions and the possible use of power against them. There are many cases, of course, when these risks are well worth taking. Sometimes, however, changing a power relationship may not be an important goal for a person and a behaviour that conforms more to social rules for that person may be more effective in attaining the central goals. Thus, an individual woman may be better served by conforming to the rules applied to her than by breaking out of them and using masculine behaviour. If she does this, however, she must also be aware that she is acting to preserve the power structure. . . . Whatever choice a person makes, social power makes a difference. (Wilson and Gallois, 1993: 176–7)

But if academic research does not exist in a social vacuum, neither does feminist therapy. Always an uneasy alliance between feminism, with its commitment to social and political change, and psychotherapy, with its emphasis on personal growth and adjustment, feminist therapy may be retreating into a 'therapy of women' analogous to the 'psychology of women' perspective in academic psychology. Consciousness-raising groups, the first form of explicitly feminist therapy, were grounded in the understanding that 'the personal is political' – that problems experienced by women were social rather than individual in origin. Over time, consciousness-raising shaded into a variant of group therapy and a means of personal change. Women's status as a class, and the possibility of political interventions, faded into the background (Kahn and Yoder, 1989; Rosenthal, 1984).

Though the ethical and theoretical principles of feminist therapy have been well-articulated (Brown, 1994; Lerman & Porter, 1990), there has been very little research on the mundane practices of self-identified feminist therapists. In a recent study involving extended interviews (Marecek and Kravetz, 1996), 20 US feminist practitioners were asked questions such as 'What does it mean to you to say that your therapy is feminist?' and 'Are there times when your professional training and your feminism are in conflict?' Marecek and Kravetz summarize their analysis of the interviews:

> Respondents spoke from within psychotherapy culture, grafting service-able elements of feminism onto its practices, language, and assumptions. Their approach to therapy privileged private meanings, feelings, and ideas. The subject of their therapy was the modern, individualized self; the goal, personal fulfillment and self-discovery. The feminist ideology that our respondents brought to their work took shape within this framework. Its core constructs, womanly ways of being, are located 'within' the individual self. Its focus of concern is mental life, not political change. It is a feminism that works within existing gender arrangements and does not challenge systems of power operating in society. (Marecek and Kravetz, 1996: 12)

Although feminism was an important part of the identities and personal histories of these therapists, all of whom were women and some of whom had long records of feminist activism, most declined to use the word 'feminist' to describe themselves or their therapeutic approaches to the public. Citing popular conceptions of feminists as 'man-haters' and 'ball-busters', they chose to conceal their values. Some justified this choice on overtly pragmatic grounds: in the current anti-feminist climate, a therapist who reveals her feminism will lose business. Others justified it in terms of their clients' misunderstandings of the term. Some invented alternative names such as 'woman's therapy' for their practices.

It seems sadly ironic that a movement that began with naming women's 'personal problems' as political and social injustices, and that channelled its therapeutic resources into raising consciousness and training women to speak assertively, should now be named only covertly and euphemistically. Has feminism gone from 'The Problem

That Has No Name' (see Friedan, 1963) to 'The Movement That Has No Name' (Marecek and Kravetz, 1996: 10)?

Creating the Space of Longing

Feminist researchers and therapists who have endorsed the AT movement as well as other forms of interventions for women need to step back from their specific techniques and methods to ask *whose needs each model serves* and *what are its social consequences*. While most social scientists are trained in the intricacies of their discipline's preferred methods, few are taught to critique their discipline's assumptions and practices. This self-reflexive political critique is essential. Because social science is a culturally privileged form of knowledge, doing research is inevitably a political act (Crawford and Marecek, 1989).

The AT movement, copiously documented in the professional and popular literature of the past two decades, provides an interesting case study of the limitations of research and therapy conducted without an ongoing political critique. Within it, women have been portrayed as victims of misguided early socialization that renders their speech inadequate and deficient. Psychologists have invented the construct of assertiveness and participated in its mass dissemination. Thus they have made available a new 'scientific' explanation of women's low social status and a new pejorative label for women. Women have been encouraged by self-help books, educational workshops and therapy groups to internalize the image of themselves as passive, inept communicators and to find a cure for this invented deficiency through psychology.

The assertiveness training movement and its offshoots – the ubiquitous workshops, videos and seminars on 'Leadership Training for Women' and 'Communication Skills for Women Managers' – function to deflect attention from the fact that women are over-represented in low-power, low-status social roles and situations. The movement has helped obscure the double bind of female authority. It constitutes an example of 'woman-as-problem' thinking in which women are blamed for the consequences of their low social status (Crawford and Marecek, 1989). Even more important, it illustrates how such thinking can contribute to the continued powerlessness of women by channelling energy into individual change efforts rather than collective action.

Its success should encourage feminist theorists to examine further the reciprocity of disciplinary perspectives and the mass media. Which psychological constructs become bandwagons, ending up on television talk shows and the *New York Times* best-seller list – and which research is never mentioned in the popular media? What are the assumptions about human nature that underlie popular psychology? The assertiveness training movement would be an interesting case study even if it were an isolated example, but unfortunately it is not. Feminist psychologists have noted many other bandwagons, such as fear of success, the Cinderella complex, androgyny, co-dependency, the different moral voice, women's ways of knowing, mother–infant bonding, and conceptions of an essentialized relational self (Brown, 1990; Crawford, 1989; Crawford and Marecek, 1989; Eyer, 1993; Marecek and Kravetz, 1996; Mednick, 1989). The discourse of difference supports existing institutions and reproduces existing power relations.

Connections between the social science disciplines and the larger North American culture are multi-stranded and reciprocal. Many traditionally trained social scientists would acknowledge that their theories 'seep' out to the larger culture and affect it. It is less widely acknowledged that the larger culture contains particular distinct types of social theory that 'seep into and mold the discipline' (Burman and Parker, 1993: 161). Feminist psychologists must do critical historical research to show exactly how cultural influences impinge on psychological research and therapy. In analysing the unexamined assumptions about masculinity and femininity that underlie the psychological construct of assertive speech and the research associated with it, I have shown specific ways in which psychology has participated in the social construction of difference and become an agent of a self-fulfilling prophecy with respect to gender. The beliefs that women as a group are uniquely in need of communication skills training, that an effective language style can be invented and taught, and that such intervention leads to a better life for women were uncritically assumed by many researchers and therapists as well as by popularizers of psychology.

In the assertiveness training movement we can see complex inter-relationships between the discipline of psychology and the larger culture in which it is embedded. When feminist critics supply a reflexive critique of these interrelationships, the way is opened to understand how social injustice can persist with no evidence of unhappiness or rebellion – the 'social construction of quiescence' (Fine and Gordon, 1989: 165).

One important area for study is women's relationship with self-help literature, popular psychology and therapy (Kitzinger and Perkins, 1993). Feminist scholars and cultural critics are beginning to ask searching questions about why particular themes arise in self-help literature at particular moments in history (Faludi, 1991); how popular psychology positions women as in need of self-improvement projects (Cameron, 1995; Worell, 1988); how women read relationship narratives and how these narratives serve social functions (Radway, 1984; Simonds, 1992). As researchers, we must analyse not only disciplinary voices but the voices of popular culture. The two form a mutually-influencing loop in the social construction of quiescence.

It is also important to name and examine women's resistance to these forms of social control. Women may use self-help books and seminars not to adjust to male norms, but to reassure themselves that their experiences of unfulfilling relationships are common, even 'normal' (Simonds, 1992). Reading themselves into the familiar, trite anecdotes of the self-help genre or the role-playing exercises of an assertiveness training seminar, women may recognize their own realities and gain reassurance that they are coping with real problems. Moreover, they may create interpretations that compete with the self-help authors' own proseletyzing. All attempts at control run the risk of engendering resistance, of provoking a critical response simply by making a particular issue salient.

Paradoxically, then, the preoccupation with women's speech style may have inadvertent advantages for feminist social change projects. By drawing attention to the way identity is created in everyday talk, the assertiveness training movement may have opened ways for women to reflect on their current identities and to imagine alternatives (Cameron, 1995).

Because of the latest wave of the women's movement, women have become more aware of external constraints on their ability to meet personal goals. Indeed, women's dissatisfaction with the status quo in gender relations and public life is what fuels the self-help industry. However, in order for feminism to realize its transformative potential, women must both become dissatisfied with the way things are and believe that they can change *social structures* by their own efforts. As Deborah Cameron (1995) points out, the quest for self-transformation encouraged by the self-help industry does, at least, give women the message that 'your life is yours to control', and this belief may be necessary and empowering for anyone committed to change.

Change, of course, involves more than personal choice. Camille Paglia's suggestion that AT can prevent sexual assault can stand as a symbol of the folly of focusing on personal transformation in the face of institutionalized power. Like the injunction to 'just say no' to drugs, it ignores the social realities of oppression.

The self-improvement projects that take the place of political action in so many women may derive their seductive power partly from academic feminism's failure to educate for critical consciousness (hooks, 1989). To the extent that feminist psychology has

awakened women to the need for change without providing substantive models and strategies for change, it has created a 'space of
longing' that can be filled, temporarily, with narratives of *The New
Assertive Woman.*

Note

Portions of this chapter were adapted from Crawford (1995).

References

Alberti, R.E. (ed.) (1977) *Assertiveness: Innovations, Applications, Issues.* San Luis
   Obispo, CA: Impact.
Bem, S.L. (1993) 'Is there a place in psychology for a feminist analysis of the social
   context?', *Feminism & Psychology*, 3: 230–4.
Bloom, V., Coburn, K. and Perlman, J. (1975) *The New Assertive Woman.* New
   York: Delacorte.
Bloom, V., Coburn, K. and Perlman, J. (1980) *The New Assertive Woman* (2nd edn).
   New York: Dell.
Booraem, C.D. and Flowers, J.V. (1978) 'A procedural model for training of assertive
   behavior', in J.M. Whitely and J.V. Flowers (eds), *Approaches to Assertion
   Training.* Monterey, CA: Brooks/Cole. pp. 15–46.
Brown, L.S. (1990) 'What's addiction got to do with it: a feminist critique of
   codependence', *Psychology of Women Newsletter*, 17: 1–4.
Brown, L.S. (1994) *Subversive Dialogues: Theory in Feminist Therapy.* New York:
   Basic Books.
Brown, S.D. and Brown, L.W. (1980) 'Trends in assertion training research and
   practice: a content analysis of the published literature', *Journal of Clinical
   Psychology*, 36: 263–9.
Burman, E. and Parker, I. (eds) (1993) *Discourse Analytic Research.* New York:
   Routledge.
Butler, P. (1976) *Self Assertion for Women.* San Francisco: Canfield.
Butler, P. (1981) *Self Assertion for Women* (2nd edn). San Francisco: Harper and
   Row.
Callahan, B. (1980) *Workshop Models for Family Life Education: Assertiveness
   Training.* Boston, MA: Resource Communications.
Cameron, D. (1995) *Verbal Hygiene.* London: Routledge.
Cheek, D.K. (1976) *Assertive Black, Puzzled White.* San Luis Obispo, CA: Impact.
Comas-Díaz, L. (1985) 'Cognitive and behavioral group therapy with Puerto Rican
   women: a comparison of content themes', *Hispanic Journal of Behavioral Sciences*,
   7: 273–83.
Crawford, M. (1988) 'Gender, age, and the social evaluation of assertion', *Behavior
   Modification*, 12: 549–64.
Crawford, M. (1989) 'Agreeing to differ: feminist epistemologies and women's ways of
   knowing', in M. Crawford and M. Gentry (eds), *Gender and Thought: Psycho-
   logical Perspectives.* New York: Springer-Verlag. pp. 128–45.
Crawford, M. (1995) *Talking Difference: On Gender and Language* London: Sage.

Crawford, M. and Marecek, J. (1989) 'Psychology reconstructs the female', *Psychology of Women Quarterly*, 13: 147–66.

Delamater, R.J. and McNamara, J.R. (1986) 'The social impact of assertiveness: research findings and clinical implications', *Behavior Modification*, 10: 139–58.

Dickson, A. (1982) *A Woman in Your Own Right: Assertiveness and You*. London: Quartet.

Eagly, A.H. (1995) 'The science and politics of comparing women and men', *American Psychologist*, 50: 145–58.

Erwin, E. (1978) *Behaviour Therapy: Scientific, Philosophical, and Moral Foundations*. Cambridge: Cambridge University Press.

Eyer, D.E. (1993) *Mother–infant Bonding: A Scientific Fiction*. New Haven, CT: Yale University Press.

Faludi, S. (1991) *Backlash: The Undeclared War against American Women*. New York: Doubleday.

Fine, M. and Gordon, S.M. (1989) 'Feminist transformations of/despite psychology', in M. Crawford and M. Gentry (eds), *Gender and Thought: Psychological Perspectives*. New York: Springer-Verlag. pp. 147–74.

Fodor, I.G. (1985) 'Assertiveness training for the eighties: moving beyond the personal', in L.B. Rosewater and L.E.A. Walker (eds), *Handbook of Feminist Therapy*. New York: Springer-Verlag. pp. 257–65.

Fodor, I.G. (ed.) (1992) *Adolescent Assertiveness and Social Skills: A Clinical Handbook*. New York: Springer-Verlag.

Fodor, I.G. and Epstein, R.C. (1983) 'Assertiveness training for women: where are we failing?', in P. Emmelkamp and E. Foa (eds), *Failures in Behavior Therapy*. New York: John Wiley. pp. 132–54.

Friedan, B. (1963) *The Feminine Mystique*. New York: Dell.

Galassi, M.D. and Galassi, J.P. (1978) 'Assertion: a critical review', *Psychotherapy: Theory, Research, and Practice*, 15: 16–29.

Gervasio, A.H. (1987) 'Assertiveness techniques as speech acts', *Clinical Psychology Review*, 7: 105–19.

Gervasio, A.H. and Crawford, M. (1989) 'Social evaluations of assertiveness: a critique and speech act reformulation', *Psychology of Women Quarterly*, 13: 1–25.

Gilligan, C. (1982) *In a Different Voice*. Cambridge, MA: Harvard University Press.

Harari, H. and Peters, J.M. (1987) 'The fragmentation of psychology: are APA divisions symptomatic?', *American Psychologist*, 42: 822–4.

Harding, S. (1986) *The Science Question in Feminism*. Ithaca, NY: Cornell University Press.

Harris, M.B. (1974) 'Mediators between frustration and aggression in a field experiment', *Journal of Experimental Social Psychology*, 10: 561–71.

Heimberg, R.C., Montgomery, D., Madsen, C.H. and Heimberg, J. (1977) 'Assertion training: a review of the literature', *Behavior Therapy*, 8: 953–71.

Henley, N. (1980) 'Assertiveness training in the social context', *Assert*, 30: 1–2.

hooks, b. (1989) *Talking Back*. Boston, MA: South End Press.

Hyde, J. (1996) *Half the Human Experience: The Psychology of Women* (5th edn). Lexington, MA: D.C. Heath.

Kahn, A.S. and Yoder, J.D. (1989) 'The psychology of women and conservatism: rediscovering social change', *Psychology of Women Quarterly*, 13: 417–32.

Kaplan, A. and Surrey, J.L. (1984) 'The relational self in women: developmental theory and public policy', in L.E. Walker (ed.), *Women and Mental Health Policy*. Beverly Hills, CA: Sage. pp. 79–94.

Kitzinger, C. (ed.) (1993) 'Special feature: "psychology constructs the female": A reappraisal', *Feminism & Psychology*, 3: 189–245.

Kitzinger, C. (ed.) (1994) 'Special feature: should psychologists study sex differences?', *Feminism & Psychology*, 4: 501–46.

Kitzinger, C. and Perkins, R. (1993) *Changing Our Minds: Lesbian Feminism and Psychology.* New York and London: New York University Press and Onlywomen Press.

Landrine, H., Klonoff, E. and Brown-Collins, A. (1992) 'Cultural diversity and methodology in feminist psychology: critique, proposal, empirical example', *Psychology of Women Quarterly*, 16: 145–64.

Lerman, H. and Porter, N. (eds) (1990) *Feminist Ethics in Psychotherapy.* New York: Springer-Verlag.

Lott, B. (1994) *Women's Lives: Themes and Variations in Gender Learning* (2nd edn). Pacific Grove, CA: Brooks Cole.

Lykes, M.B. (1985) 'Gender and individualistic vs. collectivist bases for notions about the self', *Journal of Personality*, 53: 356–83.

Manning, P. and Haddock, M. (1989) *Leadership Skills for Women.* Menlo Park, CA: Crisp Publications.

Marecek, J. (1997) 'Feminist psychology at thirty-something: feminism, gender, and psychology's ways of knowing', in E.A. Kaplan and D. Looser (eds), *Feminism and Generations.* Minneapolis, MN: University of Minnesota Press.

Marecek, J. and Kravetz, D. (1996, August) 'A room of one's own: power and agency in feminist therapy'. Paper presented at the meetings of the American Psychological Association, Toronto.

Matlin, M. (1993) *The Psychology of Women* (2nd edn). New York: Harcourt Brace.

McCullough, M. (forthcoming) *Women's Friendships across Cultures.* Cresskill, NJ: Hampton.

Mednick, M.T.S. (1989) 'On the politics of psychological constructs: stop the bandwagon, I want to get off', *American Psychologist*, 44: 1118–23.

Miller, J.B. (1984) *The Development of Women's Sense of Self* (Work in Progress Papers No. 84–01). Wellesley, MA: Wellesley College, The Stone Center.

Moriarty, T. (1975) 'A nation of willing victims', *Psychology Today*, April: 43–50.

Phelps, S. and Austin, N. (1975) *The Assertive Woman.* San Luis Obispo, CA: Impact.

Prince, J. and Hartnett, O. (1993) 'From "psychology constructs the female" to "fe/males construct psychology"', *Feminism & Psychology*, 3: 219–24.

Radway, J. (1984) *Reading the Romance: Women, Patriarchy, and Popular Literature.* Chapel Hill, NC: University of North Carolina Press.

Rakos, R.F. (1991) *Assertive Behavior: Theory, Research, and Training.* New York: Routledge, Chapman and Hall.

Rollins, J. (1996) *Women's Minds, Women's Bodies: The Psychology of Women in a Biosocial Context.* Upper Saddle River, NJ: Prentice-Hall.

Rosenthal, N.B. (1984) 'Consciousness raising: from revolution to reevaluation', *Psychology of Women Quarterly*, 8: 309–26.

Ruben, D. (1985) *Progress in Assertiveness, 1973–1983: An Analytical Bibliography.* Metuchen, NJ and London: The Scarecrow Press.

Sears, D.O. (1986) 'College sophomores in the laboratory: influences of a narrow data base on social psychology's view of human nature', *Journal of Personality and Social Psychology*, 51: 515–30.

Serber, M. (1977) 'Teaching the nonverbal components of assertive training', in R.E.

Alberti (ed.), *Assertiveness: Innovations, Applications, Issues*. San Luis Obispo, CA: Impact. pp. 67–74.

Shoemaker, M. and Satterfield, D.O. (1977) 'Assertion training: an identity crisis that's coming on strong', in R.E. Alberti (ed.), *Assertiveness: Innovations, Applications, Issues*. San Luis Obispo, CA: Impact. pp. 49–58.

Simonds, W. (1992) *Women and Self-help Culture*. New Brunswick, NJ: Rutgers University Press.

Skinner, B.F. (1957) *Verbal Behavior*. New York: Appleton-Century-Crofts.

Stanback, M.H. (1985) 'Language and black women's place: evidence from the black middle class', in P.A. Treichler, C. Kramarae and B. Stafford (eds), *For Alma Mater: Theory and Practice in Feminist Scholarship*. Urbana, IL: University of Illinois Press.

Stere, L.K. (1985) 'Feminist assertiveness training: self-esteem groups as skill training for women', in L.B. Rosewater and L.E.A. Walker (eds), *Handbook of Feminist Therapy*. New York: Springer-Verlag. pp. 51–61.

Unger, R.K. (1993) 'The personal is paradoxical: feminists construct psychology', *Feminism & Psychology*, 3: 211–18.

Unger, R. and Crawford, M. (1996) *Women and Gender: A Feminist Psychology* (2nd edn). New York: McGraw-Hill.

Wilson, K. and Gallois, C. (1993) *Assertion and its Social Context*. Oxford: Pergamon.

Wolfe, J.L. and Fodor, I.G. (1978) 'A cognitive/behavioral approach to modifying assertive behavior in women', in J.M. Whiteley and J.V. Flowers (eds), *Approaches to Assertion Training*. Monterey, CA: Brooks/Cole. pp. 141–57.

Worell, J. (1988) 'Women's satisfaction in close relationships', *Clinical Psychology Review*, 8: 477–98.

5

Dances with Feminism: Sidestepping and Sandbagging

Lise Bird

Writing a critique of work in feminist psychology is a ticklish task. I have for years been pulled towards abandoning psychology altogether as a hopeless cause, as a vestigial remnant of the 1950s Sputnik era fascination with boys' own empirical science. On the other hand, there is encouraging life from the women and men waving from the fringes of psychology. I see in these latter gestures (unlauded within mainstream psychology) the portents of a changing *Zeitgeist*, with possibilities for psychology as a significant part of the intellectual ferment elsewhere in the humanities and social sciences.

What realistic hope is there for deconstructing the edifice of positivist empirical psychology? There are a number of new strands within contemporary feminist theorizing which are handled only in the margins of psychology. The first part of this chapter contrasts two empirical programmes within the area of women and achievement motivation, using a few studies as exemplars. These research programmes can be seen as alternative reactions by psychology to questions posed by feminist thinking. I suggest these empirical practices within psychology limit the possibilities of conceptually rigorous feminist research. The second part of the chapter takes a lateral step, moving towards post-structural feminist ideas. These provide a disquieting and sometimes humourous challenge to traditional ways of doing and writing research.

A rudimentary philosophical problem for the empirical research discussed below revolves around the issue of recognizing and valuing differences among women. A difficulty for feminist movements around the world in the past two decades has been the loss of certainty which has come with the recognition that many women view feminist political movements as white and middle class. The illusion of a single unified voice for all women, expressed through a feminism of consensus, has been challenged by voices from the margin that refuse silence – voices of black women, indigenous women, lesbians and immigrant women from poor countries shunted into underpaid domestic work in affluent societies. One of the effects of this process was a concern with 'essentialism' within feminist theorizing of the late 1980s. An essentialist position (see Fuss, 1989) is an extreme position which elides differences between women of different cultures and times who may have very different needs and wants. In the psychological studies of gender difference mentioned below, strange proposals emerge when the issue of essentialism is not addressed directly.

Feminist theorists and philosophers have lately moved on from examining issues of essentialism and difference to longstanding philosophical problems such as the mind/body issue, especially for considerations of gender and corporeality, and the definition of feminist standpoints as epistemological positions (e.g. Butler, 1993). These issues are far from the concerns of much contemporary empirical work in psychology. Much of it could be labelled feminist psychology and would not be considered theoretically sophisticated in many other disciplines. Part of the problem may lie in normative paradigms and practices of empirical psychology. This chapter presents some possibilities for psychologists who are seeking to find more meaningful involvement with contemporary feminist theorizing.

Part One: Practices of Empirical Psychology

Sandbagging as damming behaviour

Feminist psychologists[1] have sometimes replicated masculinist psychology by retaining uncritically its empirical protocols. As a prime exemplar of modernism, traditional empirical psychology uses accrual of empirical data as a means for creating the warranting authority of an account.[2] Much more weight is given to testing of small-scale hypotheses than to deeper conceptual analysis. This tends to leave the big questions raised by feminists out of the picture.

The area of gender differences has already been the subject of incisive feminist critique (e.g. Bohan, 1993; Squire, 1989). A recent Special Feature of *Feminism & Psychology* was devoted to the question, 'Should psychologists study sex differences?' (Eagly, 1994; Halpern, 1994; Hare-Mustin and Marecek, 1994; Hollway, 1994; Hyde, 1994; Kitzinger, 1994). Hare-Mustin and Marecek (1994) asked whether this was indeed the wrong question, pointing out the essentialism and individualism which characterizes positivist research on sex differences. They argued that the knowledge accumulated on sex differences reveals more about the world-views of researchers in the discipline than about fundamental effects of gender. Marecek

(1995) has analysed the disciplinary issues further, questioning whether feminists have been able to influence long-held agendas of research in psychology. She suggests that feminists rebel with more vision in questioning the norms and practices of the discipline.

Experimental designs which examine differences between groups based on the variable of 'gender' tend to produce results which are limited to supporting or not supporting the existence of a gender difference. There is an unacknowledged essentialism which hides in the hypotheses of such research. Once a main effect of gender is unreplicated, there is little likelihood of a more subtle examination of gender issues. On the other hand, if gender is found to be in interaction with other variables, an unsatisfying proliferation of different gender effects may be the result. This creates not a pluralism of gender effects as much as an assortment. If there are stable effects of gender in various groups, differences can become essentialized as microsystems within particular ethnic or cultural groups. This enumeration of gender differences leaves open the racist possibility of a comparison of gender differences in white, Anglo-American groups with differences in 'other' groups, reinstating such a western difference as norm. One of the problems with the push for more and better empirical data is the tendency for variables to become more refined as the complexity of issues becomes more obvious.

There is an intriguing connection between the technological sophistication of empirical work on gender differences over time with a subtle movement towards the *de-gendering of the topic of study*. Though the focus here is on a specific area which crosses between personality, social and educational psychology, the studies encompass a large range of empirical techniques. I suspect that analogous effects can be found in many areas of psychology. There are sequences of research programme which can be choreographed as almost predictable movements of interest over time. Though I hesitate to follow a strict temporal model implying some teleological plan, the evidence seems to point to a predictable progression in certain kinds of gender-difference research.

The sequence goes something like this. Research points to a gender difference. In subsequent studies the effect seems to disappear. I think this comes about through an empirical-pursuit leaning within the discipline which encourages researchers to keep identifying more and more variables in order to attempt better to predict and control an effect. Unfortunately for the dreams of a unified empirical science, the research effect often disappears under such scrutiny. The time-honoured empirical techniques of meticulous demarcation and analysis of variables becomes instead an obfuscation. What started as a clear gender effect becomes a small sack of data hidden under a profusion of other data effects. The jumble of separately articulated findings is not the hoped-for expanding pyramid of knowledge, but an obstacle which obscures the vision of seekers left standing beside the pile. And concerns about gender disappear.

I use the term 'sandbagging' to refer to the tendency for increased empirical study to stifle the original gender effects. The hope of progress in liberal feminist research is that with more empirical facts there will be more knowledge of variables which produce inequality, which can then be targeted and controlled. Sandbagging of empirical data turns into busy activity, while the flow of oppressive social problems continues.

I first noticed the sandbagging tendency in my own research some years ago. I had found an interesting gender difference in expectations about achievement, showing that girls appeared to have even lower expectations when they were tested under private and anonymous conditions compared to the more usual test with more interaction between tester and student (Bird, 1984). In a later study I was determined to track down this effect with a complex, multiply crossed design picking apart the variables of anonymity, privacy and verbal interaction with the tester. To my surprise the gender effect 'washed out' in the midst of complex interactions between variables. Interviews carried out with each student at the end of the study turned out to be far more interesting to me than the quantitative data, which led me to change my research methods (Bird, 1986). For some time I felt guilty about having published a study of gender differences when the effect later seemed to disappear. My view some time later is that feminist research hypotheses are not neutral propositions to be confirmed or denied with a falsifiable empirical programme. As writers on feminist methods have noted in a variety of disciplines, there are many ways that research methods, conceptual systems, publishing and hiring practices can reflect masculinist practices, and ways that positivist empirical studies can reinscribe gender within a sexist world-view (Eichler, 1988).

I am proposing here a tendency within empirical programmes of gender research towards their own self-de(con)struction within a positivist framework. Within the literature on women and achievement, a sandbagging effect seems to have appeared a number of times. The combination of this effect with a conceptual problem in the area of essentialism creates an awkward duet. In the examples below, I note two ways that empirical research has become caught between increasing empirical refinement and a rigid conception of gender differences. Both approaches are responses of researchers who have been sandbagged into a corner. The two research agendas below demonstrate different ways that studies have attempted to sidestep the problem of essentialism.

Women who (don't) want to achieve

Women seemed to be a problem from the beginning in the field of achievement motivation. Women's responses did not seem to fit the paradigm created by David McClelland and colleagues in the 1950s (e.g. Sutherland and Veroff, 1985). An avenue of research which did focus on women looked at the possibility that women might have a 'fear of success' (Horner, 1972). This research 'quickly commanded both popular and scientific attention and led to an outpouring of empirical studies' (Spence and Helmreich, 1983: 36). When the initial large gender effects were not replicated in subsequent studies, attention turned to problems with the methods used to measure fear of success, and the research itself turned to other issues not so clearly associated with gender or feminist concerns (e.g. Canavan-Gumpert et al., 1978).

In concluding a summary of Horner's work, Spence and Helmreich noted: 'With greater societal acceptance of women's educational and vocational aspirations, sex differences in fear-of-success studies appear to be evaporating' (1983: 37). The quote above contrasted with earlier comments in the same article which summarized research on fear of success. The initial gender effect was described as possibly the outcome of poor scientific practices. The about-face in subsequent research towards more 'general' issues was positioned in the text as a logical step in the progress of the research. The quote above, however, leaves open the possibility of other forces at work, such as that greater liberation for women has in reality reduced women's fear of success. What is missing in this text is awareness of this contradiction. Feminist researchers have to consider and record comment on the subtle links between the research we do and the political questions of our time, even though such comments may fit uncomfortably with many textual practices in psychological writing.

The fear-of-success effect in women looks like a candidate for sandbagging. The original gender difference faded without engaging with issues such as essentialism and ethnocentrism. For some reason I always imagined that 'Anne', the heroine of Horner's projective vignette about a fictional achiever at the 'top of her medical school class', was blonde and thin. I wonder how many readers fantasized Anne as a Jamaican-born student from a poor family. The problem with these 'neutral' stimulus materials is that cultural stereotypes are less likely to be expressed overtly in responses. Though much interesting feminist research today may have been influenced by the work on fear of success, the change in subsequent research towards more general (i.e. non-feminist) concerns needs further consideration. A similar pattern can be found in another area concerned with women and achievement motivation, in the study of gendered attribution patterns.

One idea which has seeped from research into popular culture is that women are not as likely as men to take credit for their successes at school (and work) by assuming that they have 'the ability' for it. The idea comes from both US research on the psychology of gendered attribution patterns and the more critical, qualitative work of Valerie Walkerdine and colleagues in the UK. Both avenues of research on issues of women's competence are referred to below.

A major focus for feminist empirical researchers of the 1970s and 1980s was with attributions about achievement to factors such as ability, effort, difficulty of a task and luck. This work had clear links with the earlier work on achievement motivation but was expanded by techniques and concepts from the social psychology of attribution. In the area of attributions about achievement, as for research on fear of success, the sandbagging effect appears to have washed out many of the earlier gender differences. A literature search of mainstream (mostly US) psychology journals since 1975 suggests that studies of gender differences in attributions about achievement issues peaked in the mid-1980s. For example, in 1982 there was an entire issue of the journal *Sex Roles* devoted to this issue. The field has broadened in recent times to more 'applied' topics of concern to feminists such as career issues, sexual violence and alcohol use.

Research into gender differences in attribution appears to be rather moribund in theoretical development, since both empirical feminists and non-feminist writers who wish to cover gender-difference research have been caught in binarizing and essentialist discussions. Feminist theories have grappled with the issue of differences among women for some time now. I am going to create my own binary contrast here, to indicate problems both for attribution research which continues to explore gender differences, and for research which has 'moved on', beyond gender considerations. Using a 'now you see gender, now you don't' approach, I will first mention research that began with a focus on gender and then became amnesic on gender questions, in contrast to work which continues to look at gender differences by remaining with the same (superseded) paradigm first mooted in the 1970s.

Giving away her dancing shoes
In research which has now become something of a talisman of feminist folklore, attribution studies of the 1970s found evidence that girls were less likely than boys to take credit for their academic

successes as signs of their personal competence or 'ability' (Dweck and Repucci, 1973; Nicholls 1978). Girls appeared to be using a more self-defeating pattern of attributions in considering their failures as due to a presumed lack of ability. Further research suggested that teachers were crucial in creating these patterns. Dweck, Davidson, Nelson and Enna (1978) found that teachers were more likely to criticize girls than boys for academic qualities in their work as opposed to its format. In an experimental study, these researchers also demonstrated that students of both genders were less likely to attribute their lack of success to ability when given such negative academic feedback. Allusions to this gender effect are quite common in popular culture, if my observations at meetings of professional feminist educators in Aotearoa New Zealand are anything to go by.

A number of studies examined the teacher feedback effect and did not replicate the original findings (Heller and Parsons, 1981). A commentary and review by Eccles and Blumenfeld (1985) concluded that gender effects could be found in the data, but cast doubt on the links between teacher feedback and student attributions. This review suggested that more refined empirical work on the gender difference was needed.

What is the current status of work which earlier emphasized girls' debilitating attribution patterns? Following what appears to be a sandbagging effect of increasing complexity of gender effects in later studies, research by Dweck and colleagues has moved away completely from an analysis of gender effects in attribution towards a more general model of links between cognition, personality and motivation. A review of literature in the area (Dweck and Leggett, 1988) presents a theoretical model which links attributional styles to particular 'orientations' towards achievement motivation, described as either 'mastery' or 'helplessness'. 'Mastery' refers to a view of achievement similar in many ways to a McClellandian view which emphasizes challenge and persistence with striving, though ostensibly without a focus on competitive performance. 'Helplessness' is the 'maladaptive' avoidance of challenge, with a tendency for persons to perform more poorly than they could when they lose confidence in the face of obstacles. The orientations are thought to arise from people's implicit theories about the nature of intelligence, specifically whether intelligence is seen as an 'entity', a fixed potential in the person, or as a more flexible possibility of increasing intelligence in the 'incremental' model. These popular ideas about intelligence were thought to determine the sorts of goals people have in life, linked in with their motivational orientation as directed towards 'performance' (a 'show' of what the person can do) or 'learning' (a focus on knowledge and achievement for its own sake).

Throughout the Dweck and Leggett (1988) review there is a focus on the 'individual', who attempts (not always successfully) to act as a rational being in charge of reaching a goal. Their attempt to focus on 'underlying personality variables' suggests that there is some underlying truth, some deep-seated reality that 'will out' in the individual, the driving force that will work itself out in the pattern of the person's motivations. Nowhere in this analysis is there a sense of larger societal forces, of consistencies due to gender, class, ethnicity or culture that also 'will out'. Of course the review might argue that these structural features might be mappable as part of the way culture imprints itself on particular features of personality, if only more finely honed research on the relevant variables could be identified by future technicians.

The research described above has moved from a concern with gender differences in attributions to a focus on stable individual differences in personality which are not easily tied to gender. Though the early studies may still be referenced by feminist writers today, the researchers have moved into more general theorizing in personality in which feminist concerns are invisible. The point of this story is not to criticize the researchers involved for political incorrectness. Rather, I am simply referring to this story as a possible exemplar of the sandbagging effect. The early work on gender differences in attribution was stuck conceptually in a paradigm founded on over-simplified essentialist assumptions about gender. The researchers were astute in getting out of a conceptual bog. Unfortunately, as I see it, the researchers lost the possibility of feminist analysis by remaining within experimental studies of individual differences based more generally on 'adaptive' and 'maladaptive' naive beliefs about personal competence. In the final section of this chapter I will point to some research which has looked at these issues within a different feminist framework.

Gender promenade: real women achieve differently
There is still a considerable body of research work which continues to examine gender differences within the framing of the earlier paradigm. Textbooks for courses on motivation tend to have at least one section on gender differences, possibly for reasons of political correctness and marketability to increased numbers of women students as much as for empirical accuracy. One strategy is for the textbook to spotlight gender issues within a stark essentialist framework. For example, one US text (Buck, 1988) includes a section on 'sex differences' at the end of a mostly gender-blind chapter on achievement motivation. The chapter ends with a contradictory view that 'our *conception* of achievement has a distinctly masculine bias'

while undercutting its own critical analysis by referring to '[e]vidence of sex-dimorphic behavior' (Buck, 1988: 391; emphasis in original). The text thus assumes an unexamined biological primacy of sexual difference as the foundation for social structures (see Riley, 1983). The author is non-wittingly reduced to an essentialist and anti-feminist, 'biology is destiny' view.

Writers of a more feminist bent have also interpreted gender-difference studies within an essentialist framework. In a recent collection entitled, *New Directions in Feminist Psychology*, a chapter by Ayers-Nachamkin (1992) tells a strong story about gender differences in attributions. The chapter reports a 'classic' attribution study of first-year women psychology students asked to make achievement attributions after being given controlled (faked) feedback about their performance in matching geometric designs. The reported research is set valiantly against the effects of sandbagging; it keeps alive the gender-difference research of the mid-1980s, rather than turning away from gender to other variables of influence. This is done, however, primarily by creating silence around a number of key areas of attribution research. The theoretical model created by Weiner and Irene Frieze, which originally emphasized four types of attribution about achievement, is used without its later refinements. The study determinedly demonstrates that women 'can' take credit for an 'appropriate' feminine success rather than attribute their successes to luck in a self-deprecating way. The simple task of matching 'figure-grams' (a word with interesting allusions to feminine body shape) is, through the verbal instructions to 'subjects', a means of ensuring the young women's keenness to reveal their 'sensitivity . . . success in sensing other people's subtle feelings – or more generally, their capacity for sympathizing with the wants and needs of other people' (Ayers-Nachamkin, 1992: 230). The task was rather boldly described to participants as 'designed to yield information about the feminine personality' (ibid.: 230). Perhaps for these women in a small college (acknowledged to be 'Caucasian, middle class') in their first year away from home, such instructions would spur at least some semblance of interest in pleasing the female experimenter.

There is an intriguing similarity between the theoretical explanation for gender differences in attribution in the textbook mentioned above and in the latter chapter. Both explanations focus on gender as the cause of differences, though the first implicates biology and the second socialization. The Ayers-Nachamkin chapter proposes that differential socialization experiences of girls and boys define domains for the achievements on which we will focus our energies in later life, with women being just as 'ego-involved' as men when considering our performance in areas of traditional feminine competence. Socialization, tacked in place by reinforcement and modelling, were the presumed causal operators in creating the gender effects. But in contemporary feminist theorizing, conceptual explanation based on social roles just will no longer do (see Edwards, 1983). There is more scepticism these days about the idea of a 'role' as a transportable cloak of social behaviours which the homuncular inner woman may simply shake off in order to be her true, liberated self. Recent feminist philosophy takes to task the issue of the division between an inner self and outer body in western thought (see Grosz, 1994).

The feminist work just described takes an essentialist line that creates 'real women', all of whom share common features and erase those troubling differences of ethnicity, class, culture and sexuality between us. The essential woman celebrated in the chapter is one who is sensitive and feminine, in other words, as a universal help-meet who is the feminine half of a two-gendered heterosexual pair. Any work which posits gender effects that suppresses social differences is likely to reinscribe the conflation of gender and sexual orientation. The essentialist real woman is created as a glib ideal at the cost of poor, black, deaf and/or stroppy (tired of being 'sensitive') women on the margins everywhere, women who may not be looking for the male who will be their 'other half' (see Atmore, 1992).

Beyond Empirical Sandbags

The two examples of approaches to work on gender and achievement motivation create an extreme contrast. The first approach shows an avoidance of the pitfalls of gender essentialism through the Scylla of moving to excise gender as a concern for psychology. The second approach was Charybdis's story of the tenacious study of gender differences using research paradigms anachronistic in psychology and without engagement with recent feminist theorizing. Is there an alternative to an essentialist end for overly binarized studies of women and achievement issues? It is time to consider ways that feminist psychologists can broaden perspectives to get beyond the structural constraints which limit this research.

Part Two: Stepping into the Post-structural

Going beyond the gender binary
The entire social map for viewing performance in any area is located within a gendered world-view. This issue is signalled well by the

cliché that 'assertive talk from a man is aggressive talk from a woman', in other words, that the same 'speech act' is perceived entirely differently by many observers depending on the gender of the speaker. It seems a little presumptuous to assume that a girl keen on cooking makes an 'internal attribution' to her abilities in this area in a completely analogous way to a boy of the same age who makes a similar attribution (to ability) after getting 100 per cent correct on a maths test at school.

An alternative view is that gender creates the people that we are, or, to take a more post-structural stance, the positionings within discourses about femininity, or success, or competence from which our voices may speak. Judith Butler's (1993) work on gender as performative opens questions about the ways that we speak our selves into positions in social settings as particular women/men. The 'woman' I perform as I stand in front of a class of educational psychology students is not the same 'woman' who speaks to a friend from schooldays who has just been diagnosed with cancer. The words and body movements to which I have access and which are called into play in those settings are entirely different. The choreography of these sounds and movements has not required elaborate planning beforehand; performing these women has come after decades of social practices in which this body's dutiful and expressive possibilities have been shaped.

Going beyond ability hierarchies

What is silent in social role analysis (e.g. Ayers-Nachamkin, 1992) which argues for separate and equal women's knowledge is the recognition that there is a gendered hierarchy of knowledges. In this hierarchy 'cooking' may be positioned as a domain requiring little intellectual nouse compared to that of 'mathematics'. Of course the domains are not commensurable, but the fuzziness of their boundaries is usually ignored. Some skills, especially in mathematics (see Walkerdine, 1988) are seen as more indicative of an intellectual power that generalizes to other tasks; the 'intelligent' person is supposed to be able to tackle more difficult tasks of all kinds. Within the university, there is a meritocracy of the academic disciplines, with more 'abstracted', theoretical (hence less concrete or 'people-oriented') disciplines having higher status.

One area of woman's supposed achievement is related to sensitivity to other people. Though it might be possible to consider some general abstracted skill, for example to argue that some people are especially sensitive care-givers, nurturance is an obvious area in which skill is displayed in an interpersonal context and can never be considered the outcome of one person's skill in dealing with another person as object of that skill. Certainly, in some areas of public skill, such as for politicians, managers or sales representatives, it may be possible to talk of a general 'ability' that some people have in dealing with others. It is more difficult to say that a woman has a general 'ability' in nurturing or social skill. What is at stake in determining the competence of a 'true woman' is, ultimately, her 'ability' in dealing with a particular set of people, her family, a clientele with which she is in some senses stuck no matter how bad the going gets.

There seem to be contradictions in the very discourses about women's abilities that make 'attributions' about these issues rather naive. Part of the problem for psychologists is the tendency to see language as a transparent medium for the exposition of technicist problem-solving.

Going beyond language as a transparent medium
The textual styles of psychologists writing in prestigious journals of the discipline have altered little in the past 10 years, despite encouragement by the American Psychological Association for authors to remove masculine pronouns. It still appears to be more important for the academic psychologist to be able to read quantities of detailed empirical research rather than papers with greater conceptual elaboration and textual diversity.

In thinking about the linguistic impoverishment of empirical writings in psychology, including some feminist writing, it is worth remembering Sheridan's description of Foucault's historical writings as a cultivated and 'conscious rejection of the language of Reason that seeks by its grey, measured, monotonous tones to give an impression of authority, objectivity, and truth' (1980: 224). Laurel Richardson has pointed out that the language of science became, by the nineteenth century, 'objective, precise, unambiguous, noncontextual, nonmetaphoric' (1990: 14). This was in contrast to the language of the humanities, assigned the task of expressing taste and artistic judgements and feelings, using lively, highly valenced words. The discipline of psychology in its experimental and other positivist empirical programmes has clearly opted for the former at the expense of the latter. The split between rationality and passion, science and humanities, is unfortunate for feminist work and out of step with contemporary feminist theorizing, which is political, polyvocal and sometimes eloquently expressive.

An example of experimental writing comes from a study which emerged from the gender-difference literature discussed above. The following passage is taken from the 'Procedure' section of an experimental study of children's problem-solving and shows some of the textual strategies usually employed in empirical studies of its kind. The passage describes the experience planned for children at the end of a set of extremely difficult problems they have attempted as part of the researchers' controlled 'programmed failure' experience.

> A mastery experience was then given to enable each child to leave the situation feeling pleased with his or her performance. . . . Specifically, children were told that the problems they had worked on were very hard and that they had solved more of them than most kids their age. (in Bempechat et al., 1991: 17; references omitted)

The procedure just described is presumably a reflection of the ethical concerns of the investigators, a means of ensuring that children leave the testing situation with some positive comment from the adults involved. There are interesting ironies involved in attempting to produce 'mastery' beliefs in children, for research argues that 'mastery' is the most adaptive model of motivational orientation for the child at school. While educational views of 'mastery' usually do not involve competition, it is interesting that the above quote makes reference to performance of an individual relative to a distribution for a particular age-group, rather than to an individual standard of performance.

I think it is crucial that feminist psychologists consider the crafting of the language used in written texts as much as feminists in philosophy or literature. The word 'mastery' cannot be used uncritically by feminists in psychology without considering its cultural and historical implications. To 'master' a subject or a skill has links with notions of control, unusual feats of skill, authority, dominion and superiority over others. The use of such a term by researchers in a country which has a notably difficult history in its embrace of slavery in earlier centuries seems ill-considered. The term has some weight of irony, given that many African-American students may have had ancestors who were 'mastered' by enforced expatriation, immigration and work assignment, all without consideration of traditions, kinship patterns or working styles of their original cultures. Today these students may have some of the least optimistic educational outcomes, and presumably some of the least 'masterful' attribution patterns.

A different view of the rites of mastery

The work of Valerie Walkerdine and colleagues addresses some of the same issues as the empirical research outlined earlier. Their work would also no doubt support the position (in Bempechat et al., 1991) that mastery at school, exemplified by an orientation towards the successful accomplishment of schoolwork, is an adaptive winning strategy. However, these researchers would further argue that a position of 'mastery' is a predictable outcome for certain students, given certain sexist and classist social/psychic formations in western thought.

The language used in Walkerdine's (1988) account of skilful accomplishment in 'The Mastery of Reason' is quite different from that of the empirical psychological work above. The original cover of Walkerdine's book features part of a William Blake portrait of a godlike male figure, 'The Ancient of Days', leaning down from a celestial height. In Walkerdine's work, mastery is clearly an oppressive practice, resonating from colonial imperialism to domination within class and gender hierarchies. The book's cover alludes to a worldly order in which rules and hierarchies are sanctioned by god himself, the ultimate master.

Walkerdine's engaging (and often empirically iconoclastic) discourse analysis of conversations between students and teachers, or mothers and daughters, has reached a general audience in several countries. One of Walkerdine's theses is that, regardless of the actual women and men in the life of the child, the position of 'girl' either at home or at school is not one of rational mastery and competence, no matter how accomplished the girl's performance. Her work uses the psychoanalytic theory of Jacques Lacan, especially the mirror stage as reworked by Cathy Urwin (1984), to consider ways that girls are positioned in contradictory ways when they are in a classroom. According to Lacan, the child first gets an idea of coherence as a self and subject in seeing itself in a mirror in early childhood, when there is a discrepancy between the child who experiences poor motor control and the specular image of the together, functioning child. Urwin argues that the child learns the possibilities of autonomous and coherent subjecthood through interactions with adults mediated through language, not just from access to mirrored images. Through such experiences the child may begin to feel powerful as a self differentiated from the (m)other, who cannot be made to serve the child's every whim. According to Lacan (following Freud), coping with this gap between the ideal and the real creates the ego, which is a positioning of coherence and (imagined) autonomy. Like Lacan, Urwin and Walkerdine consider language to provide opportunities for the child to be positioned in a way to articulate the gap or loss experienced between desire and the fulfilment of desire.

The pivotal issue for gender is that this developing ego is enmeshed in gendered relations. The expression and articulation of a self/other difference through language is tied, in psychoanalytic thought, to an erotic economy in which the male child is positioned as the opposite/other half to the mother, in alignment (identification) with the father. The development of the ego creates a splitting along a number of dimensions for the child, especially between an amorphous fluidity of emotions that characterize the close ties with the mother and the separate, autonomous and rational position of masculinity. This latter positioning is referred to by Lacan as 'phallic' since it is more than a genital representation of male sexual desire; what the man 'has' that the woman 'lacks' is access to the public order of language, the power which controls through symbolic rather than concrete means. Lacan's term 'phallus' describes both an access to women as objects of desire and access to language as the means for taking autonomous control in the public sphere through society's laws and institutions.

Walkerdine has taken this central Lacanian tenet regarding the creation of a gendered identity and tied it to Foucault's analysis of the regulation of bodies through social structures and institutions. Through all kinds of social practices in childrearing and in the child-centred pedagogy of schooling, the 'child' is created as a position of developing autonomy and competence, especially in curriculum areas such as mathematics. The position of 'child' is interrupted by gender. Since girls' gender identity in the psychoanalytic framework is about being the object of the male gaze, the girl who wants to be a competent student is positioned as lacking autonomy and agency for her own desires. For girls who are black and/or working class (hence from a subject-position which emphasizes manual more than mental work), there is an even greater removal from positionings of autonomy and competence, and greater likelihood of positioning as objects of the eroticized male gaze.

Some of the subtlety in Walkerdine's work is in her skilful appropriation of Lacanian ideas about desire. For many feminist psychologists, Lacan's focus on the unconscious and the imaginary has provided useful alternatives to American empirical research which is rather fixed in hidden assumptions about the rational ego – whether the ego of the researcher hoping to change disadvantaged 'subjects' or that of the subjects who were being helped to get a grip on themselves and just 'think positive'. Still, Walkerdine's use of Lacanian ideas poses many questions for feminist research.

In the 1980s Lacanian theory provided a complex, convincing (masculine, French) theoretical framework for moving beyond liberal humanism. Contemporary feminist theorists have further extended Lacan's views, most recently to reconsider the heterosexual foundations of gender, sexuality and identity. In a critique of Teresa de Lauretis's book, *The Practice of Love: Lesbian Sexuality and Perverse Desire* (1994), Elizabeth Grosz concurs with the importance of Lacan's ideas to feminist theories of sexuality, referring to the theory as 'feminism's preeminent cultural discourse' in the area

(Grosz, 1995: 156). Grosz commends the book for taking the feminist potential of Lacanian ideas to their limits, while also questioning just how far the work of male theorists can be productively reworked and reappropriated towards feminist ends.

> While an immense amount of (sometimes productive and rewarding) feminist thought, ingenuity, and labor has gone into this project of stretching or extending the tolerable boundaries of male discourses so they may be useful for or amenable to feminist projects, the long-term benefits of continuing to prop up or support a discourse which has well-recognized problems are not clear. (Grosz, 1995: 167)

Recently, I have considered whether Walkerdine's analysis about gender and competence can be argued convincingly without the Lacanian foundations. In the next section I take a 'reading' of some conversations in a primary school classroom using a framework shaped by Walkerdine's analysis. My reading tends to position the girls either as active, as competent speakers and knowers, or as more pliant objects of the discourses of femininity. Since the construction of such binaries has been the subject of so much feminist critique, I am not happy to leave the stories there. A Lacanian perspective seems to lean too easily towards the evocation of such contrapuntal binaries. In contrast, Bronwyn Davies (1982) has used the more proliferate metaphor of 'jazz' to describe the extemporaneous flow of children's changing topics for play and conversation. In the stories below an ear is left attuned to themes other than the counterpoint of the assertive versus the passive. At the end I consider other readings of the fieldwork, in attempting to go beyond the binary framework of competence, towards a more open-ended feminist analysis.

Inward bound: girls and the interior
To take a closer look at the way different theoretical perspectives shape an analysis of incidents of 'mastery' in a classroom, I offer here a re-reading of some of my fieldnotes from research in a primary school in an urban area of Aotearoa/New Zealand. I consider issues of competence, using some of Walkerdine's perspectives, in interpreting actions of a group of 7- to 8-year-olds seated at a table talking and writing stories for a lesson.

Children in this classroom often discussed the plots of their stories with each other during writing lessons. They worked on these stories over several days, commenting on each other's stories and changing plots and characters with feedback from others in the class and suggestions from their teacher, Anne. My focus during this class was on a group of four girls and four boys working on their stories together. (I have described some of the dialogue of this scene in Bird,

1994, but my story has changed as I have struggled with the diverse gendered and ethnic positionings of children in this tableau.) Clothing provides an important prop in my story. On this day I noted that Sherry was wearing an unusual full, circular, red and white concentrically striped skirt (what used to be called a 'poodle' skirt.) This skirt became at one point the focus of attention of the group in the excerpt below.

> 10:20   Children are working on their stories. At a table with several girls and boys, Janet explains aloud to the group the plot of a 'MacGyver' television episode. Sherry listens. At one point Jack starts talking softly to the other boys, saying loudly the word 'knickers'. There is a moment's silence, then Danny looks at Sherry.
> *Danny*:   Once I saw you and the wind came up and it went voooooom.
> Then Carrie leans over, her head and shoulders beneath the level of the table, to look at Sherry's skirt.

A Walkerdinian analysis might focus on changing positionings for these girls between academic competence and femininity (in Lacanian terms as 'being', rather than 'having', the phallus). At the beginning of this excerpt Janet was positioned as assertively competent in her command of the group's attention to her topic in the story-writing lesson. Janet's monologue about the plot of a US television 'action' programme, which centred around a male character, further emphasized her positioning of masculine competence. There was some contradiction in Janet's position, given that the task of writing fiction may be an area of feminine expertise for women in western societies. Janet's speech was interrupted when Jack spoke simultaneously and softly at his end of the table about 'knickers'. Despite this, Janet finished her sentence with a clear voice. Then Danny took the speaking-space of the table by changing the topic to his remembered view of Sherry when the wind blew her skirt up. In this change of conversation a girl, positioned as having phallic authority, was interrupted by a boy who positioned another girl as the object of his (male) gaze, as 'having' the phallus (i.e. as the desired object of the phallus).

At this point the attention of the group of children at the table was on Sherry and her striped skirt. It was another girl, Carrie, who positioned Sherry as the object of her gaze by looking under the table at Sherry's skirt. For a child to look under a table in a class like this is not an unusual action. It would be considered a rude action if carried out by an adult, and certainly it would be more offensive for a man than a woman to look under the table at the clothing of a woman. This action of Carrie's can be read as a forbidden glimpse of the hidden beneath the rational surface of the table on which the children are writing. It is, then, a look at the hidden, the interior, the lower half of bodies which have never been a welcome part of the school curriculum. Instead of expressing demure embarrassment when Jack remarks on the undergarments of a girl, Carrie, without speech, acts to make Sherry's feminine apparel the centre of attention. Carrie is positioned presumably as female and the object of the gaze, yet expresses her own gaze. Carrie's look both reinforces the objectification of all 'girls' and creates a separate position for herself as an active viewer.

In the next moments at the table Janet reasserted her visibility as a competent performer by describing her own written work.

> *Janet*:   I've done a long story. I've written a good story.

Janet then showed the children around her how much she had written by holding her booklet up towards others so that they could see her writing as she flipped through the pages.

> *Janet*:   Look how many pages I've done. I started there and went there.
> *Debbie* (to *Carrie*):   She's done a story. She's done a whole long thing.

Debbie's response publicly affirmed Janet's achievement. When next the teacher, Anne, came to stand by Janet in order to comment on her work, Janet's position changed.

> *Anne*:   You don't have to double-space your story, Janet.
> *Sherry* (to *Janet*, putting her hands on her own work):   This is the best thing I've ever done. This is the best thing I've ever done.
> *Debbie* (to *Janet*):   You haven't done much, Janet.

Sherry had not spoken about her own work until, seemingly, the teacher's mild remark put Janet's work into some doubt. While Sherry rather joyfully commented on her own work, Debbie criticized Janet's work. At this point Janet raised her shirt to show that underneath it she was wearing a tee-shirt with a koala bear printed on it.

In the scene above, Janet began as the only person speaking, the vocal centre of attention at the table. Janet's body language, sitting forward in her chair and showing others her work, was an assertive claim to competence. Janet's positioning of competence was challenged by the teacher's brief remark about her work. Debbie followed the teacher's comment with a negative remark to Janet, casting doubt on Janet as a good girl and a good student. Janet's position then seemed to change. By lifting her shirt, Janet 'revealed' her attractive underclothing and hence her positioning of competent femininity. The femininity of this assertion was augmented by class privilege, since her gesture uncovered, under her warm woollen jumper, an item linked with an overseas trip to a warmer climate. In

Lacanian terms Janet would be seen here as jumping from being the phallus to having the phallus.

In the next few minutes at the story table, Sherry resumed her positioning as the girl with the most eye-catching clothing. Janet's next comment was to turn the table's attention back to Sherry's skirt.

> *Janet*: Your dress goes up when you talk.
> *Sherry*: It's a circle, it's made so it spins all the way round.
> *Janet*: I like those skirts and dresses.
> Sherry gets up and twirls around to make her skirt do a circular swirl.

Janet's first comment above would seem to contain a put-down, since presumably good girls do not have skirts that go up or straps that fall down when they talk. Rational talk should issue forth from a sensibly groomed body. However, Janet's next remark showed admiration about these interesting and revealing items of feminine clothing ('I like those skirts and dresses'). Sherry was very skilled in her body movements, as she had studied dance. On this occasion and later on the playground, children gathered around Sherry as she twirled elegantly on one foot, making her skirt into a rather dizzying optical illusion. This was a very interesting move, since the children watching Sherry twirl did not, on either occasion when I saw her do this, focus on the fact that her underclothing was on view. As she pirouetted 'effortlessly' so that the skirt rose slightly to make a complete circle of dizzying red and white stripes, the faces of other children around her appeared rather awe-struck. It seemed to me that the visual image of the spinning circle of fabric went beyond a possible risk of exposure, female vulnerability and objectification in the male gaze. The patterning colours left behind the everyday range of schoolroom paints and crayons. Something happened which carried a surplus of meaning, a visual image which went beyond the male gaze and Sherry's collusion with her self-presentation as object. Her movement signified a body under control for the performance.

There are pleasures involved in the wearing of clothing as a tactile pleasure, along with the visual and kinetic ones brought to play with the spinning skirt. For a stereotypical feminist of the 1970s these may be forbidden pleasures, indicating an unsavoury fascination with personal appearance, and a collusion with objectification. For Sherry, this interest in clothing could be read both as her artistic control of her own body and as her passive entrapment as object of another's gaze.

Multiple possibilities
As I signalled earlier, the focus on girls as having gendered/raced positionings of competence or incompetence, based on a Lacanian

view of access to male domains, leaves much to be desired. There must be ways to take Walkerdine's ideas further while discarding some of the Lacanian constructions of gender. One way to move is to broaden the number of possible positionings in my story.

Bronwyn Davies's work is much influenced by Walkerdine's perspectives. She has taken post-structural readings into work in classrooms and on playgrounds in collaborative work aimed at reshaping the meanings of masculinity and femininity in school practices. Davies (1990) has considered ways that our desires are contradictorily constructed by the cultural discourses and practices in which we, as subjects created by these discourses, are immersed.

To return to Moana school, Sherry's performance could lead her into a future focus on what women wear, positioning her in discourses about femininity, about what respectable women should look like, about sexiness and panache. Alternatively, it could lead her to be positioned by a teacher, a parent, a stranger on the street, as a person who might some day dance, choreograph or design what others wear. So there are no clear predictions to be made about the range and political consequences of the discourses in which Sherry and her flying skirt might be placed.

My story becomes more complicated when I move away from a tale of Janet and Sherry as 'girls' and 'reveal' that they both have ethnic minority status. Both girls were from families which immigrated to New Zealand from other Pacific Islands. Though in my fieldwork I never heard these girls describe themselves with reference to any ethnic identity markers (my 'information' came from a teacher), my story inevitably tends to create these girls as representatives of 'Polynesia'. My story becomes tied into issues of racism and colonization once these girls are positioned as members of a clearly identifiable, economically disadvantaged minority. I note how easy it is to write a story which avoids such issues if I stick to a tale of 'girls' unspecified, unmarked as 'mainstream' (white, middle-class) girls. In my altered reading, Sherry's dance movements can be viewed as stereotypic attributes of 'Polynesian Woman'. If, in Walkerdine's view, a black girl is even less likely than a white girl to be viewed as 'competent', what are the chances that Sherry's visual/kinetic art will be seen as signs of an educationally promotable artistic talent? How likely is it that Janet will continue her quest for visibility in her social group based on her references to her academic work? Could any 'girl' escape these endlessly reforming positions of incompetence?

Since writing the first drafts of this chapter, I have been surprised to discover yet another omission from my fieldwork tale. The character of Jack is a rather negative, masculine one: Jack is the 'harasser' who mentions Sherry's 'knickers' while Janet is attempting to talk about her writing project. What has been omitted is Jack's ethnicity, perhaps because Jack was described by one of the teachers as Maori (indigenous). In a country with ethnic politics as complex as those of New Zealand, I did not want to deal with the added complexity of highlighting a Maori boy's actions when they could be read as harassing. I also omitted to mention that at first I thought Jack was a girl. He had longish hair and eyelashes, and a gender-ambiguous shortening of his name. In my early fieldnotes, which used mnemonic acronyms to help me to remember particular children before I learned their names, I referred to Jack as 'BLG', or 'boy who looks like a girl'. From this small gender ambiguity I could construct quite a different story about Jack in my narrative. Rather than positioning Jack with all boys as an essentialist example of the male oppressor, I could make intertextual references to the ways a boy positioned ambiguously in discourses of gender could increase his masculinity by asserting an aggressive heterosexuality. After all, to be called a 'girl' is one of the worst slurs made to boys on the playground, a call both sexist and homophobic. The story cannot end here, however, without considering further cultural intricacies. Discourses about gender throughout Polynesia have included transsexual possibilities for men who have expressed feminine interests. My story cannot assume easily that issues of masculinity and heterosexuality theorized within a western context will have relevance for the students at this school.

Like Davies, I think there are fragmented selves. At any moment these fragments provide multiple possibilities for interpellation into a range of competing discourses, even when enmeshed in practices which are clearly sexist and racist. In my reading of the excerpts above, there is emphasis on a surplus of meaning which goes beyond the concluding wrap-up as yet another example of the oppression of women by men. It may be problematic to celebrate that moment, beyond its racist or heterosexist purview, to focus on the possibilities for change when these seem remote. But to miss that liminal moment is to forego a possibility for interrupting the structures that lead us on our predictable paths day after day.

Recently, a student asked me whether multiple readings of field-work meant that 'anything goes'. Such relativism might not be a particularly helpful path for feminist researchers. Action for change within a particular setting, such as a school, requires the kind of openness to multiple perspectives that comes from listening to many different voices expressing many different gendered positionings of competence. There are research programmes for change which begin from just such a starting-point, and proceed with a continual revoicing of possibilities from collectives of researchers and partici-pants working together (e.g. Davies 1994; Lather, 1996). There are still philosophical problems unsolved in such approaches, but for my money this is the work most consistent with an openness to diversity within a feminist approach.

Endings

This chapter has gone from the empirical social and educational psychology of gender differences to more exploratory fieldwork influenced by post-structural feminists. The change mirrors my own changing interests as a psychologist. In Part One I looked decon-structively at a few germinal texts in empirical psychology, criticizing the sandbagging techniques of psychological accounts. I found it difficult myself to avoid the dangerous pleasure of such a review, since I was once a good-girl empiricist who could summarize mounds of studies. Instead, I tried to focus on some of psychology's problems in addressing women's issues, especially the lack of reflection on the discourses which inform psychological practice.

One of the challenges for feminist psychologists is to find new ways of writing and doing empirical research that allow more possibility of joining the lively conversation among feminists of ideas outside psychology. In Part Two I looked for ideas in writings of post-structural feminists. Here I looked towards feminist research in education, since fewer feminists in psychology have been involved in such critiques. Further, the most prestigious journals in psychology seem to be those with least influence from feminist or post-structural critique. It appears that the rules of empirical psychology, like those of ballroom dancing, are questioned only at the enquirer's peril. In the rush to be a good-girl psychologist, researchers can be too exhausted from the demands of empirical busywork to reflect on the practices which their work serves.[3]

The task of the future is not to add in a few more thoughts from feminist theory into the same old empirical paradigms. Nor is there a need for a new grand (colonizing) feminist framework. The work of feminist theorists is already changing the disciplinary landscape of western knowledges. Feminist psychology will either evolve through an engagement with these complex conceptual issues, or remain as an interesting cultural formation, a vestige of a peculiar period of western beliefs about science. But this is another binary choice that oversimplifies the options. Psychology, even experimental psy-chology, is not a single, unified entity. The discipline is fragmented; there is movement at the margins interrupting the smooth, mannered expression of the good and rational. There are new feminist psychologists working more collectively, challenging authorities, and leaping over the sandbags, dancing on water. There is call for celebration.

Notes

1 My critique should be read as focusing on particular texts and empirical habits in psychology, rather than on the work of particular feminist researchers. I should also note here that my definition of 'feminist' refers to any research that could be viewed as expanding possibilities for women.

2 Several years ago a student in an advanced undergraduate course in child psychology (taught within the education faculty) was quite vocal about the limitations of empirical psychological approaches she was studying in her psychology major. I spoke to her after class, asking if she had expressed her views in psychology classes. She replied, 'I've spoken to Dr [Keen] but he always mentions studies that I haven't read. I feel as though I never know enough to be able to criticize.' In the modernist paradigm, indeed, no one can ever have read enough to be able to criticize comfortably – there is always the possibility of a crucial empirical study one has not yet read.

3 I must confess here that more recently I have felt a similar urge to be a good-girl post-structuralist, trying to incorporate the latest theoretical trends, metaphors and keywords into my writing. I am still working on it.

References

Atmore, Chris L. (1992) 'Other halves: lesbian–feminist post-structuralist readings of some recent New Zealand print media representations of lesbians'. Unpublished PhD thesis, Victoria University of Wellington, Wellington, New Zealand.

Ayers-Nachamkin, Beverly (1992) 'The effects of gender-role salience on women's causal attributions for success and failure', in Joan C. Chrisler and Doris Howard (eds), *New Directions in Feminist Psychology: Practice, Theory, and Research*. New York: Springer. pp. 226–38.

Bempechat, Janine, London, P. and Dweck, C.S. (1991) 'Children's conceptions of ability in major domains: an interview and experimental study', *Child Study Journal*, 21(10): 11–36.

Bird, J.E. (1984) 'Gender differences in expectations of children when anticipated feedback and anonymity are varied', *Genetic Psychology Monographs*, 110(2): 307–25.

Bird, L. (1986) 'Effects of help, anonymity, and privacy on children's academic expectations'. Paper presented to the American Educational Research Association, San Francisco.

Bird, L. (1994) 'Creating the capable body: discourses about ability and effort in primary and secondary school studies', in B. Mayall (ed.), *Children's Childhoods Observed and Experienced*. London: Falmer.

Bohan, J.S. (1993) *Seldom Seen, Rarely Heard: Women's Place in Psychology*. Boulder, CO: Westview Press.

Buck, R. (1988) *Human Motivation and Emotion* (2nd edn). New York: Wiley.

Butler, Judith (1993) *Bodies that Matter*. London: Routledge.

Canavan-Gumpert, Donnah, Garner, Katherine and Gumpert, Peter (1978) *The Success-Fearing Personality: Theory and Research with Implications for the Social Psychology of Achievement*. Lexington, MA: Lexington Books.

Davies, Bronwyn (1982) *Life in the Classroom and Playground*. London: Routledge and Kegan Paul.

Davies, Bronwyn (1990) 'The problem of desire', *Social Problems*, 37(4): 501–16.

Davies, Bronwyn (1994) *Poststructuralist Theory and Classroom Practice*. Geelong, Australia: Deakin University Press.

de Lauretis, Teresa (1994) *The Practice of Love: Lesbian Sexuality and Perverse Desire*. Bloomington, IN: Indiana University Press.

Dweck, Carol S. and Leggett, Ellen L. (1988) 'A social-cognitive approach to motivation and personality', *Psychological Review*, 95(2): 256–73.

Dweck, C.S. and Repucci, N.D. (1973) 'Learned helplessness and reinforcement responsibility in children', *Journal of Personality and Social Psychology*, 25: 109–16.

Dweck, C.S., Davidson, W., Nelson, S. and Enna, B. (1978) 'Sex differences in learned helplesssness: II. The contingencies of evaluative feedback in the classroom, and III. An experimental analysis', *Developmental Psychology*, 14: 268–76.

Eagly, A.H. (1994) 'II. On comparing women and men', *Feminism & Psychology*, 4(4): 513–22.

Eccles, Jacquelynne E. and Blumenfeld, Phyllis (1985) 'Classroom experiences and student gender: are there differences and do they matter?', in Louise C. Wilkinson and C.B. Marrett (eds), *Gender Influences in Classroom Interaction*. Orlando, FL: Acadmic Press. pp. 79–114.

Edwards, Anne R. (1983) 'Sex roles: a problem for sociology and for women', *Australia and New Zealand Journal of Sociology*, 19(3): 385–412.

Eichler, Margrit (1988) *Nonsexist Research Methods: A Practical Guide*. Boston, MA: Allen and Unwin.

Fuss, Diana (1989) *Essentially Speaking: Feminism, Nature and Difference*. New York: Routledge.

Grosz, E. (1994) *Volatile Bodies: Toward a Corporeal Feminism*. Sydney: Allen and Unwin.

Grosz, E. (1995) *Space, Time and Perversion: Essays on the Politics of Bodies*. St Leonard's, NSW: Allen and Unwin.

Halpern, D.F. (1994) 'III. Stereotypes, science, censorship and the study of sex differences', *Feminism & Psychology*, 4(4): 523–30.

Hare-Mustin, R.T. and Marecek, J. (1994) 'IV. Asking the right questions: feminist psychology and sex differences', *Feminism & Psychology*, 4(4): 531–37.

Heller, K.A. and Parsons, J.E. (1981) 'Sex differences in teachers' evaluative feedback and students' expectancies for success in mathematics', *Child Development*, 52: 1015–19.

Hollway, W. (1994) 'V. Beyond sex differences: a project for feminist psychology.' *Feminism & Psychology*, 4(4): 538–46.

Horner, Matina (1972) 'Toward an understanding of achievement-related conflicts in women', *Journal of Social Issues*, 18: 157–75.

Hyde, J.S. (1994) 'I. Should psychologists study gender differences? Yes, with some guidelines', *Feminism & Psychology*, 4(4): 507–12.

Kitzinger, C. (1994) 'Editor's introduction: should psychologists study sex differences?' *Feminism & Psychology*, 4(4): 501–6.

Lather, Patti (1996) 'Methodology as subversive repetition: practices toward a feminist double science'. Paper presented to the American Educational Research Association, New York City, April.

Marecek, J. (1995) 'Psychology and feminism: can this relationship be saved?', in D. Stanton and A. Stewart (eds), *Feminisms in the Academy*. Ann Arbor, MI: University of Michigan Press.

Nicholls, J.G. (1978) 'The development of concepts of effort and ability, perceptions of own attainment, and the understanding that difficult tasks require more ability', *Child Development*, 49: 800–14.

Richardson, Laurel (1990) *Writing Strategies: Reaching Diverse Audiences*. Newbury Park, CA: Sage.

Riley, Denise (1983) *War in the Nursery: Theories of the Child and Mother*. London: Virago.

Sheridan, A. (1980) *Foucault: The Will to Truth*. London: Tavistock.

Spence, Janet and Helmreich, Robert L. (1983) 'Achievement-related motives and behaviors', in J.T. Spence (ed.), *Achievement and Achievement Motives: Psychological and Sociological Approaches*. San Francisco: W.H. Freeman.

Squire, Corinne (1989) *Significant Differences – Feminism in Psychology*. London: Routledge.

Sutherland, Elyse and Veroff, J. (1985) 'Achievement motivation and sex roles', in Virginia E. O'Leary, R.K. Unger and B.S. Wallston (eds), *Women, Gender, and Social Psychology*. Hillsdale, NJ: LEA. pp. 101–28.

Urwin, Cathy (1984) 'Power relations and the emergence of language', in J. Henriques, W. Hollway, C. Urwin, C. Venn and V. Walkerdine (eds), *Changing the Subject: Psychology, Social Regulation and Subjectivity*. London: Methuen.

Walkerdine, Valerie (1988) *The Mastery of Reason: Cognitive Development and the Production of Rationality*. London: Routledge.

Part 2

FROM DECONSTRUCTION TO RECONSTRUCTION

6

Questions Concerning Methods in Feminist Research

Frigga Haug

This chapter pursues multiple but interwoven goals, arising from debates within mainstream psychology as well as the challenge from deconstruction and its problematic: the loss of a political subject, engagement and capacity to act. At the same time I try to connect a psychology and methodology that have gone through deconstruction with the most advanced positions from the past – both of a marxist, but also a methodological intervention. This is to liberate feminist articulations from the ghetto of a specialized, gendered knowledge and still retain the perspective of liberation. I want to claim that feminist interventions into the knowledge system and into research design are more advanced and far-reaching because they are related to local resources of knowledge which allow the complexity of domination to be more adequately grasped. Thus my account begins by problematizing concepts within the women's movement, which self-evidently found their way into feminist psychology. This proves to be necessary for the demand that women should not be made objects within feminist research to take effect.

This critique also holds in the field of concepts. I first present marginalized theories from the marxist tradition and some neglected ones from phenomenology to show their fruitfulness for feminist research. In the main section I introduce three very different feminist methodological proposals, all three of which start with a specific theoretical assumption and elaborate methodological considerations accordingly: that, to say the least, female individuals are fragmented, incoherent, split. This theoretical assumption must impact both on concept formation as well as for methodology, since the latter cannot be assumed to be neutral. Multiple possibilities to learn from deconstruction without losing a political capacity to act can be investigated by studying, first, the paradigm shift which Dorothy Smith proposes for sociology; secondly, by having a closer look at Carol Gilligan's more recent works, which leave behind the ethic of care; and, finally, by reading my own proposal for doing memory-work.

First I will address the question of a specifically feminist access to empirical methods. This remit permits me to avoid conventional arguments about concepts and their associated theoretical structures, and in particular to take a different perspective regarding the argument about deconstruction and the postmodern in feminism. Rather than reproducing sterile debates about the relations between feminist politics and deconstruction, my focus here instead will be on the key concepts and theories – of inequality, oppression and subjugation – that are used by feminists attempting to analyse, and change, women's experiences. My concern is with evaluating what particular concepts and theories achieve for a feminist politics. This is explicitly done in relation to the feminist models of Dorothy Smith and Carol Gilligan but also through discussion of phenomenological and marxist research on everyday life. The common ground I identify between these approaches and their bases for meaningful, liberatory feminist knowledge and methodology is formulated in terms of a critical solidarity.

By this stance towards the current contest around feminism and deconstruction, I in no way take the argument about concepts to be futile. On the contrary, each has arisen at a particular moment such that we can learn from the different biases, critiques and errors, so that each can both be 'superseded', and preserved in a new synthesis. I will suggest that what emerges from this are three propositions for feminist methodology, the theoretical assumptions of which are different. They correspondingly also arrive at different conclusions – of which no single one of these can claim the right to be a sole representative, but each of which is committed to liberation.

The description and analysis take place against the background of 'general' research of the everyday. My aim is to highlight the specificity and efficiency of a feminist approach; I will therefore structure the representation of traditional and marxist research of the everyday somewhat more extensively than is usual in feminist contexts. This is because, to my mind, it is necessary to locate feminist critiques in relation to those persons or bodies of knowledge that best represent the 'general' sciences, to take them seriously, to draw on their strengths, and to shift these by integrating a feminist standpoint.

To introduce a feminist standpoint into psychology and its methodological procedures is especially important because this body of knowledge moves from women's lives to abstract theories without any links to women's subjective experiences in the everyday world in which they live. Or else research patterns are linked to very concrete experiences of mainly men or boys – the most spectacular example beside Kohlberg (or perhaps his inspiration) was Piaget and his marble-playing boys inventing democracy while developing morally.

Concept Formations and their Consequences for Methodology

Feminism has a political project: women's liberation. In this context, there is a series of well-established concepts – inequality, women's oppression and women's subjugation – which, in a little-reflected-upon manner, regulate stances on methodology just as they do political practice. For instance, when we speak about *inequality* of gender, or of suing for equal chances, positions, etc., we utilize – because they are the most effective – quantitative procedures, by which we count how often, how frequently, and to what extent, equality is lacking. The statistics and tables that are so constructed certainly provide necessary and informative material for political practice, but they in no way disturb conventional academic life. They take over the academy's methods, and only add further, similar information to the existing level of knowledge; such women's research can without any difficulty be annexed as a special section of existing individual subject areas, leaving the rest intact.

I formulate the following as a first thesis: *the more necessary the elevation of data and facts is to the situation of women, the less women's research – which restricts itself to such action – will be in a position to really comprehend the existence of women, to make it understandable and to intervene. So it follows that the concept of inequality is not sufficient to theorize this.*[1] The accumulation of data on such topics as unemployment, income, marital status, on the share of housework, on the percentage of high-school graduates, etc., has indeed the strange effect that the living women themselves remain external to it even when they are directly affected. One can, in discussions with women, and in their biographical narratives, easily detect how even in collecting data of direct importance to everyone (e.g. on the average level of women's incomes), this will nearly always be heard as if one is not a part of it. Women as subjects have escaped, in that the research is always about the 'other'. Doubtless the subjective reasons for such escape are diverse and are themselves worthy of research. It is as if the classificatory concepts have an independent existence, with their own meanings beyond the lives of women, whose experiences will anyhow be discerned in another way.

In the sweeping changes and condemnations out of the reunification of the two Germanies, it becomes even clearer that the experiences and realities of women from the five new federal states still lie outside the conceptual framework of our sociological and psychological thinking. Even the most usual concepts that seem so safeguarded, secure and well-known that a closer definition of what is meant appears superfluous, wrest themselves from simple understanding in an uncanny way. I will take as an example the evaluation of 'the family' by a 'western' sociologist, and an 'eastern' one (who now lives in England). Ilona Ostner (1993) writes about the former GDR:

> Totalitarian societies with enforced conformity are characterized by a deficiency of differentiation of their social structure; by the lack of subsystems having their own logic, which fulfil specific functions with regard to the respective society. Thus, these subsystems were also lacking in the institutions of marriage and the family. There was marriage, children were born and lived with mother and partner(s), but marriage and family were, in the sociological sense, functionless. (Ostner, 1993: 253, trans. A. Godfrey)

About the same institution (the family) in similar conditions (states of former state socialism), Peggy Watson (1993) says:

> In the neotraditional society of eastern Europe, the family, the household, the personal and the private are of central significance. . . . The family is the source of autonomy – an autonomy, not in the sense of demands of the individual, but rather that which is defined in separation from the state. Although there is a formal and spatial distinction between public and private areas, these areas are in fact not comparable with those of the free market economy. (Watson, 1993: 869, trans. A. Godfrey)

These contrasting evaluations are based on opposite experiences. The covering over of that which was unknown with existing concepts spanned large areas of ignorance and let them disappear unrecognized into history. Therefore, in the two Germanies, commonalities in women's oppression were also urgently looked for and tentatively secured by means of the concept of the *double burden* of women, that was assumed to hold generally. Meticulous calculations of time allow Christina Klenner to arrive at the following results:

> Per day, women do, on an average, 4 hours 41 minutes in the area of reproduction (that is, domestic work, time for childcare, and care of the sick, taken together) . . . as against men, with only 2.38 hours. (Klenner, 1990: 867, trans. A. Godfrey)

It is further calculated that men average 1.18 hours longer in gainful employment, and that women have a bare hour less leisure time. It is certainly useful to study carefully such expenditure of time. However, it seems to me as if the proof – that it is therefore a *double burden* which has afflicted women in the east as it has those in the west – is insufficient. Should we really take it for granted that, in two hours a day, patriarchy is existentially and comprehensively asserted? Nevertheless, these attempts to transfer such concepts – which are fundamental to western women's research – on to the past of the state socialist federal countries, have the favourable effect that we must also reflect anew on the adequacy of such concepts (as family, and the double burden of women).

I will try a second, familiar concept: *oppression*. The word indicates the weight that lies upon women, and appears to recommend that this be dismantled, and in dismantling oppression, claims 'to make women visible', audible, public.[2] In terms of method, it is about re-reading; about a discovery of women in history, literature, science etc.; about the recording of their actions in the official history of our societies; and, sociologically, about the procedure which registers the 'voice' of women in the canon of science up to now. This locus of questions, opened through such a metaphorical concept, struggles with essentialist presumptions. The previous methods and analyses of science do not get off entirely scot-free. In the end, it is thanks to their orderings and lines of vision that women remained invisible, a blind spot. Nevertheless, the assumption is that it is largely possible to work in the usual canon of science, and solely to shift the emphases.[3]

The third of the concepts I now discuss, *women's subjugation*, by contrast, reveals a different dynamic site. Protagonists, relations, move into view: a battle field. The scene is the entire society, including the sciences and their methods. The 'suspicion' that up to now the so-called 'general' has had the gender of the historical victors of history – therefore also the suspicion of engenderedness of science – promotes criticisms of methods, concepts and theories. Reason itself, in so far as it determines our thinking and ideas about life, comes under the charge that it is a masculine construction. To liberate 'science' from masculine bias, and consequently from power relations and relations of ruling, needs a comprehensive deconstruction and corresponding reconstruction of all usual procedures up to now.

In this context, I would like to present some experiments to reorganize science. Here I concentrate on one area, on empirical procedures and preliminary theoretical considerations, to attain knowledge about the socialization processes of women. At the same time, I examine how far conventional scientific procedures have come, in this area: their possibilities and boundaries. This is especially crucial, since traditional psychology has managed successfully to neglect women's socialization and experience. This is not only a problem of adding data to the existing body of knowledge, but of questioning the theories as well as the methods which have been used up to now.

On the Problematic of the Everyday – Ethnomethodology and Marxism

It needed the political women's movement, inside as well as outside the academic arena, to discover that the conventional theories were, or rather are, conceived without the inclusion of women. This exclusion is not only as creators of theory, but also as its objects. The prevailing theories, on balance, get by without the *experiences* of women. (That men were also conceived in this way – that is, without experience – was again a later result of critiques of reason.) This discovery addresses that site in which experiences were made – a site still quite incomprehensible, though understandably immediately called *the everyday*. In fact, this critique from the women's movement came more or less at the same time as the general turn of science disciplines towards so-called 'everyday life'.

Since around the middle 1970s, the turn towards the everyday has also become something of a vogue (Alheit, 1983); but from the start it was always combined with critiques of conventional social science research. This work advocates a turning to the trivial, and thereby accuses other research of not taking the lives of human beings seriously. But at this point something odd happens: while everyday occurrences, as something other than that which especially sociology but also psychology have concerned themselves with up to now, are emphasized and described with an extra term (trivial) as such, they are thereby made exotic.

For Alfred Schütz, the father of phenomenological sociology, 'the world of everyday life [is] . . . the region of reality in which the human being can intervene and that which they can change' (Schütz and Luckmann, 1979: 25). One sees that the turn towards the everyday also involves the concession that 'the human being' cannot change the world at large. What is largely missing in the lengthy discussions about the everyday as possible object of science is the mediation between everyday actions and society as a whole. A consequence of this, among others, is that theories (and rules) concerning the everyday become the objects of study, rather than how society itself is daily reproduced. The study of working/living conditions, everyday culture and, finally, everyday knowledge became the main focal points. The everyday – as the subject of ethnosociology and methodology – is thereby constituted as a kind of field or area of research that traverses the usual areas of the logic of sociology. The everyday is both in industry, and in the family, as well as in the school, etc., but it has its own logic, which can be looked at from the outside, and whose order can be ascertained. In short, ethnomethodology constitutes the everyday as a research field towards which it is indifferent, a standpoint which has to be overcome by feminists in the first place. Consequences from the turn towards the everyday for methodogical action were, essentially, linked to the fact that the curriculum vitae, biography, and narrative and its structures, as well as media analyses, were added to observation and interview.

By contrast, a far earlier analysis of the everyday originates from Marx. In *The German Ideology*, Marx outlines his research programme with repeated references to the 'language of real life', the 'actual life-process' of people, 'actual living individuals', 'lively human beings':

> This method of approach is not devoid of premises. It starts out from the real premises and does not abandon them for a moment. Its premises are humans, not in any fantastic isolation or abstract definition, but in their actual, empirically perceptible process of development under definite conditions. As soon as this active life-process is described, history ceases to be a collection of dead facts as with the empiricists (themselves still abstract), or an imagined activity of imagined subjects, as with the idealists. (Marx and Engels, 1942: 15)[4]

Again, Marx emphatically stresses: 'Where speculation ends – in real life – there real, positive science begins: the representation of the practical activity, of the practical process of development of men' (ibid.).

In the works of Marx and Engels one always finds further studies about everyday life – about dwellings, nutrition, theft of wood, alcohol, etc. In the official philosophies that were crystallized as marxism, or marxism-leninism above all, the theorum that being defines consciousness remained. However, that itself was not taken as a turning towards the study of the real 'being' and 'consciousness' in daily life. Rather it worked to censor empirical research; to keep under lock and key anything else that was reflected in a way other than the officially asserted 'socialist way of life' – for instance, alcoholism, rebellious youth cultures, yearning for jeans, etc.

Like erratic signs, admonitions, such as those of Rosa Luxemburg, to write historical research as a work of active everyday human beings, are reminiscent of the above-reiterated directive of Marx.

The entire human culture is a work of social interaction of the many, a work of the masses. . . . This history (of humanity) teems with heroic sagas, with great individual feats that resound with the glory of wise kings, bold commanders, foolhardy discoverers, ingenious inventors, heroic liberators. But all this varied and beautiful individual hustle and bustle is only the external, flowery dress of human history. At first sight, everything – good and evil, the happiness of the people, like their distress – is the work of individual rulers, or great men. In reality it is the peoples, the nameless masses themselves, who manage their fate, happiness and pain. (Luxemburg, 1970: 206, trans. A. Godfrey)

. . . the pyramids are in reality the work of thousands upon thousands of patient slaves, who, in heavy forced-labour, with loud groans, erected the stony pieces of evidence of their own enslavement. (ibid.)

Accordingly, Luxemburg formulated a revolutionary 'realpolitik' which, among other things, starts with the everyday experiences of human beings and the experienced contradictions this involved; the goal of the 'real politik' is therefore to make these contradictions evident to those affected, so that these might be addressed.

Brecht takes up her vivid propositions in his *Questions of Reading Workers* (cited in Luxemburg, 1970: 656f.): 'Who built seven-towered Thebes? . . . Did the kings drag the boulders over there? . . . Where did the bricklayers go to, on the evening when the Chinese Wall was finished?', etc. In part of a project about Rosa Luxemburg that he called *Conversation about the Everyday Struggle*, the choice between pure abstractions – like those produced, for instance, in mathematics, which Luxemburg had first studied – and integration into the everyday, is the particular leitmotiv. At this time, Brecht wrote about 'everyday theatre' as a new task:

> You artists, who make your theatre
> In big houses, under artificial sunlight
> Before the silent crowd, visit sometimes
> That theatre, which happens on the street.
> The everyday, thousand-faceted and inglorious
> But so very lively, down-to-earth theatre
> Fed by the co-existence of the people
> That which happens on the street.
> (poem from the *Messingkauf* 4, 171, trans. A. Godfrey)

A further, explicit, turn towards the everyday as a critical social-science programme can already be found on the margins of marxist theory (which often are valuable resources for feminist thinking), in reflections on the experiences of fascism and stalinism in the 1930s and 1940s – thus there is a suspicion of economic determinism, for instance in Antonio Gramsci and Henri Lefebvre, whose formulations I turn to now.

Gramsci's point of departure was the disruption of everyday common sense in a contradictory society. Out of his project of the *Philosophy of Praxis* (1995), one can decipher emerging ideas of research for a critical, empirical method concerning the everyday life:

> We are all conformists of some conformism or other, always man-in-the mass or collective man. The question is this: of what historical type is the conformism, the mass humanity to which one belongs? When one's conception of the world is not critical and coherent but disjointed and episodic, one belongs simultaneously to a multiplicity of mass human groups. The personality is strangely composite: it contains Stone Age elements and principles of a more advanced science, prejudices from all past phases of history at the local level and intuitions of a future philosophy which will be that of the human race united the world over. To criticise one's own conception of the world means therefore to make it a coherent unity and to raise it to the level reached by the most advanced thought in the world. . . . The starting-point of critical elaboration is in the consciousness of what one really is, and is 'knowing thyself' as a product of the historical process to date which has deposited in you an infinity of traces, without leaving an inventory. (Gramsci, 1995: 1376)

The 'actual people' therefore exist under intellectual subjugation and subordination, but at the same time they also follow another practice. In short, their everyday common sense is contradictory. They have at least 'two theoretical consciousnesses', one emerging out of the determinant practice, and one which they have uncritically absorbed from the past. Thereby, the individual comes to the point 'in which the contradictory state of consciousness does not permit of any action, any decision or any choice, and produces a condition of moral and political passivity' (Gramsci, 1995: 1384).

It is necessary that individuals themselves work their way out of such unliveable decay and incoherence (sometimes currently attributed to postmodernity); that they become people who realize themselves and therefore are capable of action. Gramsci calls that 'to turn one's own action in a conscious direction' (1995: 1375). For that, people must become – as he terms it – 'philosophers'. For him, that means to reach an interpretation of the world with which they can be in agreement. The only way to do this, is as a common social project which is directed towards social change. This is because the problematic of their covertly overtaken, disrupted being is also a result arising from the fact that individuals have no share in the societal project – or if they have – only as underlings. The above fact conditioned the necessity of organic intellectuals in this project, who prepare the way, so that anyone can be an intellectual. It is not their task to introduce 'from scratch a scientific form of thought into everyone's individual life, but of renovating and making "critical" an already existing activity' (Gramsci, 1995: 1382). This position is most fertile for feminist intervention, as I will show later.

I now turn to another author, whose views on the everyday have been influential for contemporary social theory. Without reference to Gramsci, Henri Lefebvre comes to quite similar conclusions.

> The consciousness of the worker involves – together with the content of his own practical experience – numerous ideological elements, some justified, others illusory; some atavistic (coming for example from the peasant or artisan classes); others deriving from objective but partly out-moded conditions of capitalism (the 'free' labour contract in competitive capitalism, the 'classic' forms of the class struggle); still others derived from the new conditions within capitalism (monopolies, and new content contradicting the monopolistic form of capitalism; trade union action and new forms of class struggle); others deriving from socialism, and finally others coming from individual limits or the limits of the group the worker in question belongs to (corporatism, professional solidarity, etc.). If we consider the overall life of the worker, we will see that his work and his attitude towards work are linked to social practice *as a whole*, to his experience as a whole, his leisure activities, his family life, his cultural and political goals, as well as to the class struggle. What is more, this 'whole' must be taken in the context of a specific country and nation, at a specific moment of civilization and social development, and as involving a certain set of needs. And this brings us back to the critique of everyday life. (Lefebvre, 1977, I: 96)

Lefebvre's project – wholly analogous to the marxist critique of political economy – was to write a critique of everyday life as contradictory motion; both as the site of the movement of alienation, and as the struggle against this (cf. 1977, II: 77). In the middle of the text there is, in capitals: 'THUS MARXISM, AS A WHOLE, REALLY IS A CRITICAL KNOWLEDGE OF EVERYDAY LIFE' (1992, I: 148). For this, Lefebvre's point of departure is Marx's project in *The German Ideology*. This he understands as a directive to research everyday life, to lay bare the dormant and awry energies within it, to use critique as revolutionary weapon: '*Thus the critique of everyday life involves a critique of political life, in that everyday life already contains and constitutes such a critique: in that it is that critique*' (ibid., I: 153; emphasis in original).

Lefebvre's central concepts are alienation and appropriation. He draws both out of their historical–philosophical application to the everyday. Through critique of the everyday life, he deciphers the split of the public and private – even private life itself as common expression for the reversal of everyday life, the role of ideology, its entry into the everyday, and its simultaneous reproduction in this. The theoretical framework is still valid for feminist research.

Lefebvre undertakes analyses of the press, and formulates as a general hypothesis for research, that:

everyday life [is] the place, in which and out of which actual *creations* are wholly made; those which produce *the humane*, and – in the course of their humanization – human beings: *the actions and works.* (Lefebvre, 1977, II: 52, trans. A. Godfrey; emphasis in original)

In accordance with Gramsci, he argues that the everyday must be coherently worked on by the individual. With its point of departure in everyday life, it follows that recognition will be connected with changed practice, and a theory of social change with a paradigm change, linked with the sciences. (This interlocking of social change and shifts in theoretical paradigms will show up in almost all serious feminist interventions.) From the practices of human beings, conventional structures of theory will be able to be decoded as interesting representations, ideologies and speculations.

Lefebvre's research led him to critiques of ideology in the media as well as to the study of alternative films and theatre pieces (Chaplin and Brecht). Among other matters, he researches changing technical conditions in households and attitudes to leisure. However – significantly – his analyses do not lead him to an inclusion of the everyday human being in the research frame itself. In this way the individual is again seen as an outcome of economic and technological relations, not as an agent on his or her own. This last has to be the absolute base for a feminist psychology.

Situated in between ethnosociology and marxist positions, Habermas claims that there is a rupture in everyday life, when the communicative everyday world is undermined through systemic structures, when a 'systemically induced reification' (Habermas, 1989, II: 327) takes place and the lifeworld is 'cut off from the influx of an intact cultural tradition' (ibid.).

In the deformations of everyday practice, symptoms of rigidification combine with symptoms of desolation. The former, the one-sided rationalization of everyday communication, goes back to the growing autonomy of media-steered subsystems, which not only get objectified into a norm-free reality beyond the horizon of the lifeworld, but whose imperatives also penetrate into the core domains of the lifeworld. The latter, the dying out of vital traditions, goes back to a differentiation of science, morality, and art, which means not only an increasing autonomy of sectors dealt with by experts, but also a splitting-off from traditions; having lost their credibility, these traditions continue along on the basis of everyday hermeneutics as a kind of second nature that has lost its force. (Habermas, 1989, II: 327)

Habermas, unlike Lefebvre and others, does not take counter-reality to be anchored in the everyday; rather, he argues that the ruling reality system itself subverts everyday life, which we should imagine as defined through familiarity and understanding. Having outlined some of the foremost intellectual resources and political rationales for studying the everyday, I now move on to explore how feminist work engages with and comments upon these.

Feminist Interventions

From a feminist standpoint, there is a blind spot in all of the above attempts, worthwhile though they might be. The design of the research is – even if the public–private split or the household are explicitly mentioned – framed in a way so that women's lives are invisible. This happens whether, as with Habermas, the subversion first takes place with penetration out of the system worlds, instead of seeing lifeworlds and their loci like family, privacy, intimacy, and proximity itself, as sites of struggle; as places of subjugation, power and control. Or, as also happens with Lefebvre, where the problematic is conjectured exclusively between alienation and liberation from capitalist relations of exploitation – even if now the everyday life is understood as the place where such a struggle is carried out – and not only in the workplace.

Or, even in the work of Luxemburg and Brecht, where the concentration is directed towards the producers, and the attack validated by the historical tradition of the big names. Finally, women's lives have been invisible in the search for general structures concerning both the everyday and appropriate communicative processes (e.g. Garfinkel, Schütz, Luckmann), as if here one does not have to start first from particular power and control – or subjugation processes, with corresponding consequences for gender-specific everyday actions and for methodological procedure, respectively. Although Gramsci's intervention is better by far than the other propositions – methodologically as well as theoretically – his framework is not sufficient to include women's experiences in scientific research, and, correspondingly, in the subsequent methodological breaks.

A further change concerning questions of the everyday happened through the women's movement. The catch-phrase 'the personal is political' means thinking of the everyday as a site of political struggle. But it also invites us to see the everyday in two ways: as a source out of which knowledge is elaborated into various hidden dimensions of female socialization, the production of femininity, the effect of ideology, of power and control; and, simultaneously, as a field from which reconstructions are to be made, including alternative methods of gaining knowledge.

In the rest of this chapter, I outline three feminist projects which in their different ways are also paradigm shifts for conventional procedures, or indicators of ways sociology or psychology can be differently pursued, drawing from the terrains of contest around the everyday life discussed above and shifting them at the same time. I review the projects of Dorothy Smith, of Carol Gilligan, and my own memory-work. I will describe these approaches and consider their usefulness for the construction of new forms of psychology and sociology.

A sociology for women – the project of Dorothy Smith

In ethnosociological and methodological reflections – incidentally including Habermas's ideas of the always other rationalities of system and lifeworld – the same problem emerges again and again. This is that, for the everyday activities (and knowledge), different logics, structures and concepts must be used other than those in the conventional science system. What is conceptualized here as juxtaposition, or as just being other, Dorothy Smith reformulates as a problem of gender relations and as a general critique of sociological knowledge and the corresponding systems and concepts. Out of experiences in the women's movement, and the rapid, radical learning processes that were possible there, she draws the conclusion that the estrangement and emptiness that she, as a woman in sociology, experienced were not located in her own inadequacy, but in the absence of women and, along with that, of bodily existence generally in the construction of science itself and its central assumptions and conceptualizations.

From this realization that the conventional sociological concepts about women's lives, actions and feelings do not fit, Smith does not elaborate new, more fitting concepts and theora out of women's experience in such a way as to develop an empirical research project. Rather, she comes to the conclusion that the ruling systems of the sciences, the state bureaucracies, the ruling societal apparatuses, and bureaucracies, not only operate with concepts and systems to exclude women, but that these concepts/systems themselves function in regulatory ways in the societal order; in this way, they intervene in women's lives. Thus, out of the estrangement constituted by sociological theora for women's own everyday lives, Smith outlines an empirical project which finds the disjunctures between general 'precursory' practical experiences of women and other experiences which they make with concepts that both regulate society and which are indigenous to sociology, and which define women's perceptions (i.e. they thereby also experience certain strange perceptions determined by sociological concepts). Smith's aim is to make the connection between everyday experience and the level of societal regulation understandable for those who are affected by it – in this case, women. The procedure/method itself has a universal validity claim.

This project is based on three points of critique:

1   The fact that female experiences are not integrated into the language of sociological concepts and its thought systems signified – for Smith as sociologist – that she had to effect an equivalent separation from herself, with all the consequences that this has for scientific fantasy and use.
2   While the consciousness-raising groups in the women's movement generated a new impetus for the question of realization, such experiences are mediated by higher social levels of regulation (i.e. because it is impossible to understand ideology within your experience if you only remain at the level of experience).
3   Science, including that produced by women scientists, is questionable in so far as this does not make its competencies and tools usable for those with whom they nonetheless deal, and who live, so to speak fatefully, in an unrecognized world.

The paradigm shift Smith proposes applies to two dimensions:

1   Scientific procedures should make the world as social production understandable for those that live in it; and therefore should contribute to people's everyday capabilities for action. This is relevant both for the standpoint of scientific work and its integration with a social/political project.
2   A displacement of the line of vision: the subject of Smith's sociological research is – although this is perhaps to exaggerate it – concepts (texts) as interventionary and regulatory powers in the lives of human beings.

I will elucidate the procedure by two examples. First, in recent times in Germany (as probably elsewhere), a series of what had previously been rather private acts have been moved into the glare of the public: the sexual abuse of children, particularly girls, in addition to the overall neglect and disregard of children; violence towards women within marriage (general physical violence, for example rape); devaluation and violence towards the aged. All these acts which let the family – that place of intimacy and trust – be made into an inhospitable space of brutality and control in need of being publicly remedied, in fact frankly demanded the following: to find a common concept for what had happened. In collaboration with feminists, the concept of 'familial violence' was suggested. The concept became substantive. The Ministry for the Family took this on, and funded (naturally not with much money) a department. As a result of this financial backing, different civilian initiatives suddenly became fierce opponents. The Association for the Protection of Children fought the claims of the feminists who, like 'Wildwasser' in this country (Germany), concentrated mainly on the sexual abuse of girls; and, self-evidently, both had to play down the significance of the maltreatment of the aged as a secondary problem. This example thus demonstrates that concepts – as abstractions from concrete everyday life – both intervene in people's relationships, and regulate the practices of these.

A second, different empirical project, concerns displacements of perception with regard to the individual person, as when, in the processes of guardianship, mothers learn that they have to give their views on the concept of the 'best interests of the child' to determine with which parental party the child is in better hands (this is, at any rate, an advance on prior conventional practice: that of deciding according to the question of 'guilt'). Questioned in such a way, a mother may assume it to be in the child's best interests that it gets told a goodnight story, that she answers its questions, that she is present in general, or conversely, that it should often be with friends, even that it should stay away from home overnight, etc. In this process, a mother is told that income and moral life-style are decisive; therefore she is henceforth obliged to look at herself and to judge herself in such a way, as well as considering what she had thought beforehand as being insignificant. The intervention is directed at individual self-esteem and at previous experience.

Empirical research begins with a conflict, finds the conceptual frame, and re-articulates the different experiences which are combined in the concept, and from which it is abstracted. This research shows that abstraction is a specific act of power and displacement, as illustrated by the concept of material violence, with which the original participants find it difficult to live. Concepts like 'familial violence' or 'what's best for the child', even if their formulation were constructed with the help of feminist psychologists, can be abstractions which become all of a sudden the reason why certain initiatives have to fight for money in competition with their former friends. In both cases the abstractions resulting from those concepts did not include or were not really grounded in women's experiences, and in their institutionalization in policy and state-funded resources, gave rise to strange contradictions. This is not only a theoretical problem but also a practical, material one. What is needed, therefore, is the development of different concepts and strategies for practice.

Both a central assumption and result of such research is the idea of rupture, of violation, of the improper, of seizure. An important field of research is a critique of ideology; ideology understood as categorization and strategies of normalization – such as psychology is comprised – which guarantee, or at least help safeguard and support, the functions of society. In this sense, up to now the sciences are ideology in so far as they form and regulate the experiences of human beings, but do not really start out from the latter. It is therefore understandable that this project of critique becomes powerful from a feminist standpoint.

On the dissociation of women – a proposal from Carol Gilligan

Carol Gilligan is known in Germany – as elsewhere – through her book, *In a Different Voice* (1982), in which she maintains that Kohlberg's seven levels of moral development are an androcentric construction and – in opposition to his ideas of justice as the highest principle that guides action – identifies a morality of women that is relationship-oriented and based on care. The following discussion, as well as the colonizing practice of Kohlberg, who could effortlessly incorporate her proposal into his research,[5] prompted Gilligan to construct her research frame as a paradigm shift. In her new works, her starting point is that women in this society are principally split – she terms it 'dissociated'. As adolescents, girls have experiences which have an interpretation that is socially other than is clear to them practically. In the crisis of adolescence, girls come up against decisions concerning whether they 'want to know', or be 'accepted' as belonging to their peer group. Or, differently put: the socially valid mental images of a good woman, a good girl, a good mother, a good relationship, etc., are not in accordance with individual insights about social contexts. So girls get to a point where they do not (want to) know what they know. Put in another way: they must give up their personality, in order to keep it. In the course of negotiating such paradoxes they therefore 'dissociate' themselves.

After these theoretical assumptions, Gilligan goes on to develop a methodological procedure which we could perhaps describe with the phrase 'the reading of traces'. She searches in women's literature for this dissociation and its description; she has conversations with adolescent girls on a particular question: how knowledge is unlearned and its place taken by ignorance – how this is seen in the fast-growing number of 'I don't knows' in the answers, which, the moment the situation is identified as more secure, alternate with 'but you do know', etc. The project has the intention of strengthening the level of social classification of previous experience and social awareness. As a result, it is also a social project of liberation, taking as its starting point the alienation of women in our society.

At this point, Kohlberg's frame of the continuing advancement in moral development, with corresponding integration into society is left behind. According to Gilligan's message, women cannot integrate without losing themselves. Revolt is only a question of time. Women have to share their experiences with each other and listen to one another in order to enable them to undo the alienation from themselves. In this process, they will not find any support in the ruling social culture. Thus, the title of Gilligan's first book, *In a Different Voice*, has strangely shifted. The different voice is not the voice of women as different from that of men; rather, as it were, a second voice, one which – beneath the accustomed, normalizing voice of adult women – wants to be heard.

Dissociation, rupture, split – what feminist interventions have in common is that they start from here: that, under relations of control and power, one undergoes damage which aggravates the active effort for changing such living conditions, to the point of making them impossible. Women are split, underestimate their knowledge and do not recognize the powers which silence them. This makes them incapable of action. Interventionary analysis – in so far as it is connected with a project of liberation – can help to make the silenced speak. Consequently, feminist psychologists understand themselves – as Gramsci would have expressed it – as organic intellectuals in the women's movement.

Dorothy Smith's ideas to develop a sociology that makes structural connections understandable to women (which, from the place where the latter are situated, are not observable for systemic reasons) and also Carol Gilligan's assumption of the lack of unity, indeed, the disunity of women, are both compatible with Gramsci's proposals above for working with common sense. (Though both Smith and Gilligan were unable to work sufficiently with his ideas, since a complete edition of the *Prison Notebooks* has only recently started to appear in English, 1994, ed. Buttigieg.) However, a specific differentiation and displacement is revealed with the question of gender relations. Gramsci's idea – that it would be valid to reach a conscious relation to one's own history, and to participate together in the social project, the 'societal future' – only starts from *one* relation of domination. Gramsci enlarges simple assumptions about all determinant relations of production, with the notion about an unconscious, non-simultaneous relation to one's own past that can only be coherently worked on in social participation. But there is still no frame for the problem that, even with such non-simultaneities, the subjugation of women is rendered normal and this also has consequences for reconfiguring the project of social participation. The restrictions against the possibility, even against the wish, to attain knowledge because the costs are too high (as, for instance, Gilligan has shown), make a different intervention necessary for women.

Memory-work – about the context of an ability to act, and research the everyday

From similar observations to those informing the previous ideas, I, together with others, have similarly developed a project for women's research: *memory-work*. The point of departure here is also the *absence* of experience, as empirical data, in science – at least, concerning the everyday lives of women – and the lack of concepts about experience. The different positioning of women researchers – as people able to make the world understandable for the many who live in it – was, in a way, a result of methodological and theoretical considerations.

Thus, first of all, I have not taken the same route as Dorothy Smith, to research what these big concepts of sociology – such as the state, the law, society, the economic, notions of interest, organization, institution, etc., do with the everyday experiences of women. Rather, I have worked the other way round: I have searched for what the orientating meaning is for women themselves, in their lives, which areas and phenomena are intensified in women's day-to-day living, and therefore which conceptualization women's experience and female practices can grasp, from the bottom up, so to speak. By such means I came upon recognized phenomena that existentially move and drive human beings, such as, for example, morality, guilt and fear, experience of time, happiness, love, power, daydreams, sexuality, achievement, learning, the desire to work, and laziness. What is characteristic of such areas and phenomena is that, since they are essential for social conduct and socialization, they can in fact be immediately and consensually recognized. Their strained relation to sociological concepts does not mean that they are, as it were, everyday, and therefore belong in a subsystem of intermediate theory formation. Rather, the opposite holds: they are very strongly engaged theoretically, but have fallen elsewhere in the division of our science disciplines – in the theories of psychology and psychoanalysis that are close to persons, and also in the extensive realm of philosophy.

We too carried out empirical, qualitative research with women, concerning the aforementioned big themes, research through which we suddenly came to a discovery that, despite being one we had imagined all along, was nevertheless also strange. Even with those concepts that obviously directly affected women, we saw that women's experience and action are again either not included – or only very speculatively – in the theoretical articulations in philosophy and psychology/psychoanalysis concerning such existential phenomena like morality, guilt or fear, etc. The concepts are bisexual (have two genders); thus the women's share of these needs to be ascertained in order to be theoretically comprehensible. It seems what is needed therefore is a different type of theory formation.

This circumstance makes research work diverse, For now it is not only that sociology or psychology must reorganize, and the boundaries of the sciences cross, to enable the social actions of women to be generally theorized, and for women themselves to make this conceivable. More than this, female experiences themselves have to be the source of such recognition, and as such are thereby contradictorily defined. They are, after all, experiences in a society in which, practically and theoretically, women are simultaneously granted a *general* position in so far as they are perceived as human beings, and a *particular* one in so far as they are women. Put briefly, women in our societies thus have various experiences, which can be in contradiction to one another, the harmonization and balance of which concerns individual awareness and processing. Orientation offers norms and values, socially recognized meanings that, for women, form a subsystem under a general, valid orientation system. Just as, for example, morality for men, in the main, refers largely to politics and business, for women it refers to the body and sexuality (although women also know that it is immoral to falsify a cheque). (See Chapter 6 for a critique of Gilligan.)

The proposal to do memory-work likewise assumes an incoherence of the person involved that is hard to live with for the individual. The initial question is to look for women's capabilities to be autonomous, active subjects within society. One of the theoretical prerequisites is that femininity is a social construction; consequently, becoming a woman is an historical and cultural process, the study of which has as its requirement a knowledge of the structure and organization of society. However, the research question is: how do girls incorporate societal structures and thereby form these, so that, in this respect, they themselves are capable of, and see sense in, action. The formulation of the question in this way seeks to avoid two problematics with which we easily get caught up in empirical research: either to think of everything as determined or defined, and derivable from social relations, and to reduce it to these accordingly; or, conversely, to regard action and conduct all too subjectively, in any way one wants to, as arising solely from individuals. Instead, the subject under discussion is *what* is taken from relationships, from society, from the individual, and *how* it is perceived, provided with meaning and built into the individual's life.

We do not get to female experiences from theories; rather, to start from the former means to make them available theoretically, to decode their intersperson with ideologies, heteronomy and self-determination. The only ones that 'know' how they themselves are inserted into society are those affected, the women themselves. They are thus, sociologically speaking, the epistemological material. The process is more complicated, because experience does not speak, it cannot be collected as knowledge. What must be researched is *how* one has learnt out of some experiences, and how one could not learn out of other ones; *which* ways have been chosen as useful and overlaid with subjective meaning, and which have been turned down. In short: how the social construction of femininity, as the main target, was automatically acquired, transformed, rejected, reproduced and produced. To try this deciphering of the construction itself in an analysis of society shifts the research objects – women – into the status of subjects, making them into researchers of their own socialization.

The process is more complicated than it sounds. The feminist methodological postulate – not to do research about women as though they are insects (see in particular, Mies, 1978), but to resolve the subject–object question in favour of collective research – becomes here the inner necessity of the process itself. Both movements, to make oneself object and to be subject – one who researches oneself – require competence. In memory-work we try, as a possible way, to start with the problem by assuming a different objectification. We do not take women as those fragile, incoherent, 'dissociated' personalities, who enter into the research process, who themselves research or are researched, but rather, we start from their written *texts*, the remembered scenes in their lives.

A theoretical premise that underlies such action is the view that the past, that is the way we perceive it, has a meaning both for our action and behaviour in the present, and for the way in which we proceed into the future. By this, we do not suppose that the different parts simply lie around in individual personalities in a disorderly manner. Rather, following the opinion of Leontjew (1973), we assume that the personality has a memory (see also Holzkamp, 1983). That is to say, the past is by no means totally stored in the memory, but a selection has been made and, so to speak, there is a set of pieces relevant to be remembered that is assembled; it is these pieces that determine us as personalities, that is first construct our perception of ourselves as a relatively consistent person, free of contradictions. (For example, we can feel ourselves failures and have corresponding scenes at the ready that cover this as such; or, conversely, as always successful, since without that, few 'could dispose of' both experiences.) The past, even our own, is therefore not easily at our disposal as such. Rather, it is again already a construction, a selection; it has a defined meaning that is of importance for our personality today.

To examine the historico-cultural being that we have become in all its complexity, it is advisable to distance oneself from experience, in the form of a remembered, written-out text. This is written as a scene about a particular situation, in which details – diversely assembled in accordance with the premises – allow one to decode a series of ways of construction. By a reversion to linguistically and discursively analytical procedures, these texts are deconstructed in the group, to decipher the ways of construction as self-made, as constructions of the self and society, and the subjectively perceived correlation of these. The assumption is here similar to that of Gilligan – that different voices occur in the text out of dissimilar experiences and societal expectations – and that they are decipherable as contra-dictory to one another as ruptures and inconsistencies with the overlying meaning. Incidentally, this is not a process that only produces insecurity, as perhaps could be assumed; rather, it is frequently pleasurable, because one can catch oneself out by making adventurous constructions of plausibility, which can never be maintained against one's own theoretical view. So the memories prove themselves to be not only a treasure trove of knowledge about socialization, but also a mixture of ideologies, theories of the everyday. That mixture being a jumble composed of submerged bits of theory and common sense, and containing elaborate eliminations of contradictions in favour of a capacity for action.

This complexity and involvedness of experience and the construction of memory in society, positions those taking part in a research group in diverse ways. The women – everyone in the group – whose insertion into societal structures it concerns, experience themselves less as fated and tossed around, or ordinarily without any alternatives; rather, much more as beings that achieved autonomy in definite practices, with definite perceptions, meanings, harmoniza-tions, selections, etc. That means that, in order not to lose the capacity for action, they must change.

Therefore, memory-work is, or is aimed at, a critique of praxis and a critique of social perception; it is also a critique of theory. The researcher – if there is only one in the research group – also does not remain exempt from change: she herself is likewise not only subject–object of the research, one among others, but is also called upon to be a theoretician, one who provides the instruments of deconstruc-tion, who knows the theories that occupy the field, and who acceler-ates critical change in these. She plays a part as 'organic intellectual' in the Gramscian sense, and is furthermore challenged through the necessary crossing of disciplines – a sacrilege in the conventional scientific canon. Her critique is levelled a second time also at sociology. The fact is, that one cannot advance from the central concepts of sociology (if one attempts to acquire these as it were, out of a concise dictionary) to the social experience of women; and, conversely, that one comes from existentially fundamental experiences to other sciences – like for example, psychology or philosophy. This fact allows one to suspect that, under the circumstances, sociology is in no way a science of experience; that the supply of experiences is thanks to an everyday – therefore, is one, in itself – in a world of disembodied, artificial existence. To call this 'experience' indicates that it has the negation of women's everyday life as one of its bases – as Dorothy Smith (and with her, many feminist theoreticians of reason and rationality critiques) maintains.

Does such a critique mean that women researchers in sociology should now become philosophers or psychologists? I would like to give a short example out of the research concerning fear and its psychoanalytical treatment to demonstrate that such a choice is not the consequence. Rather, I will suggest that the former critique is directed at the splitting-up in the disciplines and advocates the overstepping of boundaries – not to abandon them, but to call for an extension of the forms of sociological and psychological questions.

Fear is certainly a feeling which orients actions, and blocks, makes impossible, and determines, social relations. Philosophical considerations generally make a connection between fear as a primary feeling and with the mortality of human beings, and assert the fear of death as a primeval fear (e.g. Kierkegaard, 1984). However, one can see women are specifically and variously entangled with the fear of life. Fear orients their steps in the public sphere, in darkness, at work and in the time dimension. Freud suggested that a feeling on such a massive scale, as he found it to be with his female patients, should be closely linked with an inverted social practice of the masses; later he assumed that fear originates in a contradiction that individual people cannot solve alone. This view is one-sidedly directed towards sexual practices; he overlooked the frankly unavoidable: that all social practices in which women are involved are contradictory. He also neglected – in looking at these contradictions for women solely in the relations of the ego/id/super-ego – that societal organization itself is, for women, perceived as contradictory, and thus arouses fear.

Feminist science starts from the standpoint that people neither simply experience society (or the state or the economy), nor that their feelings have had no significance for social awareness, behaviour and action. The broadening of sociological question-formation makes feminist research, among other things, into a science of culture. By culture or, better, by the cultural, I understand thereby – again following Gramsci, Irene Dölling, CCCS, W.F. Haug, and others – the ways in which individuals acquire society, transform the conditions, infuse these with life, and thereby find a sense to confirm themselves as people. To research this process sociologically as historico-cultural, one must, I think, begin with the subjects themselves: their experiences in society, their solutions for their own capacities for action. By capacity for action, I mean the capability to influence the conditions of individual action.

Individuals, like society, are thus interpreted as historical products – as made history – able to be comprehended and, inasmuch, also to be criticized and changed. Therefore, memory-work is *one* proposition for a methodical empirical procedure. It has the advantage of connecting together critiques of ideology, language, the everyday, theory, society and culture. It has the disadvantage that an organizing researcher, with a knowledge of structure and organization, theory and ideology in possibly many areas of the research work, is of importance herself – and at the same time, has to behave as an equal at the level of the experience. This contradiction has still to be worked on. The only way of doing this is via the learning process in the group. Whether sociologist or psychologist, the researcher's project is to try constantly to make herself superfluous by supporting the progress of all. This is as much of an illusion as it is a necessary methodological step. In doing so, far from hiding her methodological steps as a professional secret, she has to explain and legitimize every move.

This marks a decisive difference from Gilligan's method, which fails to treat the 'research-objects' as agents, and therefore has to maintain the existence of a knowing researcher. It also differentiates memory-work from Dorothy Smith's approach. Although this approach is much more radical in its criticisms of social conditions, and in her taking up of a feminist standpoint, she does not systematically include women as agents into her research plan either. Instead, she insists on the researcher including herself as part of the research, thus allowing her to bridge the gap between subject and object at the beginning of each research.

Once there was an argument about whether there were feminist methods at all, or whether women's research simply concerned the application of recognized, tried-and-tested methods around women's lives and societal situation. In so far as it is possible for such arguments to come to a decision, it turned out favourably for the neutrality of the methods (see e.g. Becker-Schmidt, 1987). In this chapter, I have tried, among other things, to demonstrate through this analysis of different feminist interventions that, on the contrary, a more far-reaching paradigm shift is needed.

Feminist research is tied to a socio-political project; it arises out of contradictions and ruptures; it changes the positions of the researchers and those of the research 'objects'. At the same time, disciplinary boundaries need to be systematically overstepped; the construction and function of the sciences will be displaced; diverse methodological approaches will alternate – to form, as it were, a methodological grid or formation; method itself remains in development. Both social change and also change in the self are implicit in feminist research. The extent to which the new proposals will be able to move on to enter the general scientific canon still remains open. However, on the whole, it shows, among other things, that feminist science is itself a civil society project; an attempt consciously to connect the individual with realization, and thereby to expand this from below and drive it forwards.

Notes

Translated by Andy Godfrey, with thanks to Claudia Hillman for her invaluable assistance.

1 See also the extensive discussion about equality and difference, for example in Ute Gerhard et al., 1990.

2 An example here is the critical incorporation of a feminist critique of science in the course of history (Sandra Harding, 1990).

3 See, among others, new debates in feminist ethics in which masculine ethics theoreticians themselves, as authors, also speak with a female voice. See, for example, Annette C. Baier on Hume, in Nagl-Docekal and Pauer-Studer, 1993.

4 It is worth noting here that in the original German Marx and Engels talk about 'humankind': it is only when translated into English that such formulations become gender specific (EB).

5 See Nunner-Winkler, 1991; also, *Social Research*, 50(3), Autumnm, 1983.

References

Alheit, Peter (1983) *Alltagsleben: Zur Bedeutung eines gesellschaftlichen 'Restphänomens'*. Frankfurt-on-Main: Campus-Verlag.

Baier, Annette C. (1993) 'Hume, der Moraltheoretiker der Frauen?', in H. Nagl-Docekal and H. Pauer-Studer (eds), *Jenseits der Geschlechtermoral: Beiträge zur feminstischen Ethik*. Frankfurt-on-Main: Fischer-Taschenbuch-Verlag. pp. 105–34.

Becker-Schmidt, Regine (1987) 'Frauen und Deklassierung. Geschlecht und Klasse', in Usrula Beer (ed.), *Klasse und Geschlecht*. Bielefeld: AJZ-Verlag. pp. 187–235.

Gerhard, U., Jansen, M., Maihofer, A., Schmid, P. and Schultz, I. (eds) (1990) *Differenz und Gleichheit: Menschenrechte haben (k)ein Geschlecht*. Frankfurt-on-Main: Helmer.

Gilligan, Carol (1982, trans. 1984) *Die andere Stimme: Lebenskonflikte und Moral der Frau.* Munich: Piper.

Gramsci, Antonio (1994) *The Prison Notebooks* (ed. J.A. Buttigieg). New York: Columbia University Press.

Gramsci, Antonio (1995) *Philosophie der Praxis (Philosophy of Praxis)* (Vol. 6, Books 10 and 11) (ed. K. Bochmann and W.F. Haug). Hamburg: Argument-Verlag.

Habermas, J. (1989) *The Theory of Communicative Action* (Vol. 2). Boston, MA: Beacon Press.

Harding, Sandra (1990) *Feministische Wissenschaftstheorie: Zum Verhältnis von Wissenschaft und sozialem Geschlecht.* Hamburg: Argument Verlag.

Holzkamp, Klaus (1983) *Grundlegung der Psychologie.* Frankfurt-on-Main: Campus-Verlag.

Kierkegaard, Sören (1984) *Der Begriff der Angst.* Frankfurt-on-Main.

Klenner, Christina (1990) 'Doppelt belastet oder einfach ausgebeutet? Zur Aneignung weiblicher Reproduktionsarbeit in DDR-Familien', *Das Argument*, 184(6): 865–74.

Lefebvre, H. (1977) *Kritik des Alltagslebens* (3 vols). Munich: Hanser.

Lefebvre, H. (1992) *Critique of Everyday Life* (Vol. I). London: Verso.

Leontjew, A.N. (1973) *Probleme der Entwicklung des Psychischen.* Berlin: Volk and Wissen.

Luxemburg, Rosa (1970–75) *Gesammelte Werke* (5 vols). Berlin/DDR: Dietz.

Marx, K. and Engels, F. (1942) *The German Ideology.* London: Lawrence and Wishart.

Mies, Maria (1978) 'Methodische Postulate zur Frauenforschung', *Beiträge zur feministischen Theorie und Practice*, 1(1): 41–64.

Nagl-Docekal, Herta and Pauer-Studer, Herlinde (eds) (1993) *Jenseits der Geschlechtermoral. Beiträge zur feministischen Ethik.* Frankfurt-on-Main: Fischer-Taschenbuch-Verlag.

Nunner-Winkler, Gertrud (ed.) (1991) *Weibliche Moral. Die Kontoverse um eine geschlechtsspezifische Ethik.* Frankfurt-on-Main: Campus-Verlag.

Ostner, Ilona (1993) 'Die Beschränktheit der Totalen. Anmerkungen einer empirischen Soziologin', *Ethik und Sozialwissenschaften*, 4(2): 252–4.

Schütz, Alfred and Luckmann, Thomas (1979) *Strukturen der Lebenswelt.* Frankfurt-on-Main: Suhrkamp.

Social Research (1983) 'Editorial', 50(3), Autumn. New York School for Social Research, Albany, NY.

Watson, Peggy (1993) 'Osteuropa: Die lautlose Revolution der Geschlechterverhält-nisse', *Das Argument*, 202(6): 859–74.

7

Moving Beyond Morality and Identity

Lenora Fulani

In the 1960s, Lawrence Kohlberg formulated a theory of moral development that mirrored Piaget's six stages of intellectual development. Kohlberg's initial research, from which the theory was derived, was a longitudinal study of 84 boys whose responses to hypothetical moral dilemmas were coded in terms of the type of reasoning they used. Subsequent to the original study, Kohlberg and others extended his research model and stage theory to women. Results showed that men consistently reach a higher level of moral development than women. Carol Gilligan, a graduate student working with Kohlberg at the time, initiated a challenge to his findings and claims. According to her, Kohlberg's method was fraught with bias. Further, the ethic relative to which he postulated stages of moral development was itself male-biased. With the publication in 1982 of Gilligan's *In a Different Voice: Psychological Theory and Women's Development*, a full-blown controversy about the gendered nature of ethics and moral development erupted.

Throughout the 1980s, critiques, refutations and counter-critiques appeared regularly, not only in the psychological literature but in philosophical and feminist journals and texts as well. Gilligan's research became the paradigmatic case of exposing male bias in scholars' claims about 'the norm'. Nearly 15 years later, the battle within academia shows no sign of abating (the March 1995 issue of *American Psychologist* revisited the debate). According to some (e.g. Hyde and Plant, 1995), Gilligan's theory no longer holds such sway among feminist psychologists, although it continues to be popular among women's studies scholars in other disciplines. While Kohlberg's position has lost influence within academic circles, it remains a force within social policy. By placing moral development on a par (pseudo)scientifically with Piaget's well-respected (and, to me, equally problematic methodologically) stage theory of cognitive development, Kohlberg 'became the major speaker for the importance of understanding moral development in educating children in the moral attitudes for a mature citizenry in a democratic society' (Larrabee, 1993: 3). Some efforts to address 'the moral deficiencies of youth' in the USA, such as the character education movement currently gaining popularity, are based on Kohlberg's work (Bates, 1995). As one commentator, feminist philosopher Alison Jaggar (1991), puts it, studies of what Gilligan identified as an ethic of care have become a 'minor academic industry'.[1]

On the one hand, those located within the positivist, empirically-based, rationalist philosophical-scientific paradigm argue Gilligan's relative success in modifying the dominant paradigm. On the other hand, there are readings of Gilligan that see her as attempting a break with positivist science and providing the framework for a new epistemology.

Despite the limitations of this (or any) academic debate, in my view the controversy over morality, moral development, feminism and the dominant psychology that has been raised in the literature since Kohlberg's initial study is of enormous theoretical and practical significance. Moreover, I think it is undeniable that, regardless of the limitations of Gilligan's own research study (and her original intentions), her project not only served to put gender on psychology's agenda, but has contributed to the postmodern effort to deconstruct and reconstruct how we humans know ourselves.

In this chapter I will concentrate initially on the methodological problems I see in how the issues have been framed and what I believe are serious flaws in the psychological–political–philosophical paradigm being employed. Following this critical examination, I will offer a different vantage point – my reading as an African-American female postmodernist of social constructionism and activity-theoretic practice – from which to re-examine the debate. I will focus on two concepts central to Gilligan's work and the controversy it has generated – morality and identity. My intention is to point out the ways in which these modernist conceptions hold us back and to suggest how, by moving beyond them, we might advance a new epistemology and a new psychology.

The Limitations of Inclusive or Alternative Moral Systems

Let us begin by reviewing the work of Gilligan and listening to the diverse voices of her critics and supporters in relation to the following questions: Has the positing of a uniquely female developmental process advanced the effort to create a human science and/or a more humane (developmental) world for women and men? Has Gilligan's new 'ethic of care' feminized and/or humanized psychology? Has the academic debate about morality, moral purpose or imperative, and moral activity (these terms are far from equivalent, as I will show) impacted on ordinary people's everyday activity (moral and otherwise)? More generally, has *identity psychology* been any more successful than *identity politics*? Perhaps by exploring these questions, we can come to see more clearly the extent to which 'feminist psychology' functions 'to reproduce the conceptual and political difficulties of psychology' (see Burman's introduction).

I mean two things by identity psychology. First, I am referring to theories and practices that are constructed out of, reflect, and are designed to foster, a specific cultural identity, for example, black psychology, feminist psychology, and so on. Secondly, I am referring to the pragmatic approach in which psychological descriptions are seen as naming particular societal uses. According to Newman and Gergen (1995), this pragmatic view is at root identity-theoretic; while rejecting the view that words, language, descriptions and so on have an identity relationship with 'reality', it posits an identity relationship with use and, as such, is abstracted from, and obscures the prominence of, relational activity.

Gilligan's challenge to Kohlberg was clearly within the framework of identity politics and identity psychology. Her goal was 'to expand the understanding of human development by using the group left out in the construction of theory to call attention to what is missing in its account' (Gilligan, 1982: 4). She sought to extend the existing psychological thinking about development and morality to include the experience and voice of women: 'Only when life-cycle theorists divide their attention and begin to live with women as they have lived with men will their vision encompass the experience of both sexes and their theories become correspondingly more fertile' (Gilligan, 1982: 23).

Should Heinz steal the drug that will cure his wife's cancer? Kohlberg presented his subjects with hypothetical moral dilemmas such as this one, and scored their responses according to the reasoning they verbalized in reaching their conclusions. Whether the subjects said yes or no was not as important as how they came to the conclusion they did. Kohlberg's scoring placed respondents in one of six stages of moral development, depending on how closely their reasoning approximated an ethic of justice. The higher stages represented reasoning based on criteria of fairness, impartiality and the capacity to apply appropriate universal principles to a particular situation. Kohlberg found that men tended to reach level four, the capacity to think legalistically, that is, in terms of 'what is right', while women rarely scored beyond level three, in which one conforms to the conventional notion of what is good.

In her critique of Kohlberg's theory and method, Gilligan pointed to the male bias inherent in presenting subjects with hypothetical situations. This places a high premium on abstract thinking which, in turn, is characteristic of the kind of morality he is investigating. His exploration was determined by a preconceived ethic; his evaluation of moral development was essentially an authoritarian imposition of that morality on his subjects.

Gilligan's corrective was to include in her interviews open-ended questions about her subjects' own experience with moral conflicts. Her data consisted of interviews with different groups of adults who participated in three studies: the college student study (exploring identity and moral development); the abortion decision study (with pregnant women considering abortion); and the rights and responsibility study (exploring conceptions of self and morality, experiences of moral conflict, and judgements of Kohlberg's hypothetical moral dilemmas). From her analysis of her subjects' language (and 'the logic of their thought' (1982: 2)), Gilligan postulated another ethic or moral voice, the 'different voice' of women. According to Gilligan, men tend to employ an ethic of justice while women tend to employ an ethic of care. The ethic of care is characterized by a sensitivity to the individual, a focus on the particularity of the situation and concern with providing safety and security. It is a contextual morality. Gilligan believed that her subjects' utterances revealed the existence of two different moral imperatives. She says:

> The moral imperative that emerges repeatedly in interviews with women is an injunction to care, a responsibility to discern and alleviate 'the real and recognizable trouble' of this world. For men, the moral imperative appears rather as an injunction to respect the rights of others and thus to protect from interference the rights to life and self-fulfillment. (Gilligan, 1982: 100)

Gilligan's urging that the experiences of women be included in psychological research, her developing a less abstract, more open-ended system of data collection, and her positing of a 'different' female ethic are elements of her attempt to go beyond Kohlberg and to feminize a male model of development. She criticizes his exclusion of women as subjects and his elevation of a particular ethic that is male-dominated and male-dominating. She does not, however, challenge the fundamental character of the moral system.

In my view, there is a methodological problem with attempting to include women and substituting one moral system for another. It is also likely to fail. The approach Gilligan takes is reminiscent of the fight against racist IQ tests in the 1960s and 1970s, an intellectual–political effort in which I took part. Our cry was for culture-fair or even culture-free tests. We pointed out the race and class bias of test items. We created tests based on 'the black experience' and published results showing that white children were 'dumber' than black children based on these test results. Regardless of our good intentions and the validity and reliability of our empirical data, we could never win the fight because we had implicitly accepted the biased scientific paradigm. We never challenged the racist bias of testing, but only revealed the racist nature of particular tests and test items. But test performance as the measure of intelligence is itself ideological (as is the very conception of intelligence as measurable). The very people who excel at testing – by virtue of having every culturally constructed advantage to become good at this culturally biased behaviour – are the ones who defined intelligence in terms of test performance. Testing continues, 30 years later, to do great harm to children and adults. It is testing – not biased tests – I believe, that is anti-developmental.

And so it is with moral development. The notion that a moral system (Morality, if you will) is necessary in order for people to function in an ethical manner is, in my opinion, a product of a male-biased culture and a deterrent to development (moral and otherwise). Morality is an abstraction, a wrenching out of the continuous cultural-social life process of certain behaviours, acts, values and beliefs which are then reified into a code or system of conduct. As I hope to show, moral activity is a very different kind of thing.

The Missing Woman

Before going further, it is important to explore the varying meanings of male-biased. When we speak of male-biased culture, are we referring to the fact that certain cultural products (e.g. morality, testing, language, political systems, and so on) – or even the culture in its entirety – are discriminatory and oppressive towards women? Or are we referring to the fact that the *historical process* of producing the culture excludes women? Within identity politics (and psychology), male-biased culture generally refers to the ways that varied cultural products discriminate, exclude and oppress women and favour men. By contrast, the relational, activity-theoretic view I am taking locates male bias in the history of the production of the culture. In this view, even if men somehow happened to produce a culture not oppressive to women, it would, nonetheless, be male-biased. This is because products are inseparable from the process of their production. Morality, then, is male-biased by virtue of men having historically excluded women from the productive activity of discussing and making decisions about moral issues (including whether or not morality was needed or even existed).

What conception of male bias underlies Gilligan's research enterprise? On the one hand, if male bias refers to the ways the current society oppresses women, then how would it have been possible for women to have developed an alternative morality? On the other hand, if male bias refers to the historical process of creating the institutions of the society (including the institutionalized exclusion of women from the very process), then how could the bias be eliminated by including women even if they somehow did manage to create an alternative morality? While either conception of male bias is thus problematic, I think that Gilligan locates male bias in the alienated products that oppress women. Her lack of historical perspective can be seen in the formulation (above, p. 142) of her goal: she wants to 'use the group left out in the construction of the theory to call attention to what is missing in the account' (Gilligan, 1982: 4). Apparently, what is important for Gilligan is that women are missing from *the account*, rather than that women are missing from *the historical process* of the production of the culture. She wants to use the group left out to eliminate the male bias. But male bias as historical process of production (which includes 'the product' at any given moment in time) cannot be eliminated by including women in the continuation of one of the products – morality – that, by virtue of women's exclusion, is male-biased.

The majority of critiques and defences of Gilligan's work share her historical, non-dialectical view of male bias. Most focus on the ideological–political impact of her conclusions, or the reliability and validity of her data. I will briefly review some of them to illustrate what I see as their limitations.

Some have argued that Gilligan's studies establish the voice of white middle-class women as the norm, are thus racially and class biased, and recommend that the voices of non-western women be included if we are to develop an accurate picture of women's morality (e.g. Nicholson, 1993; Stack, 1993). In my view, this strategy still accepts the traditional research paradigm and philosophical tradition which clings to the notion that a moral system must govern human action.

Gilligan is also criticized for reinforcing the female stereotype of women as nurturing and caring, but not rational. One response has been the attempt to formulate a theory of care that does not relegate women to traditional roles (see Puka, 1993; Tronto, 1993). Gilligan responded by deploring any use of her work to rationalize oppression and urging that women not settle for being defined by men: '. . . I do not see it as empowering to encourage women to put aside their own concerns and perceptions and to rely on a psychology largely defined by men's perceptions and thinking about what is of value and what constitutes women's development' (Gilligan, 1993: 214).

Both responses are, to me, consistent with traditional (male-biased) methodology which demands a systematic causal explanation for human subjective-social phenomena. Women might be more caring than men. The problem is not located here, but in insisting that there must be some *accounting* for it. To claim that women's caring grows out of a moral imperative, as Gilligan has done, is an idealistic assertion of the primacy of the cognitive, for it makes human activity temporally and causally conditional on certain kinds of mental acts. It has the effect of creating the kinds of defensive response and denials of difference that we see occurring not only in relation to moral development but many other issues.

There are those who have re-examined the moral development data and found no empirical basis for positing a gendered difference in an ethic of care and an ethic of justice (see Broughton, 1993 for a summary of such studies). (It is noted in almost every article in the Gilligan–Kohlberg debate that Gilligan consistently denies she is positing such a difference, even though her book as a whole makes that claim.) Gilligan's response in her 'Reply to critics' raises another methodological point relevant to the limitations of identity politics and psychology:

> To claim that there is a voice different from those which psychologists have represented, I need only one example – one voice whose coherence is not recognized within existing interpretive schemes. To claim that common themes recur in women's conception of self and morality, I need a series of illustrations. In counterposing women's conceptions of self and morality to the conceptions embedded in psychological theories, I assume that psychological literature filled with men's voices exemplifies men's experience. Therefore in listening to women I sought to separate their descriptions of their experience from standard forms of interpretation and rely on a close textual analysis of language and logic to define the terms of women's thinking. (Gilligan, 1993: 20)

The interesting issue raised by the critique and response concerns how difference is understood and used as a basis for generalities and the construction of a moral system. In a culture with a history of institutionalized sexism, clearly men and women are socialized differently. The differences this creates need not, cannot – indeed, should not (to use a moral term) – be justified by research which reduces this social–cultural–historical process of construction to a particular piece of data or a new category.

As an African-American woman, I have come over the years to appreciate the distinction between 'the female experience' and the 'experiences of women' and between 'the black experience' and 'the experiences of black people'. The experiences of blacks and the experiences of women are infinitely varied. By exploring and expressing these experiences in a variety of ways, it is possible to gain a deepened understanding of women, blacks, society and history.

Certainly, generalizations can be made from this creative activity. But transforming these generalized experiences into institutionalized identities – the black Experience, the female Experience (with a capital E) – does a good deal of damage. The remarkable and non-measurable particularity of human experience becomes invalidated. When our experiences are turned into a marketable commodity – an identity – official representatives of blacks, women and other left-out groupings now find a niche, yet most of us are oppressed by still another category and standard. I am urging we move away from this unfortunate consequence of identity psychology to a more relational psychology of developmental activity.

Likewise, it is a shift from ideological critique to methodological critique. Positing a women's morality may expose the ideological biases of the traditional theory of moral development but, as I have attempted to show, it does little to expose its methodological biases. Arguing that feminist theory can provide both an ideological and methodological critique of moral philosophy and moral develop-ment, Susan Hekman (1995) suggests alternative readings of Gilligan. She carefully lays out a reading of Gilligan's research project as an instance of feminist empiricism (Harding, 1986), that is, correcting the masculine tradition of science by adding the experiences of women. Her own more radical reading is informed by Gilligan's later works. In Hekman's view, Gilligan is attempting 'an alternative conception of scientific analysis . . . introducing a new interpretation of the moral realm . . . [defining] truth as a function of theoretical perspective' (Hekman, 1995: 5). What is significant about Gilligan's work, to Hekman, is that she offers an alternative framework for science – theory is linked to method and to epistemology – and for looking at morality – morality is interpretive. Her narrative-based methodology is relational rather than objectivist. The self is rela-tionally constituted.

Hekman's analysis is helpful, for it shows how far one can take Gilligan's methodology. For even if we accept that one of her key contributions is the postmodern relational self, we still have the modernist conceptions of morality and identity to contend with. We need to question seriously whether acceptance of these abstracting and reifying social categories is, however unintentionally, a collusion with mainstream psychology.

Beyond Morality (Beyond Accounting for What We Do)

In my view, we have no need of an alternative morality. We have no need of morality at all. In saying that we do not – as a society, culture and species – need morality, I am making a philosophical–

methodological distinction between *morality* and *moral activity*. Morality is the systemization of ethical beliefs and practices. As such (as a system, a code, a set of criteria and rules and roles), it thwarts moral activity. Moral systems both reflect and perpetuate authoritarianism – a code is set up and people are judged by how well they conform to it.

Given that morality *is* male, men are necessarily more morally developed than are women. Kohlberg was right. His findings accurately reflect western culture. Men are moral. Women are immoral. Gilligan's findings (or interpretations of her findings) support the gendered distribution of morality as institution and behaviour. The women interviewed tended to reason about so-called moral issues in a manner less impartial, less utilitarian, less based on abstract principles – in a word, less morally – than men.

In a patriarchal society it could hardly be otherwise. Morality, a cultural institution produced over hundreds and hundreds of years by men, through a process that excluded women, is an essential element of patriarchy. Morality is the codification, rationalization and legitimization of a certain perception of women as innately good and virtuous (in the Aristotelian sense) or innately bad and sinful (in the Biblical sense), but not moral or just (in the Kantian sense of being capable of reason). Historically seen as incapable of entering the male domain where justice is dispensed and rights and obligations are determined in an impartial and utilitarian manner, women have been barred from those institutions which define reality and morality, make moral decisions and enforce justice/morality. Only in recent history have women voted, served on juries, entered the legal profession, or participated in government in western cultures, while many cultures and nations still prohibit women's participation. Religious institutions, the ultimate guardians of morality, lag even further behind legalistic and governmental ones.

The moderately transforming history in which women have fought for and won some rights and responsibilities includes, of course, the history of morality. Positing a women's morality does not challenge the *institution* of morality. Gilligan's work, addressing the sexist *content* of morality, is a partial deconstruction or, perhaps, a rearranging of the decor, leaving the foundation, the paradigm, intact. The issue relevant to human development is not which is primary – right or good, justice or care – or creating a synthesis of the two. It is the methodological bias inherent in the acceptance of the deductive paradigm and the positivistic conception of understanding – in which the establishment of generalizable rules and the imposition of these rules on particulars comes to define what is meant by understanding – that we need to take issue with.

The relationship between official Morality (morality with a capital M) and ordinary, everyday moral activity or morality-making was addressed recently by Newman:

> We have yet to see that point in human development where the process of creating morality, the moral activity, the meaning activity, is self-consciously continuous. If you study the history of morality as well as the history of all production, you see that what has traditionally happened is that at a certain point in the process, what is produced is taken away from, ripped out of the hands of, the producers, and the continued unalienated activity of producing – the production of morality – turns into something else. Suddenly we have abstractions and authorities who are given life beyond what we actually created. No longer do we have the imposition of our own creations on ourselves, but rather the imposition of others on us. That's been a real part of the tradition of morality making. The process of creating morality has invariably been undermined by the authoritarian patriarchal model which puts it in the hands of those – or is taken by those into their hands – who now use it to impose on others. (1993: 13)

Newman identifies the morality-making activity as one in which morality is the process-and-product of creative human activity. This kind of product is not a commodity or a finished item or system, but is continually produced and continually developing (unless it is thwarted by Morality). The social–cultural productive activity of morality-making is an instance of 'meaning making'.

The human joint activity of making meaning is critical to development. As Newman and Holzman put it:

> Meaning is to be located precisely in the human capacity to alter the historical totality even as we are determined (in our societal particularity) by it. The activity of making meaning is a fundamental expression of 'revolutionary activity' which 'reorganizes thinking/speaking and much else (potentially everything else)'. (1993a: 49)

They thereby challenge the idealism and dualism of the dominant philosophical–psychological paradigm that takes ideas, thoughts, beliefs, and so on, as prior to, necessary for, and explanatory of, action: 'It is the meaning in the emerging activity, not the pre-conceived imagining followed by its realization, which is transformative, revolutionary and *essentially* human' (1993a: 52).

Morality-making, then, occurs in the everyday, moment-to-moment, continuous meaning-making activity of human beings engaged in living their lives. It is part of the seamless historical totality, the 'potentially everything else' that is transformed and continuously created and recreated by revolutionary meaning-making human activity. What I find especially compelling in this argument is its challenge to the authoritarianism and judgementalism which permeates moral philosophy and moral development research.

There is no evidence that human beings require Morality (a predetermined ethic system) in order to know what to do. (Whether a society needs a legal code to function is another issue altogether.) Human beings no more need a moral code to act morally than children need rules of grammar to speak. Children learn to speak by actively participating in a socio-cultural speaking environment – well before they know how to speak, or any rules of language, or even that there is a such a thing as language (Newman and Holzman, 1993a, 1993b). They engage in revolutionary activity; that is, through joint activity with others, they reshape the existing environment, creating something new (their development). When there is no longer the support for revolutionary activity, then people stop developing.

In my view, what is identified as a moral breakdown in the postmodern world is not due to a lack of moral teaching. It is not a cognitive or educational problem. It is not a behaviour issue. What we are dealing with, in my opinion, is the fact of decreasing opportunities for women, men and children to engage in revolutionary activity, to participate in creating developmental environments, thereby developing themselves in all ways, including what we might identify as morally.

The authoritarian reification of the morality-making activity into an abstract moral system is the opposing force in the history of morality and moral development. The imposition of such a system stops revolutionary activity. It is one way ordinary people are deprived of participating in creating developmental environments. Rather than morality and 'potentially everything else' being continuously created, it becomes a non-changing ideal (indeed, its *raison d'être* is its non-changing universality) to which we must strive and by which we are judged.

This kind of reification of human activity is characteristic of the dominant philosophical method that has greatly influenced the social sciences and the social policies to which they provide rationalization. One of the twentieth century's most influential (anti-philosophy) philosophers, Ludwig Wittgenstein, takes philosophy to task for its reification. According to Wittgenstein, philosophy obscures rather than clarifies life (not just for the philosophically sophisticated but also for ordinary people) in its very attempt to explain, generalize and account for life. It is mythological: 'In philosophy one is constantly tempted to invent a mythology of symbolism or of psychology, instead of simply saying what we know' (Wittgenstein, 1974: 56).

In the past several years, some psychologists have come to find Wittgenstein's anti-foundationalism helpful in developing a strong critique of the traditional psychological paradigm (Gergen, 1994; Holzman, 1997; Jost, 1995; Newman and Gergen, 1995; Newman and Holzman, 1993b, 1996, 1997; Shotter, 1993; Van der Merwe and Voestermans, 1995). He raises fundamental methodological questions for us: we seek causes, correspondence, rules, parallels, generalities, theories, interpretations, explanations for our thoughts, words and verbal deeds (often, even when we are not trying to). What if, Wittgenstein asks, *there are none*? (Newman and Holzman, 1993b: 8).

It is our language in particular, according to Wittgenstein (1953, 1965, 1980), that creates confusion, gives us 'mental cramps' and hides the fact that speaking is a 'form of life'. In his later writings, Wittgenstein identifies as metaphysical obfuscations characteristics of ordinary discourse and thinking, such as the 'craving for generality', the cognitive bias, the dominance of the practical syllogism, and the hegemony of deductive scientific explanation. These 'permeate our ordinary thinking and experiencing; seeming "natural", they are hardly noticed, still more rarely questioned' (Newman and Holzman, 1993b: 38).

There is, of course, a close relationship between morality, on the one hand, and rules, codes and explanations on the other. They are, in some sense, the same kind of thing. Both abstract from the ever-transforming developmental life activity. They are *accountings* of life. Moral philosophy and moral development research are accountings for life. For Kohlberg, morality lies not in what we do but in accounting for what we do (a very different sort of doing). Gilligan offers a different means of accounting, but does not question that we must give an accounting in order to understand. Despite her emphasis on contextuality and her claim that it is no longer possible to say what morality is, she nonetheless formulates moral imperatives and ethical codes, thus remaining within the cognitive, deductive tradition she is trying to escape.

In addition, Gilligan is not sufficiently sensitive to the philosophical (male-biased) presuppositions concerning development. She appears to accept uncritically the traditional conception of development in utilizing a neo-Freudian theoretical model *without reflecting on its social–historical–cultural construction*. Further, there is no acknowledgement that in so doing she is creating another hierarchical model system of development. As Broughton has pointed out, her approach – substituting phases for stages – keeps her 'tied to a hierarchically ordered structural system' (1993: 130). She has merely produced a variant on the developmental model of Kohlberg and Piaget. Development, to Gilligan, is still understood non-dialectically and as measurable in terms of levels of cognitive ability and transitions in between.

By contrast, the activity of creating developmental environments/ development (rather than an accounting of it) is continuous and life-long. It has no beginning or end points. It is not measurable. We do not need to measure development in order to develop. Similarly, I believe we do not need to explain, systematize, measure or interpret moral acts in order to engage in them. There is no evidence that people care for the sick and run into burning buildings to rescue babies, dogs and cats because they have a moral position or imperative. More than likely, human beings do such things simply because such things must – not should – be done. No doubt many will think this is simplistic at best and tautological at worst. Stripping away meta-level accountings for our deeds often has this effect. (That is the experience one has in reading Wittgenstein.)

An Activity-theoretic, Relational Account of Human Development

As a developmental psychologist, psychotherapist and political activist, I have been working for many years to formulate in practice a methodology for social change that, while building on the psychological and political movements of the 1960s, breaks with many of its conceptual and methodological presuppositions. My effort has been to reinitiate people's capacity to create their own growth and development. In contemporary terminology, my approach can be described as an evolving synthesis of elements of social constructionism and activity theory.

In relation to social constructionism, it is Kenneth Gergen's attempt to formulate a positive (but anti-positivistic) methodology grounded in relationship that I find most compatible with my own thinking. In relation to activity theory, of the many followers of Lev Vygotsky (and, to a lesser extent, Mikhail Bakhtin), the work of Fred Newman and Lois Holzman (with whom I have worked closely for the past 15 years) holds the most promise for creating a non-cognitively-biased (with all the gendered and Eurocentric biases that entails) psychology of *developmental activity*.

What I am proposing, following Gergen, Holzman and Newman, is a *psychology of relational activity*. While not feminist in its origins, this emerging synthesis is, I believe, compatible with the most epistemologically radical perspectives within the feminist tradition. To the extent that Gilligan's ongoing research project is a deconstruction of positivist science and moral philosophy, these two reconstructionist efforts can be of significant value in moving the anti-positivist feminist agenda along.

First, the *theory of development* of Newman and Holzman (Holzman, 1995, 1996, 1997; Newman, 1991, 1994; Newman and Holzman, 1993a, 1993b, 1996, 1997) offers an activity-theoretic account of human development. It is, at the same time, a practical critique of current developmental theory. As articulated first by Vygotsky (following Marx), activity theory offers a different orientation from which to view human–social phenomena from the dominant perspective that models social science on the natural sciences. For Vygotsky, human beings learn, develop, speak, write, play, solve problems, think, feel, and so on, as socio-cultural–historical activity (Vygotsky, 1978, 1987). Development is not, as it is for Piaget, Kohlberg and most developmentalists, accounted for by an appeal to mental structures. Nor is it the process (or product) of a disembodied knower or autonomous subject. Nor is it gradual, linear, or stagist. In joint activity, we create/construct/transform the unity 'mind in society' (Vygotsky, 1978) or 'individual-in-society-in-history' (Newman and Holzman, 1993a).

Vygotsky emphasized the need for a new science activity: one could not study human beings with a science constructed to study stars and plants; one could not study activity with a science constructed to study behaviour. The results of trying to do so are summarized by Holzman:

> While theories vary in their specifics, development in psychology (and the disciplines upon which it has major influence) is what happens to an individual as s/he comes to 'know' or 'construct' the world. Development is understood as a gradual unfolding of internal, individual capacities, affected in significant ways by environmental factors. Within the traditional framework, development refers to a process that has a beginning, an end point (for example, adolescence, adulthood or death), and a relatively smooth trajectory in between (often identified as 'stages of development'). In the view of recent critics, this conception of development is fraught with biases. They claim it is hierarchical, elitist and ideological rather than scientific (Bradley, 1989; 1991; Broughton, 1987; Burman, 1994; Cushman, 1991; Morss, 1992; 1993; Walkerdine, 1984), and for these reasons some urge abandoning development altogether. While I agree with much of their critique, in my view, a more positive route is to reconceptualize what development is. (Holzman, 1995: 200)

Vygotsky's goal of creating a new psychology and some of his findings suggest a more creative, open-ended and less Eurocentrically biased concept of development. For example, his identification of activity, not behavioural use, as the critical feature of uniquely human development raises the possibility of a less cognitively-overdetermined and passive approach. The difference between activity and behaviour is the difference between changing totalities and changing particulars, between qualitative transformation and quantitative accumulation (Newman and Holzman, 1993a). Human beings do not merely respond to stimuli, acquire societally determined and useful skills, and adapt to the determining environment. The uniqueness of human social life, according to Newman and Holzman, is that we transform through our activity the very circumstances that determine us:

> For human beings are never fundamentally changed (i.e., never develop) except insofar as, by our revolutionary activity, we change the totality of our continued historical existence. This we accomplish not by the humanly impossible act of materially altering all the elements of history, but by the uniquely human activity of materially reorganizing what there is to create a new meaning for everything. (1993a: 90)

Development, then, is the *tool and result* of developmental activity, rather than the outcome (in means–end or tool for result fashion) of something prior (Newman and Holzman, 1993a, 1993b). From an activist perspective, the question becomes how do we help support people to transform the circumstances that determine us?

The psychotherapeutic, educational and cultural projects Newman, Holzman and their colleagues (including myself) have created over the past 20 years function as an effective environment for advancing beyond the current state of cognitized, theoretic intellectual thought. These projects are the building of a broad community where people practice the methodology of creating developmental environments, that is, environments for carrying out a developmental critical practice as human activity.

My perspective is also informed by the recent emphasis within the social constructionist movement on relationship and relatedness (see Gergen, 1992, 1994, 1995 and Shotter, 1993). Especially useful for the current discussion is the distinction Gergen makes between identity politics and relational politics. In a recent essay, he links the relational turn in constructionist theory with what he sees as a necessary and promising transformation of identity politics. While he credits identity politics with contributing significantly to broadening the arena of the political, Gergen also shows its limitations. In particular, he highlights the ways identity politics is rooted to the traditional psychological paradigm:

> In important degree, identity politics is a descendent of western, individualist ideology. No, it is not the single individual who commands our interest. Rather, as we have seen, individual identity is conflated with group identity: individual and group interests (and rights) are one. In this

way, the group replaces the individual as the center of concern, but the discourse of individuality is not thereby disrupted. Rather, the group is treated in much the same way discursively as the individual: imbued with good and evil intent, held blameworthy, deemed worthy of rights, and so on. In spite of the shift toward the social, we thus inherit the problems of individualism yet once again – simply one step removed. (Gergen, 1995: 14–15)

According to Gergen, shifts within the constructionist movement towards what he calls a relational sensibility expose the limitations of identity politics in effecting social transformation, and suggest a new direction:

There are no necessary or natural distinctions among persons or groups. Rather, identity is a relational achievement. Individuation is only one of many ways in which we might describe or explain the world. And such forms of discourse obscure the more essential domain of connection. . . . Societal transformation is not a matter of changing minds and hearts, political values or the sense of the good. Rather, transformation will require unleashing the positive potential inherent in relational processes. In effect, we must locate a range of relational forms that enable collective transformation as opposed to alienated dissociation. (1995: 16–17)

Creating the Possibility of Continuous Moral Activity

Earlier I tried to show why creating an alternative morality is a futile effort. What then are women to do? Are we doomed to being immoral? No, I think we have another choice. In the existing male-dominated, patriarchal culture, the only alternative to being immoral is to choose to be amoral. We can reject the codification (by men) of what is 'right' – not merely the historically specific codification but *the very act of codifying*. As women, we can make the difficult choice to not submit to that which oppresses us (it might still – indeed, probably will – continue to oppress us, but there is a difference between submission and non submission). The way to reject morality, to be amoral, is through engaging in ordinary, mundane revolutionary life activities unimpeded by generalities, explanations, codification and systemization (which includes so-called scientific psychology). The women I most admire have indeed been amoral. They have been revolutionaries, creating through their activity an articulation of who they are that is not overdetermined by patriarchy/ Morality – even as they continue to live in a society and culture in which such patriarchy/Morality oppresses and humiliates.

In the current period of developmental crisis, I believe that the historically-specific revolutionary activity we need to engage in is building community – not a women's community, a black community, a therapeutic community or any other kind of a community.

We need to create *community* as continuous, historical, dialectical environments where all kinds of people – black, Latino, Asian, white; women and men; gay and straight; working class and middle class – are able to go beyond themselves as defined by the existing political, cultural and psychological institutions to create something new together. Anything less than this, such as creating an alternative (e.g. feminist, black, gay) psychology or an alternative moral system, is to capitulate to the existing power arrangement which insists upon and determines *identity*. Regardless of whether that identity is considered inferior (as in racist theories of intelligence or sexist theories of morality) or superior (as some black nationalists and feminists suggest), it nevertheless reinforces the discourse and experience of possessive individualism (Sampson, 1993; Shotter, 1993), as yet another patriarchal psychological product.

The kind of for-itself activity I am referring to and have been involved in for many years – creating a new practice and theory of human development, new ways of doing politics, schooling, therapy, theatre, new ways of doing all kinds of things – can be seen as the beginning, in Gergen's words, of 'a relational politics that will be incorporative, pervasive, collaborative, and unceasing' (1995: 25). Moving beyond identity politics to relational politics and beyond identity psychology to *a relational psychology of developmental activity* (which may turn out to be more a cultural phenomenon than a psychology) can, I believe, create the possibility for continuous moral activity.

Notes

I gratefully acknowledge the assistance of Lois Holzman and Hazel Daren in the formulation and articulation of my arguments and analysis.

1 The situation reminds me of Marx and Engel's caustic comments about the Young Hegelians in *The German Ideology*:

> As we hear from German ideologists, Germany has in the last few years gone through an unparalleled revolution. The decomposition of the Hegelian philosophy . . . has developed into a universal ferment into which all the 'powers of the past' are swept. In the general chaos mighty empires have arisen only to meet with immediate doom, heroes have emerged momentarily only to be hurled back into obscurity by bolder, and stronger rivals. It was a revolution besides which the French Revolution was child's play. . . . Principles ousted one another, heroes of the mind overthrew each other with unheard-of rapidity, and in the three years 1842–45 more of the past was swept away in Germany than at any other time in three centuries. All this was supposed to have taken place in the realm of pure thought. (1973: 39)

References

Bates, Stephen (1995) 'A textbook of virtues', *New York Times*, IV–A, 1:1 pp. 16.

Bradley, B.S. (1989) *Visions of Infancy: A Critical Introduction to Child Psychology*. Cambridge: Polity Press.

Bradley, B.S. (1991) 'Infancy as paradise', *Human Development*, 34: 35–54.

Broughton, J.M. (ed.) (1987) *Critical Theories of Psychological Development*. New York: Plenum.

Broughton, J. (1993) 'Women's rationality and men's virtues', in Mary Jeanne Larrabee (ed.), *An Ethic of Care: Feminist and Interdisciplinary Perspectives*. London: Routledge. pp. 112–39.

Burman, E. (1994) *Deconstructing Developmental Psychology*. London: Routledge.

Cushman, P. (1991) 'Political uses of the self in Daniel Stern's infant', *American Psychologist*, 46: 206–19.

Gergen, K.J. (1992) *The Saturated Self: Dilemmas of Identity in Contemporary Life*. New York: Basic Books.

Gergen, K.J. (1994) *Realities and Relationships: Soundings in Social Construction*. Cambridge, MA: Harvard University Press.

Gergen, K.J. (1995) 'Social construction and the transformation of identity politics'. Paper presented at the New School for Social Research, New York.

Gilligan, Carol (1982) *In a Different Voice: Psychological Theory and Women's Development*. Cambridge, MA: Harvard University Press.

Gilligan, Carol (1993) 'Reply to critics', in Mary Jeanne Larrabee (ed.), *An Ethic of Care: Feminist and Interdisciplinary Perspectives*. London: Routledge. pp. 207–14.

Harding, S. (1986) *The Science Question in Feminism*. Ithaca, NY: Cornell University Press.

Hekman, Susan (1995) *Moral Voices, Moral Selves: Carol Gilligan and Feminist Moral Theory*. Cambridge: Polity Press.

Holzman, Lois (1994) 'Stop working and get to play', *Lib Ed*, 11: 8–12.

Holzman, Lois (1995) 'Creating developmental learning environments: a Vygotskian practice', *School Psychology International*, 16: 190–212.

Holzman, Lois (1996) 'Newman's practice of method completes Vygotsky', in I. Parker and R. Spears (eds), *Psychology and Society: Radical Theory and Practice*. London: Pluto Press. pp. 128–38.

Holzman, Lois (1997) *Schools for Growth: Radical Alternatives to Current Educational Models*. Mahwah, NJ: Lawrence Erlbaum.

Hyde, J.S. and Plant, E.A. (1995) 'Magnitude of psychological gender differences: another side to the story', *American Psychologist*, 50(3): 159–61.

Jaggar, Alison (1991) 'Feminist ethics: projects, prospects, problems', in C. Card, *Feminist Ethics*. Lawrence, KS: University of Kansas Press. pp. 78–104.

Jost, John T. (1995) 'Toward a Wittgensteinian social psychology of human development', *Theory and Psychology*, 5(1): 5–25.

Larrabee, Mary Jeanne (1993) 'Gender and moral development: a challenge for feminist theory', in Mary Jeanne Larrabee (ed.), *An Ethic of Care: Feminist and Interdisciplinary Perspectives*. London: Routledge. pp. 3–16.

Marx, Karl and Engels, Frederick (1973) *The German Ideology*. New York: International Publishers.

Morss, J.B. (1992) 'Making waves: deconstruction and developmental psychology', *Theory and Psychology*, 2(4): 445–65.

Morss, J.B. (1993) 'Spirited away: a consideration of the anti-developmental Zeitgeist', *Practice*, 9(2): 22–8.

Newman, Fred (1991) *The Myth of Psychology*. New York: Castillo International.

Newman, Fred (1993) 'Some more spoken thoughts/actions on psychology and morality', *Practice*, 9(1): 3–15.

Newman, Fred (1994) *Let's Develop*. New York: Castillo International.

Newman, Fred and Gergen, K.J. (1995) 'Diagnosis: the human cost of the rage to order.' Paper presented at the annual convention of the American Psychological Association, New York.

Newman, Fred and Holzman, Lois (1993a) *Lev Vygotsky: Revolutionary Scientist*. London: Routledge.

Newman, Fred and Holzman, Lois (1993b) 'A new method for our madness', *Practice*, 9(2): 1–21.

Newman, Fred and Holzman, Lois (1996) *Unscientific Psychology: A Cultural-Performatory Approach to Understanding Human Life*. Westport, CT: Praeger.

Newman, Fred and Holzman, Lois (1997) *The End of Knowing: A New Developmental Way of Learning*. London: Routledge.

Nicholson, Linda J. (1993) 'Women, morality, and history', in Mary Jeanne Larrabee (ed.), *An Ethic of Care: Feminist and Interdisciplinary Perspectives*. London: Routledge. pp. 152–68.

Puka, Bill (1993) 'The liberation of caring: a different voice for Gilligan's different voice', in Mary Jeanne Larrabee (ed.), *An Ethic of Care: Feminist and Interdisciplinary Perspectives*. London: Routledge. pp. 215–39.

Sampson, Edward E. (1993) *Celebrating the Other: A Dialogic Account of Human Nature*. Boulder, CO: Westview Press.

Shotter, John (1993) *Cultural Politics and Everyday Life: Social-constructionism, Rhetoric and Knowing of the Third Kind*. Toronto: University of Toronto Press.

Stack, Carol B. (1993) 'The culture of gender: women and men of color' in Mary Jeanne Larrabee (ed.), *An Ethic of Care: Feminist and Interdisciplinary Perspectives*. London: Routledge. pp. 182–201.

Tronto, Joan C. (1993) 'Beyond gender difference to a theory of care', in Mary Jeanne Larrabee (ed.), *An Ethic of Care: Feminist and Interdisciplinary Perspectives*. London: Routledge. pp. 240–57.

Van der Merwe, W.L. and Voestermans, P.P. (1995) 'Wittgenstein's legacy and the challenge to psychology', *Theory and Psychology*, 5(1): 27–48.

Vygotsky, L.S. (1978) *Mind in Society*. Cambridge, MA: Harvard University Press.

Vygotsky, L.S. (1987) *The Collected Works of L.S. Vygotsky* (Vol. 1). New York: Plenum.

Walkerdine, V. (1984) 'Developmental psychology and the child-centered pedagogy: the insertion of Piaget into early education', in J. Henriques, W. Hollway, C. Urwin, C. Venn and V. Walkerdine (eds), *Changing the Subject: Psychology, Social Regulation and Subjectivity*. London: Methuen. pp. 153–202.

Wittgenstein, L. (1953) *Philosophical Investigations*. Oxford: Blackwell.

Wittgenstein, L. (1965) *The Blue and Brown Books*. New York: Harper Torchbooks.

Wittgenstein, L. (1974) *Philosophical Grammar*. Oxford: Blackwell.

Wittgenstein, L. (1980) *Remarks on the Philosophy of Psychology*. Oxford, Blackwell.

8

Towards a Communicative Feminist Psychology

Gordana Jovanović

Perceiving, thinking and researching are processes taking place in a context in which at least two focuses can be differentiated: first, a psychological agency, which has the role of subject; secondly, the objects of its perception or thinking. This subject–object model expresses a common experience in different activities ranging from dreaming of something to social interaction with somebody. It can also cover changes of the same activity over time and under various socio-cultural conditions. Such an epistemological function of the subject–object model allows for treating it as a general model.

This general model is a starting point for my approach to the theme of this book – deconstructing feminist psychology. The theme identifies an object of investigation – psychology, here specified as feminist psychology. An additional matter at issue is deconstruction. This invitation to deconstruct feminist psychology has been delivered in this case to a psychologist, a woman living and working in a society labelled as a transitional society, in a country which is usually designated as 'former Yugoslavia'. Thus the general and abstract subject–object model becomes specified: female psychologist in a transitional society in a former country is dealing with the deconstruction of feminist psychology. The general model can incorporate further specifications concerning myself as a psychologist (it includes my understanding of psychology and self-understanding as a psychologist), concerning a transitional society (transition from what towards what, the status of different traditions in this process, including also the status of socialist achievements in women's liberation, then the status of sciences, particularly psychology). Each of these signifiers (woman, psychology, transition) has a plurality of changing connotations.

These changes occur at a crossroads of different developments ranging from global world processes to a personal transformation. As a kind of change tending towards globalization, I see the growing awareness of the woman's position as a changeable one. If this awareness reaches an individual, it is experienced as a personal change. Another widespread tendency concerns recognition of the growing importance of psychology as a science in modern societies. On a personal level this tendency could be experienced as an invitation (or even obligation) to act.

This range from global processes to personal position defines the context in which I am writing. What I am going to present here is my point of view developed at a crossroads of the global and the local. Thus the abstract global is constitutive for my approach.

Facing rather dramatic changes in the society where I live – in Yugoslavia – I can understand them only in a broader context which necessarily includes such global developments as modernization, but also local resistance to modernization grounded to a great extent in a still socially valid patriarchal order. I recognize the same dynamics in many particular spheres of social life. Out of such dynamics arises also the thinking of woman's position or even a regressive turn (after a quite liberal socialist ideology which advocated a wide social affirmation of women).

This is a sketch of the hermeneutic context from which I am going to approach the deconstruction of feminist psychology. It is hermeneutically necessary that my understanding of the deconstruction of feminist psychology depends on my broader gender, sociopolitical and professional context. In that context (meaning among psychologists in Yugoslavia) there is still no feminist psychology as an academically differentiated and articulated women's psychological standpoint (although there is a group of women, including psychologists, dealing with women's studies).

The absence of feminist psychology in this sense draws greater attention to the existing psychology. Courses given at psychology departments in Yugoslavia represent mostly mainstream psychology which has still not appropriated social reflection on the origin and function of psychological knowledge as its methodological task. Taking into account this state and adding experiences (and difficulties) which feminist psychology is facing elsewhere, I am going to suggest an alternative approach. It is based on a reflection of assumptions necessary for elaborating a psychology which develops feminist psychology as its own theoretical need. In this way it can respond to the needs already articulated in other social settings, but can also participate in the constitution of the new ones. I think it is reasonable to expect that, on this kind of basis, feminist psychology could avoid the impasses of either reproducing traditional biases rooted in the patriarchal order, or of advocating a radical isolation or separatism.

I am aware – and I want to make clear – that the ideas on feminist psychology I am defending here arose out of, and derived

their meaning from, the context in which I live. This context includes
– fortunately – many symbolic communities which offer tools to
construct meanings and to build values. Thanks to these communities, I can transcend the limits of the present local community.
Again, the global is constitutive for my understanding of the local.

A cognitive and practical interest which motivates my choice of
focus and determines my arguments concerns the realm of warranting conditions of communication. There are general logical reasons
in favour of communication as an aim of activities undertaken in
society: society consists of processes of communication and is built
upon the achievements of communication. Without a certain amount
of successful communication society could not exist. There are also
psychological arguments confirming the last statement: without
communication with an adult a newborn could not survive, and
without a certain amount of successful communication a child
cannot develop into a competent individual.

I will also touch on how life experiences can prove in a dramatic
way what the consequences of lack, or impossibility, of communication are. As the most striking characteristic of the social context in
which I live I see a dissolution of the previous societal bounds and
communicative patterns. Communication as a formative paradigm
has been replaced by isolation – from others in various senses – as a
means of self-definition. This leads to the reinforcing of naturalizing
attitudes which then generate another turn in the process of desocial-
ization, or, radically speaking, sociocide. These dramatic experiences
drew my theoretical attention to the genesis of communicative
patterns, especially their psychological foundations. The communicative focus – underlined both by theoretical position and life
experiences – defines my framework in dealing with feminist
psychology.

I will try to deconstruct the deconstruction of feminist psychology
by offering a reconstructive approach. This attempt follows deconstruction's claim of decentration to its extreme point: it decentres
deconstruction itself. Since the results of deconstruction cannot be
pure, isolated elements, but rather networks building new perspectives, it is clear that reconstruction is still a necessary procedure which
enables us to understand patterns subjected to deconstruction. In
accordance with this approach, in the first part of my contribution I
am going to reconstruct transformations in the conceptualizations of
the psychological subject which led to the purification of the psyche of
historical, social, cultural connotations. It is logically evident that a
feminist psychology cannot be based on such a conception of psyche
– either as a theoretical or as a political project. I think it is necessary
to know the genesis of the structures that we are criticizing in order to

be able to project alternative ways. Feminist psychology is part of these alternatives, as well as being in need of deconstruction.

Psyche in Polis

One way of describing our time could be by using the label 'a psychologized age'. This summarizes both the institutional break-through of psychology (in the form of psychology departments, research centres, psychological books and journals, or scientific meetings) as well as the contribution of psychological attitudes and sensitivity in defining and answering many problems of modern life (including such 'hard' fields as economy and state organization). Such psychologization of life has usually been closely associated with the process of modernization. But far from being a discovery of modern times, it is rather a peculiar renaissance of an old paradigm which originated in ancient animism. Animism presupposes a universal presence of souls which populate the whole world. Souls are proper agents of life courses. As personified agents they become partners with whom people interact, trying to influence them. In these first mythical images, souls were omnipresent and omnipotent, participating in all kinds of activities, and interacting also with the sort of souls which were located in individual human beings, who became in the later development the only 'seat' of the soul.

In the first ancient Greek philosophies, the soul remained an important heuristic means. Philosophers from Miletus, when comparing cosmos and humans, spoke of the world soul. Heraclitus shares the same general view, conceiving that the cosmos and the soul consist of a common element – fire. This substantial identity was a necessary condition for the soul to know the being. According to the epistemological principle of similarity, knowledge is possible only through means which are similar to the object of cognition. In Plato's *Phaedo* we find the following argument:

> . . . the soul, too, like the forms, since it is not perceptible and is concerned with what is unchanging, is itself unchanging and incomposible, and therefore indestructible. . . . These objects you can touch, see and perceive with the other senses, but the things that are unchanging cannot be grasped by anything except the mind's reasoning. (*Phaedo*, 78b; 79a)

This epistemological principle has been used in developing models which parallel the order of cosmos, the state and the human being. As is well known, Plato builds his theory of the state by using the structure of the human soul as its model. Since, according to his conception, the individual soul is divisible into three parts – reason, which rules over the all, a spirited element and the bodily desires –

the ideal state possesses three classes: rulers, soldiers and farmers (Plato, *The Republic*, book IV). The diversity of the soul's capacities was preserved in Aristotle's conception which also presupposed a relation between the soul's particular capacities (parts possessing rationality or not) and objects of knowledge (see Aristotle, *Nicomachean Ethics*).

The most striking characteristic of these ancient views of the soul is their inclination to recognize the soul as a universal principle, explaining first life motion and maintenance of life, the possibility of perceiving and knowing the outer and the inner world and ethical foundations for the construction of an ideal state form. Thus the soul participates at three levels: biological, psychological and socio-political, embracing the whole life experience. The soul is considered as a subject-matter which has high dignity – with these words Aristotle starts his first book on the soul (402a 1–4).

A political context of human affairs was recognized as an important subject-matter of knowledge and practice. To be a 'zoon politikon' means necessarily to partake in *res publica* (in the literal sense of the word: public issue). Consequently, the soul was conceptualized by using notions derived from political practice, shaping in turn the prevalent para-political myth. We read in Ryle's *The Concept of Mind*:

> Minds and their Faculties had previously been described by analogies with political superiors and political subordinates. The idioms used were those of ruling, obeying, collaborating and rebelling. They survived and still survive in many ethical and some epistemological discussions. (1949/1973: 24–5)

Such conceptions of the ancient soul belong to that long past of psychology which Ebbinghaus (1908) expressed in his famous statement that 'psychology has a long past and a short history'. What remained hidden in this statement could be added as a critical comment: psychology has not made history from its past, meaning that it has not appropriated heuristic values contained in the previous views. One of these insights concerns a very broad life-embeddedness of the soul.

Michel Foucault, who defined his field as 'the history of thought', located the roots of the modern concept of the self in Greek philosophy, more specifically in its principle 'the care of the self'. This presupposes care for the activities of the soul. In this way to be concerned with oneself also included political concern. 'The precept "to be concerned with oneself" was for the Greeks, one of the main principles of cities, one of the main rules for social and personal conduct' (Foucault, 1988: 19). Foucault interprets Plato's *Apology* so that: 'in teaching people to occupy themselves with themselves [Socrates – G.J.] teaches them to occupy themselves with the city' (Foucault, 1988: 20).

Following the later development of the principle of 'the care of the self', Foucault discovered very important transformations in forms and organizations of subjectivity, the most significant of which is probably the substitution of the care of the self by knowledge of oneself. This inward turn also brought a loosening of the relationship between the self and city, expelling political concerns from those of the individual's subject-matter step by step. The same 'shrinking' of the self has been repeated in the framework of the scientific development of psychology. But this has not reduced the expectations of the people who wanted to possess a powerful knowledge about their own psychical states and to have insights into the souls of the others. The question is, to what extent academic psychology can fulfil these expectations.

To sum up so far, I would say that with the disappearance of the original socio-political context of the emergence of the ancient soul, the insights into the constitutive relationship between soul and society were also forgotten. The aim of this brief reconstruction of the original concept of the soul in the first western philosophical conceptualizations was to draw attention to some neglected, forgotten, repressed connotations of the soul experience as derived from the socio-political context, a real context in which soul activities (so to speak) occur. In this context the soul generates the multiplicity of activities and values which became divided (and gendered) in later times. Thus the ancient soul was concerned with a 'masculine' knowledge, and also with a 'feminine' care, with Eros and with discipline. The soul was, as its reflection, fully representative of life. Only within this original context does it make sense to undertake an 'archeological' examination of the inherited beliefs and value-orientations, including those with gendered connotations. On one hand, this context allows us to decentre from imposed dualisms: thus the interest in knowledge could be understood as a consequence of care, rather than as opposed to it. Or, on the other hand, care of oneself could also mean care for one's community. These insights can be used as a starting point in constituting a psychology, including a feminist psychology, whose subject-matter is fully representative of life.

How Psychology Inherited the Soul

Psychology has built upon the heritage of the subject-matter of these ancient views of the soul. Yet, to inherit does not mean to continue and preserve a given object, but to construct it by some other means. The means is not a neutral device or mediator, but is itself constructed in relation to the subject-matter examined and the methods used in accomplishing this task. In the case of psychology, methodological claims were borrowed from the epistemological doctrine applied in natural sciences in order to constitute psychology as a science. These claims are limited, however, as was expressed by Harré and Secord (1972):

> Much of experimental psychology and other empirical approaches in behavioural science are based upon three assumptions: (a) that only mechanistic models of man satisfy the requirements for making a science, (b) that the most scientific conception of cause is one which focuses on external stimulation and which excludes from consideration any treatment of the mode of connection between cause and effect, and (c) that a methodology based on logical positivism is the best possible approach to a behavioural science. All three are mistaken. . . . One of the most important consequences of these views is that they encourage unwarranted assumptions about the degree to which people are alike, so person parameters are allowed to vary at random in experimental studies, a mistake that vitiates much of the experimental work and makes generalizations to the life situations dubious. (Harré and Secord, 1972: 5)

A new technology – the scientific one – has been invented to produce and shape the scientific subject-matter. One of the first consequences of this process of scientification is that the soul has been banished from psychology and replaced by psychic processes which are involved mostly in cognitive relationships to the outer world. Inner-psychological as well as socio-political contexts of the cognitive activity have been excluded from experimental design and theoretical models.

Psychology puts forward its achievements as promoting scientifically proved knowledge of psychic states. But, by the same achievements, psychology makes all these experiences, which remain outside of its methodological network, invisible. Harré and Secord point out that 'the experimental set-up destroys the possibility of the study of the very features which are essential to social behaviour in its natural setting' (1972: 44). These 'invisible' features contain many experiences which were once ascribed to the soul, many of them being gendered as feminine. By division and isolation of cognitive and emotional processes, and the lower evaluation of the latter, psychology has committed a first masculinist fallacy: it has taken *pars pro toto* and then neglected the lower or even invisible *pars*. Thus it reproduces power structure by selecting what could be spoken of.

In this way psychology became a new place where the knowledge was used as a means of constituting and reproducing patterns of power. Political rights of expressing one's own opinion (to speak of) or of having access to the public domain have their counterpart in psychological conceptualizations which highlight certain realms and neglect or repress the other ones. For example, in the whole development of psychology, emotions belonged to the 'other' side. A metaphor for emotions used by T. Ribot as 'the gypsies of our mind' (quoted in Vygotsky, 1932/1987: 326) transmits easily recognizeable connotations of marginalization of emotions (as well as essentializing structural conditions for the lives of minoritized groups). Such marginalization is also reproduced at meta-theoretical levels.

These and similar procedures have provoked objections from those interested in making the invisible visible, in revealing hidden biases which intervene in methodological designs and theoretical generalizations, and in questioning ideology and the hierarchical structure of institutions, including academic ones. Feminists, as a matter of course, share this interest and partake in critical deconstruction of the psychological *toto* 'universalized on the basis of limited perspectives' (Nicholson, 1990: 1).

Psychology's Texts

It is reasonable to take textbooks as representative for mainstream psychological thinking, since these books are accessible to more people than other psychological literature and can therefore most inform psychological understanding. In that sense they are very relevant for socialization. If we look at general psychology textbooks, we can see that over many years they have had a very similar structure: they start with biological aspects of psychological processes and then continue with sensation, perception, learning, memory, thought and language, motivation and emotion, personality, interpersonal behaviour and group influences. Such a structure reflects a still prevailing logic of psychological thinking which could be described as linear in two senses: it supposes a linear development from basic elements towards more complex structures (first sensation and then personality and group behaviour) and also a linear development from a biological base to a social psychology.

However, even within a person it is not possible to prove this elementary linear assumption: 'Most probably, the attributes of people are not logically independent, but are interactive, and the most important ones of all may not even exist in isolation. Yet the idea of experimental design relating independent variables to dependent ones requires the assumption of logically independent attributes' (Harré and Secord, 1972: 16).

Psychological textbooks transmit an unhistorical and very weak version of social psychology which is very suitable for reproducing biologically biased prejudices. As gender is a construct which relies on notions of biological male–female differences, it can easily be used to support sexist prejudices which, as a rule, take masculinity as a source of both defining and evaluating standards. For example, a very elaborated hermeneutics has been built around a male bio-logical characteristic – the penis (in the form of phallus). This became a universal symbol which stands for psychological, social, political issues as if they were a direct consequence of the original biological fact. At the core of this transfer occurs a very simple operation which reduces meaning to visible and ostensible characteristics. This type of thinking belongs to the lowest stages of cognitive competence – as does every other kind of prejudice. As such it is suitable to reinforce the inclination towards dependence on immediate and unreflected actions.

A socio-historical form of such a masculinist transfer is known as patriarchy. It is a social order and thought system that is built on masculinity as a universal organizational principle: it defines the social position and future perspective of the newborn, inheritance law, economic chances, family structure, heterosexual pattern and political claims. Actually, the whole world has been constructed to do justice to the pure fact that there are two biologically different forms of human being.

We read in the *Encyclopedia of Feminism* (Tuttle, 1986): 'Femin-ists began to point out that all societies, whatever their economic, political or religious differences, are patriarchies' (quoted in Westerlund, 1990: 16). Some aspects of modern North American womanhood, under the auspices of patriarchy, are briefly sketched by Kerstin Westerlund in her book *Escaping the Castle of Patriarchy*:

> Patriarchal ideology stipulated full-time motherhood and wifehood as the fulfillment of female identity, and opportunities for professional progress were clearly obstructed. After the mid-1960s, in particular, social, economic, political, and psychological struggle has indeed altered, if not revolutionized, women's lives. A greater awareness of women's estate has undoubtedly been achieved. Recent research shows that women's attitudes toward gender equality . . . have changed in a feminist direction. Nevertheless, it is mainly the lives of professional women that have been more visibly affected by transformations within the work force. Women continued to predominate in occupations that were extensions of their traditional tasks within the home. Their relative economic powerlessness was apparent in a wage gap, with women earning only approximately two thirds as much as men. At the close of the 1980s, wages were still far from

equal. Furthermore, an alarming feminization of poverty was taking place
. . . and the continued stereotyping of sex roles in the media were other
backslashes against feminist hopes. (Westerlund, 1990: 16–17)

Yet, just as changes within patriarchy are possible and patriarchy
is not the only form of social organization, so it is clear that
biological maleness can be interpreted in different ways. In other
words, what makes a difference is a social construction of the
biological fact. Once this has been acknowledged, we can open our
minds to imagine other possibilities rather than those which have
been insisted on as the naturally given and legitimate ones.

If academic psychological thinking were socially reflected, it would
not maintain naturalistic biases in its conceptualizations. The
assumption still prevails that there is perceiving, learning, and
thinking before social influence starts. There is also an inclination to
accept an individualistic bias that sociality is a constraining, limiting
factor which intervenes within a natural psychological course.
Starting from such assumptions, psychology cannot grasp the real
dynamics of psychological processes.

How can psychology conceive and understand the invisibility of
feminine interpretation of experience, and claim to make this visible
as a subject-matter of its investigations, if it has no conceptual links
to any context of perceiving or thinking? If perception is understood
as a neutral process occurring in an isolated, bodiless, asocial
monad-like mind, then there is no room to recognize in it either
men's or women's way of perceiving. For an historical, social and
cultural context for psychological processes is a real life-context of
their functioning. If psychology should be considered as a science
dealing with the human psyche, it has to establish conceptual and
theoretical links with these contexts by using any specific social
construct – be that a broad one such as collective mentality or
gender, or a narrower one such as pre-school children in a war-
affected situation.

By recollecting the forgotten experience, a necessary, but only first,
step has been taken. For to recollect does not mean just to add a new
experience to the old, known one; it means to construct a whole
new story in which also the former visible and speaking part gets new
meaning by recognizing what has been overlooked. Using psychoanalytic insights, this also could be expressed as follows: repression
damages the repressing instance also. In gender terms: the masculine
position has disadvantages which should also be reflected upon. To
take just one example: we could reinterpret psychological knowledge
as implying that to be split off from emotional and social background
is a very serious deprivation.

By elaborating and implementing an approach – I call it a socio-historical reconstruction of psychology – we could certainly avoid simply repeating naturalistically biased constructs – now with a feminine label. These constructs could widen the field of psychological knowledge. On the other hand, they would contribute to the fixation of those beliefs which are targets of feminist critics – for they would just offer a complementary view and not a deep re-thinking of underlying presuppositions.

Towards a Sociogenetic Psychology

Psychology as an academic discipline has already more than a hundred years of history behind it. But historical psychology does still not shape the mainstream development of psychology, although there are some attempts to reconceptualize psychology in this sense (Danziger 1991; Rose 1988; Staeuble, 1991). Historical understanding of the psychological subject would mean that psychic processes are not taken for granted, that they are conceived as constituted and developed in a context that bears historical traces. These historical conditions invite a long-term perspective in relation to psychic structures. Only from this perspective is it possible to detect changes which occur in patterns of perceiving, knowing, feeling and behaving. Once the social genesis has been recognized as the *definiens* of a phenomenon, the social world becomes constitutive for psychological functions. Thus social psychology becomes the core psychology, and not just one among many psychological branches.

Through social psychology a whole network of social interactions becomes the subject-matter of psychological investigation. In these networks gendered interactions occur, with different meanings and functions: they transmit socially inherited constructions of law, labour division, family patterns, socialization models, affectivity exchanges, and so on. All these phenomena have a social origin, social genesis and function. They are answers to needs which appeared in social life through its historical development. By satisfying these needs they contribute to the maintenance of existing structures.

Even elementary needs such as food, sleep and clothes have undergone a profound socio-historical shaping, embedded especially in gendered meanings and relations. Thus, around food consumption, for example, a whole culture of cooking, serving and behaving has been built (see Elias, 1939/1978). As woman is traditionally perceived as close to nature, her role in this pattern has been put close to 'biological' needs and interpreted as biologically rooted. In the next step these supposedly biological roots are used to legitimate claims against any changes. Fortunately, in spite of resistance against claims to change woman's inherited position, there are changes in the meanings of gender in relation to elementary needs, which partake in the broader socio-historical process. An historical example can confirm social insights into 'biological' need: cooking outside of the home has always been socially more appreciated than cooking at home, and this outside cooking has been mostly performed by men. What matters in the unavoidable social sense is not the fulfilling of a so-called biological need, but a complex social arrangement built around these needs. Changes in social settings transform our attitudes even to the supposedly invariable biological needs, transforming both the personal attitude of an individual and the generalized attitude of the social groups.

Yet in modern societies scientific knowledge, and advice derived from it, is also involved in this process. Due to its subject-matter psychology has an important role in this process. It goes without saying that psychological concepts are involved as real co-producers of the perception or behavioural schemes. This is reason enough to reflect on psychological concepts – their difference makes a real life-difference.

Historical, social and cultural contexts are included in the genesis of the individual which traditionally has been the primary topic of psychological interest. Decentring of the individual, accomplished through taking into account historical and social contexts, does not mean a neglect of the individual. On the contrary, it is intended to contribute to the affirmation of the individual and her/his life-history. The social and the individual are not opposed. The individual is the most mediated form of organization of sociality. As George Herbert Mead (1934) said, it is society which provides the basis for the self. And there are already some theoreticians who reject the objection that such a study of psychical states cannot be considered to be scientific: 'the idea of men as conscious social actors, capable of controlling their performances and commenting intelligently upon them is more scientific than the traditional conception of the human "automaton"' (Harré and Secord, 1972: v).

Although there is no general sociogenetic psychology, there are already many works dealing with the social formation of psychological functions. As socio-genetic psychologist Jaan Valsiner puts it: 'psychologists have been talking about the relevance of the social world for the formation of the psychological functions of persons for over a century, but still there is very little progress in building explicit theoretical models that could explain how the individual becomes a person via social relationship' (Valsiner, 1994: 47).

Socialization is a general process concerning the construction of psychological patterns which are the necessary equipment of individuals in their life activities in societies. This process starts even before the birth of the child, through the relationship of women to men, through social norms which regulate expectations and behaviour in that relationship. Piaget has shown that a child's cognitive competences cannot be developed without a cooperation with peers. Vygotsky (1931/1981) claimed:

> the very mechanism underlying higher mental functions is a copy from social interaction; all higher mental functions are internalized social relationships. These higher mental functions are the basis of the individual's social structure. Their composition, genetic structure, and means of action – in a word, their whole nature – is social. Even when we turn to mental processes, their nature remains quasi-social. In their own private sphere, human beings retain the function of social interaction. (Quoted in Wertsch, 1981: 164)

A long-term view is needed, together with the social conditions conducive to the development of autonomous personhood, social identities and responsible action. 'Everything which is unique and personal about our identity does not radiate from within the self as something pregiven or innate. Rather, the basis of human difference and individual identity is to be found within society, in the social relations that exist between individuals' (Burkitt, 1991: 189). In a word, humans are social selves.

In considering the theoretical and socio-practical problems of our time, it is my view that there is a pressing need for the return of grand theory in the human sciences. Psychology can follow this quest by offering a general socio-historical theory of the individual. Drawing attention to the socio-historical factors in the constitution of individuality will improve the theoretical competences of psychology. For these reasons I argue for reconstruction as a necessary procedure in acquiring socio-psychological insights. After all decentrations and decompositions there still remains a psychological agency which has no 'imperial self' (Lash, 1984) anymore, which is not unified and does not raise universal claims, but it is still a perceiving, thinking, feeling, caring and interacting agency taking part in the processes of society reproduction. As society needs a psychological vehicle, psychology – and perhaps especially feminist psychology – needs 'a core subject' (Widdicombe, 1992: 491). Moreover, this socio-genetic shift can also involve the political consequences of increasing sensitivity to social issues, including feminist issues, as well as possibly being responsible for them.

Psychological Representations of a Feminine Regard

In the remainder of this chapter I am going to analyse some phenomena of our contemporary life which could be labelled as psychologized (subjected to psychological criteria, shaped on the basis of psychological knowledge). Bearing in mind that psychology on the one hand, due to its subject-matter, has to be open to a 'feminine regard', but on the other hand has not fulfilled this expectation, I shall consider these phenomena as markers of a crossroads at two levels: one level is the main/malestream psychology; the other level represents female patterns in the background. The aim of my analysis is to make this background visible, to understand the meaning it bears and then to deconstruct the 'double bind' that lies behind and inhibits the development and recognition of other possible meanings which can motivate changes in beliefs and attitudes. I will now address six areas that inscribe naturalized definitions of gender, and suggest how all these rely upon both the positioning of a (unitary) feminine nature and the feminization of nature.

1 Politics

The first phenomenon is the unavoidable politics. At first glance psychology is again unavoidably returning to political milieu in contemporary life. We are bearing witness to, and participating in, a political mode in which psychology has a very striking role. Politics is becoming psychologized. How is psychology represented in these contemporary political scripts? How does psychology represent a feminine regard?

To psychology has been ascribed a power to shape individuals' thinking, feelings and acting in accordance to given or chosen goals, including political ones. These fabricated social characters, which are supposed to be manageable in a short time, are expected to inform relevant public opinion to support political decisions. Icons and images are the main means of political representation and of psychological shaping. Such images are invested with strong basic emotions. Due to media dominance in our everyday life, politics is also subjected to media mediation: thus a very important political influence on individuals occurs through television while we are sitting in the privacy of our homes watching 'objective' live reports.

The whole script is a mixture: a masculine–feminine hybrid. Politics was traditionally the province of dominant men. Modern life has brought some important changes by also opening this field, with delay, to women. However, these changes have not removed men's supremacy – either in a quantitative sense or in a qualitative one.

But the visible political life has been shaped according to a model which has elements that still retain strong traditionally feminine connotations. Many elements of this script bear connotations which are usually strongly associated with feminine features: emotionality, image-dependence, family privacy as the main place of life-activities, other-directedness, submissiveness, and so on. This model seems to be very successful – unfortunately, not in the sense of solving political problems in a legitimate and satisfactory way, but in the sense of fulfilling psychological/ideological tasks: the expected products have been fabricated. And at whose expense or benefit are these fictions?

An important aspect of this fabrication concerns the suggested self-understanding: it is supposed that these direct short social mediations should be forgotten, repressed. Instead of social insights, a naturalistic belief has been promoted which says that what has been happening is just a natural reaction of an autonomous moral agent. Here we have again a mixture: a 'feminine' treatment and 'masculine' legitimization.

2 Nationalism

Another issue in contemporary politics which exhibits a specific form of feminization concerns the definition of nation and related problems of nationalism. Originally, 'nation' was designated to the Roman goodness of origin (Habermas, 1991). Besides the notion of origin, the classical concept of nation includes territory and language, being used as a base for the classical form of national state. But this culturally and historically founded notion of nation is not a satisfactory base for a contemporary state. Taking only the great mobility and dynamics of the modern life, it is clear that the traditional concept of nation does not fit into the contemporary way of life. Its content represents experiences and norms which belonged to past life patterns. The contemporary states cannot be deduced from a common origin and language of their inhabitants. The competences needed to live in a contemporary state belong to tasks of socialization – they must be available through learning and not by birth. But in spite of changed facts, there are still legal regulations which try to impose this outdated concept, instead of advocating a pure political concept of nationality as acceptance of a political form (Habermas, 1991).

Nowadays, especially in the 1990s, we are witnessing a massive regression to the previous concept of nation grounded in shared origin, history, language and territory. The nation is becoming a refuge for troubled people. This construct has been shaped on the model of a grand mother – the woman who guarantees protection on the basis of the common origin, the warmth, belongingness to a community of equals (Eisenstein, 1995). Behind the widespread metaphor of mother-nation, lies an elaborated ideology once described as 'blood and soil' and associated with fascism. It is clear that such a concept of nation has strong naturalistic roots which presuppose an idealized notion of nature. Thus the nation gets a deeper feminine foundation in nature.

Here it is worthwhile noting that some feminist movements, for example ecofeminism, elaborate their ideas drawing on such an idealization of feminine nature. They derive societal features from characteristics of female biology which appeal to a sense of boundness and cooperation. These ideas are offered as a kind of salvation, as it is demonstrated in Lenz and Myerhoff's book *The Feminization of America* (1985): 'This book glowingly visualizes woman's warm, empathetic, humanizing hand infusing feminine values in all areas of American life, bringing inspiration for peace and genuine prosperity to a community of future beings of "hybridized identity"' (Westerlund, 1990: 25). In contemporary political life mixtures are made of two old patterns. We can see these mixtures as a good starting point to analyse underlying presuppositions, cognitive operations, affective preferences and models of actions. A particular masculine standpoint acquires its complementary counterpart in the particular feminine model. They reinforce each other by reproducing the constraints of one's point of view. Thus the visible feminization of politics has not brought a new and better politics – far from it, as our current experience shows.

Nor has this feminization brought an emancipation in ways of conceiving women, since it subscribes to a patriarchal view of woman. In the same way as patriarchy shapes both pictures – of the man as well as of the woman – a project of feminist psychology also necessarily shapes the way of looking at the man. But if feminist psychology conceives the man just as a residual category (reversing the patriarchal model), it imposes constraints upon its own development, limiting its experiential sources which lie in interaction. Thus, if the project of feminist psychology should be affirmative of women's experience, it has, in my opinion, to establish links with men's experience and to foster their mutual communication on the basis of new meanings.

I do not share a belief in solutions which use the same models as those they intend to replace. These kinds of claim of feminization just mentioned represent the same biased way of thinking as does masculinization. I would rather advocate another standpoint which would allow for a 'joint venture' where different standpoints are coordinated on the basis of their dynamic mutual relationships. This means that one standpoint does not have the franchise on rationality or superiority; the strength or the warmth can move from one to another side, depending on the concrete contents.

3   Empathy

I will try to make clear my argument taking empathy as an example. As empathy is supposed to be a precondition for modernization (Lerner, 1958), it must obviously be needed for and by both sexes. But the traditional sex-typing still prevails (reflected also in psychological conceptualizations) according to which empathy is ascribed to women and is consequently feminized. In this view, empathy remains mostly oriented to private relations, restricted in its relevance and inhibited in its possibilities of development. But empathy, as the 'capacity to see oneself in the other fellow's situation' (Lerner, 1958: 50), presupposes psychological processes derived from interactions which are shaped by elementary rules of exchange. There is no reason to exclude male members of society from these exchanges. Actually, they are not excluded, but their participation in these exchanges is not explained by using the concept of empathy. In this case (male) empathy remains excluded from a masculinist point of view, thus invisible, repressed and theoretically neglected. Reasons for this exclusion could be understood only within the global social setting, its value system and legitimization sources.

The example of empathy, I hope, makes clear the mechanism of sex-typing: an interest rooted in existing power-structures (in this case patriarchal order) is a motivating source which influences the perception, the scope of its subject-matter (what will be seen and what overseen) and the meaning of the seen phenomenon. In the next step what has been seen is taken for granted as natural (women are empathic), which accords this quality both legitimacy and exclusion from change. The reconstruction of this process uncovers what was invisible and repressed (men can also have a capacity of empathy). Without reconstruction it is not possible to get insight into the original setting in which the selection of visible and invisible issues occurred. This insight allows for the shaping of a possible alternative model which can recognize the contributions of both sides. In terms of our example: empathy is a capacity available to, and expected from, both sexes in their roles as citizens living in a modern society, which necessarily demands participation in rapidly changeable settings. Differentiation of this general capacity occurs through the specificity of another's situations which consist of different roles with respectively different behavioural patterns.

Returning now to our first example of politics, we can conclude that the mere addition of a feminine perspective is not enough. A preparatory step, consisting of decomposing the first norm-generating standpoint, is needed. After decomposing the prevailing masculine model it would be possible to elaborate a common ground of human needs from which different orientations then could be developed. In that case these different orientations (including sexual orientations) would not be understood as deviations from one supposed normal case, but as different interpretations of that need. This could, I hope, contribute to a tolerance towards plurality and educate a non-hierarchical thinking and sense of common interest, where the similarity lies in the acknowledged starting point, not in the expected results which must be forced.

4 Public and private

The institutional and conceptual differentiation of life activities into public and private spheres is an achievement of modern times. As a differentiated sphere, the private life has become the subject of both social attention and regulatory practices. To be private does not mean to be of no social importance. Private life is a specific part of social life, as well as a necessary condition of its reproduction. It always had this function – the difference concerns mechanisms which are used in fulfilling this function, in contents ascribed to it, in meanings expressed through it.

Besides this function, private life depends on public life in a complementary way: changes in public life consequently affect private life. To mention one familiar historical example, as production moved from the family and started to be organized in special places outside of the home (industrialization), this change affected family life, the relationship between members, and their roles very significantly. These changes gave private life more importance in people's self-understanding. Private life became a field where new sensitivity, new ways of thinking and new skills were developing. Family relationships started to be grounded on an emotional basis. The discovery of the child in the Europe of the eighteenth century (Ariès, 1960) was possible due to this rising importance of family life. As sexuality started to be dissociated from reproduction, new possibilities for providing personal pleasure were opened and new expectations were correspondingly invested in sensuality. A culture of intimacy elaborated a new field of personal expression and actualization. This was also shaped by literature – novels were a very influential means in shaping affectivity patterns, following the historical predecessor of medieval court literature (see Luhmann, 1983).

All this is already known, but we shall recall that this general division of public and private is constructed around that of male–

female difference. On the basis of the prevailing sex-difference, a whole culture was built, a system of norms, attitudes, and expectations attributed to women or men. Though not all feminists insist on the cultural construction of gender difference, some of them argue for the future revelation of yet unknown features of gender. In the opinion of the latter, phallocentric culture has repressed even a possibility of seeing the specificity of feminine configurations (as discussed in the writings of the French feminist Irigaray).

Still, private life has been seen as the proper domain for woman where she can fulfil her identity as care-giver who provides warmth and support without expecting and asking for reciprocity. These roles of motherhood and womanhood are imbued with a 'feminine mystique'. Complementarily, woman is kept away from the broader social life. For a long time it was denied that she had either the need or the competence to participate in social life outside the family. Her sociality was limited to the family realm.

5 Female sociality

What is this feminine sociality like? First of all, it has been stated that female identity is of a relational character, meaning that women experience and understand themselves in relationships and not primarily as separate entities (Gilligan, 1982). An ontogenetic explanation of female relational preferences has been suggested: while both sexes start with a strong relation to mother, the boys turn to relation to the father (after Oedipus complex), while the girls retain the mother as object of identification. Feminine sociality is grounded on a personal relationship to the other and has a strong emotional value. It follows particular rules valid in this particular situation and does not need any universal legitimation. It grows out of supposed natural needs (sometimes called instincts) and does not leave much room for personal choices.

If family sociality is split off and isolated from the broader social life, that is if one is just exposed to that type of interaction which is grounded in family sociality, these interactions become a means of socialization which reproduces features attributed to the so-called feminine character: dependence on others, strong affectivity, rejection of any rational legitimation and a fatalistic attitude. With such a social character women are not considered equipped to take part in other social settings which are founded on impersonal relationships, which demand universal legitimizing procedures and respect for universal norms. It is not a question of the natural incapability of women, but a question of having or not having adequate opportunities to develop certain competences. It is worth recalling that 'early liberal feminists such as Mary Wollstonecraft and John

Stuart Mill . . . attempted to prove that women's rationality was equal to that of men, although not developed to the same extent since women had been deprived of educational opportunities and been confined to the home' (Westerlund, 1990: 24).

It is theoretically and politically wrong to universalize the feminine character as the proper and best women's choice because it is in accordance with supposedly natural needs. The so-called feminine character is just a product of socialization developed under conditions of the traditional family form. But even when this family form has already undergone very significant changes, the model of feminine character has survived. It is used, for example, in the elaboration of a 'different voice' in ethics, the ethic of care in contradistinction to the ethic of rights (see Fulani, this volume).

Paradoxically, this ethic, which is intended to respond to women's specificity, reproduces stereotypes concerning feminine character. For women's voice in morality does not come from their biological characteristics but from the social conditions under which the majority of women live. The interaction pattern determines thinking and feeling schemes which are the substance of moral judgements. It goes without saying that if the dominant interactive pattern of women's lives is the care of others, this will influence their *Weltanschauung*, a part of which is also ethical. Moral norms included in this version of ethics certainly deserve more attention and social support, but they cannot be the only source of moral criteria.

Can we imagine what would be the consequences if we substituted empathy with the ethic of rights? We have enough historical experience of what the life of ordinary people was like before the universal moral claims were put as legitimizing sources of modern institutions. There is no doubt that care cannot and should not be expelled from the modern welfare state. At the same time, care cannot be a substitute for universal moral norms and equality before the law.

This issue exemplifies my thesis in this chapter: since gender is a social construct, the first task in deconstructing feminist psychology is the deconstruction of general psychological conceptualizations about the social. It means revealing hidden, overseen or repressed social mediation in the functioning of psychological structures as a prerequisite for any further examination. Without conceptual links with social mediation as a general mechanism of the individual's development it is not possible to reflect on gender as a social construct. Without social reflection gender schemes have been naturalized and taken for granted.

The first attempts at correction concerned a more positive evaluation of those activities and features usually charcterized as feminine.

At first glance this can be seen as a contribution to the affirmation of the other, neglected, invisible side. But, in my opinion, this is an unsatisfactory, superficial affirmation which does not reach the source of discrimination. That source lies in the ways of understanding the constitution of every phenomenon, in this special case, gender phenomena. If, instead of the reconstruction of social genesis, a naturalization of these phenomena had been undertaken, there is little room left for change. In this case, the dominant masculine standpoint has been legitimated on the basis of the accomplished naturalization. Even if a feminine standpoint has been added, this does not question the underlying naturalistic foundation which is a strong source of legitimization. Only after the deconstruction of naturalistic assumptions down to their social roots, and consequently ideological functions, has been done, can we start a new conceptualization where both standpoints have social roots and therefore could undergo changes. The example of the constitution and operation of the public–private divide reminds us of the mechanisms of the naturalization of gender as a conceptual means of repressing potentials for a different development.

6   Emotions

My final example concerns the conceptualization of emotions. The sphere of affectivity has, in a traditional view, strong feminine connotations, as it is perceived as close to nature. In such an understanding we can recognize the same epistemological patterns: repression of social mediation in the constitution of phenomena and knowledge about them and, consequently, their naturalizations. A biologistic conception of emotions still prevails. Consequently, it is believed that humans are not sovereign over emotions. Irrationality of emotions and their closeness to a natural basis are additional mutual bonds that link us with traditional femininity.

Cross-cultural research shows a great variety of emotions – in their arousal, meaning, social function – which corresponds to the variety of social patterns in different societies. As Rosaldo concludes: 'Feelings are not substances to be discovered in our blood but social practices organized by stories that we both enact and tell' (Rosaldo, 1984: 143). In the symbolic interactionism of George Herbert Mead, the cultural-historical school of Vygotsky, ethnogenics of Rom Harré and sociology of Norbert Elias, we find a common paradigm shift in understanding emotions: emotions are socially created and historically variable. Bodily states are interpreted within a linguistic framework which yields meanings for these states. Without a meaning which contains social heritage, moral regulations and group preferences there would be no psychical states called emotions.

These insights invite a rethinking of the traditional psychological understanding of emotions. Once emotions become understood as social constructs which conceptualize that aspect of the interaction between the individual and the environment which expresses a general positive or negative evaluation, emotions lose their closeness to nature and consequently shed their feminine connotations. Instead, they become a specific communicative code available to both sexes and used by both. This will widen the previous narrow conceptions of emotions and allows for the emergence of new emotional possibilities. Such an understanding of emotions can contribute to the re-evaluation of other phenomena which have been traditionally associated with emotions and their prevalent feminine attributes. A key candidate for this is the dualism of rationality and irrationality which parallels the masculinity–femininity binary. Once affectivity is dissociated from natural links to femininity, it also brings about a dissociation between natural femininity and irrationality.

Towards a Communicative Feminist Psychology

All the phenomena I have analysed as examples of hybrid patterns where the feminine regard is either invisible or naturalized are very important in the assessment of competences needed for participation in global social life. It is thus obvious that the re-evaluation of these phenomena concerns the global image of women in society. I have put the case forward for a new framework of evaluation, one which starts from the life-embeddedness of particular processes which are parts of this global image. By this procedure both perspectives are constantly present in considerations – the particular embedded in the global, and the global founded in the particular.

I think that our attempts to make those particular experiences which are feminine visible should not make invisible the global perspective which includes others' perspectives, also including a male one. This would not be the same global perspective as the previous one – neutralized, purified of historical, social or cultural connotations. The global perspective I am arguing for in this issue should be founded in the historical, social, cultural and gendered context of life-patterns. If the particular standpoint cannot be related to a global perspective, it will remain simply an isolated, inaccessible point of view. It will be split off from the other particular standpoints which can be accessible only through a global standpoint in which different particular standpoints have their common aspects. The necessity of a global standpoint comes from the necessity of communication as a procedure of the constitution, development and legitimization of experiences represented in the particular perspective.

To the same extent as it is necessary to recognize a particular standpoint, it is necessary to recognize and build up paths towards a global standpoint. This is because the particular standpoint can be made visible only if it is expressed in a common code, by common means. Thus it could be said that for the sake of the particular standpoint it is necessary to preserve the global standpoint too. I want to claim that this general argument also holds for the feminist point of view as a particular standpoint. If the 'feminine' voice wants to be listened to and recognized and understood, it should be expressed in a code which allows for other points of view (including the masculinist one among others) to be heard and acknowledged.

In the end, after working out my argument patterns, I hope my thesis – that a deconstruction of feminist psychology presupposes a general deconstruction of psychological theoretical and methodological assumptions – has a solid legitimization. A complementary thesis states that a well-founded feminist psychology is possible only if it can develop (multiple, particular) paths towards a global, general psychology. A psychology which cannot reconstruct a feminine experience is not representative of the psychology of human experience. A feminist psychology which cannot communicate its experience and make it understandable to other points of view is an autistic project. I am arguing for a communicative feminist psychology.

References

Ariès, Philippe (1960) *Centuries of Childhood.* New York: Knopf.

Aristotele (1941) *The Basic Works of Aristotle* (Trans. and ed. R. McKeon). New York: Random House.

Aristotele (1983) 'Von der Seele', in *Vom Himmel, Von der Seele, Von der Dichtkunst* (*On the Soul, on the Heavens, on the Poetry*). Munich: DTV.

Attia, Iman (1991) 'Wider die Verherrlichung des Weiblichen: Kritik des Ökofeminismus' (Against the idolatry of the feminine: critique of ecofeminism), *Psychologie und Gesellschaftskritik*, 3–4: 91–120.

Beck, Ulrich (1986) *Risikogesellschaft. Auf dem Wege in eine andere Moderne* (*Risk Society. Towards a New Modernity*). Frankfurt-on-Main: Suhrkamp.

Buchholz, Michael (ed.) (1989) *Intimität. Über die Veränderung des Privaten* (*Intimacy: On the Changes of Privacy*). Weinheim: Belz.

Burkitt, Ian (1991) 'Social selves: theories of the social formation of personality, *Current Sociology*, 39(3): 1–229.

Danziger, Kurt (1991) 'Editorial introduction', *History of the Human Sciences*, 4(3): 327–33.

Ebbinghaus, Hermann (1908) *Abriß der Psychologie* (*Outline of Psychology*). Leipzig: Feit.

182   Deconstructing Feminist Psychology

Eisenstein, Zillah (1995) 'Feminist psychology'. Paper presented at Belgrade University.

Elias, Norbert (1939/1978) *The Civilizing Process* (2 vols) (Trans. E. Jephott). New York: Urizen Books.

Foucault, Michel (1988) *Technologies of the Self* (A seminar with Michel Foucault edited by L. Martin, H. Gutman and P. Huton). London: Tavistock.

Gilligan, Carol (1982) *In a Different Voice: Psychological Theory and Women's Development*. Cambridge, MA and London: Harvard University Press.

Groneman, Carol (1994) 'Nymphomania: the historical construction of female sexuality', *Signs: Journal of Women in Culture and Society*, 19(2): 337–67.

Habermas, Jürgen (1991) *Staatsbürgerschaft und nationale Identität* (*Citizenship and National Identity*). St Gallen, Switzerland: Erker Verlag.

Harré, R. and Secord, P. (eds) (1972) *The Explanation of Social Behaviour*. Oxford: Basil Blackwell.

Harré R. (ed.) (1986) *The Social Construction of Emotions*. Oxford: Basil Blackwell.

Lash, Christopher (1984) *The Minimal Self: Psychic Survival in Troubled Times*. New York: W.W. Norton.

Lerner, Daniel (1958) *The Passing of Traditional Society. Modernizing in Middle East*. Glencoe, NY: Free Press.

Luhmann, Niklas (1983) *Liebe als Passion* (*Love as Passion*). Frankfurt-on-Main: Suhrkamp.

Martin, Jane R. (1994) 'Methodological essentialism, false difference and other dangerous traps', *Signs*, 19(3): 630–57.

Mattenklott, Gert (1988) 'Körperpolitik, oder das Schwinden der Sinne' (Body politics, or disappearance of the senses), in P. Kemper (ed.), *Postmoderne – oder der Kampf um die Zukunft* (*Postmodernity – or the Struggle for Future*). Frankfurt-on-Main: Fischer. pp. 231–52.

Matthews, Gwynneth (1972) *Plato's Epistemology and Related Logical Problems*. London: Faber and Faber.

Mead, George H. (1934) *Mind, Self and Society* (Ed. C. Morris). Chicago: Chicago University Press.

Meyer, Ursula (1992) *Einführung in die feministische Philosophie* (*Introduction to Feminist Philosophy*). Aachen: ein-Fach-Verlag.

Morawski, J.G. and Steele, R.S. (1991) 'The One or the Other? Textual analysis of masculine power and feminist empowerment', *Theory & Psychology*, 1(1): 107–31.

Nash, Kate (1994) 'The feminist production of knowledge: is deconstruction a practice for women?', *Feminist Review*, 47: 65–77.

Nicholson, Linda (ed.) (1990) *Feminism/Postmodernism*. New York: Routledge.

Parlee, Mary Brown (1983) 'Psychologie und Frauen' (Psychology and women), *Psychologie und Gesellschaftskritik*, 2–3: 87–107.

Plato (1937) *The Dialogues of Plato* (Trans. B. Jowett). New York: Random House.

Plato (1941) *The Republic of Plato* (Trans. F.M. Cornford). Oxford: Clarendon Press.

Plato (1972) *Phaedo*, in G. Matthews (ed.), *Plato's Epistemology and Related Logical Problems*. London: Faber and Faber. pp. 61–82.

Renchowsky Ashley B. and Ashley, David (1986) 'Sexualität und Gewalt: Der pornographische Körper als Waffe gegen Erotik und Nähe' (Sexuality and violence: the pornographic body as weapon against erotics and closeness), *Psychologie und Gesellschaftskritik*, 2: 7–36.

Rosaldo, Michelle (1984) 'Toward an anthropogy of self and feeling', in R. Shweder and R. Le Vine (eds), *Culture Theory*. Cambridge: Cambridge University Press. pp. 137–57.

Rose, Nikolas (1988) 'Calculable minds and manageable individuals', *History of the Human Sciences*, 1(2): 179–200.

Ryle, Gilbert (1949/1973) *The Concept of Mind*. Harmondsworth: Penguin.

Schwalbe, Michael (1992) 'Male supremacy and the narrowing of the moral self', *Berkeley Journal of Sociology*, 37: 29–54.

Staeuble, Irmingard (1991) '"Psychological man" and human subjectivity in historical perspective', *History of the Human Sciences*, 4(3): 417–32.

Tuttle, Lisa (1986) *Encyclopedia of Feminism*. London: Longman.

Ussher, Jane M. (1994) 'Sexing the phallocentric pages of psychology: repopulation is not enough', *Theory & Psychology*, 3: 345–52.

Valsiner, Jaan (1994). 'Bidirectional cultural transmission and constructive socio-genesis', in W. de Graff and R. Maier (eds), *Sociogenesis Reexamined*. New York: Springer. pp. 47–70.

Vygotsky, Lev S. (1931/1981) 'The genesis of higher mental functions', in J. Wertsch (ed.), *The Concept of Activity in Soviet Psychology*. Armonk: M.E. Sharpe. (Russian edition, 1960)

Vygotsky, Lev S. (1932/1987) 'Emotions and their development', in R.W. Rieber and A.S. Carton (eds), *The Collected Works of L.S. Vygotsky* (Vol. 1). *Problems of General Psychology*. New York: Plenum Press. pp. 325–37.

Wertsch, James (1981) *The Concept of Activity in Soviet Psychology*. Armonk: M.E. Sharpe.

Westerlund, Kerstin (1990) *Escaping the Castle of Patriarchy: Patterns of Development in the Novels of Gail Godwin*. Upsala: Upsala University.

Widdicombe, Sue (1992) 'Subjectivity, Power and the Practice of Psychology', *Theory & Psychology*, 2(4): 487–99.

9

Through a Lens, Darkly

Ann Levett and Amanda Kottler

Taking feminism to mean asserting opposition to male power and privilege, what, more particularly, has 'feminist psychology' to offer women in South Africa (SA)? We explore this as it has, and has not, been evident in our own experience at our university, and viewing the recent historical and current status of South African psychological studies of issues related to women's oppression in the local literature. Against the background of major socio-political change, the paucity of feminist ideas in psychology, even in progressive sites, is remarkable.

It has been uncomfortable criticizing the work of our colleagues and friends. However, in noticing what others have and have not done we are forced to recognize and acknowledge our own roles and have been alarmed at the extent to which we have disempowered ourselves. It is tempting to censor what we say. However, since this chapter is about silences and collusion at a particular time in the South African history of psychology, we have tried to adopt the role of the praise poet: the one who takes a position outside the terrain of power in order to comment on what transpires within it. Saturating our discussion is the question of silences: absences, silencing, being silenced and silencing ourselves. Unlike the praise poet, who represents the 'common view', our view is particular and limited: one lens. When writing this chapter, we often felt as though we were groping in the dark; increasingly discovering the effects of having been silenced and of our own collusion, we also experienced feelings of isolation, frustration and anger: dark feelings. At the same time, SA women are beginning to enjoy the fruits of feminist challenges – in spite of contradictory interests and inevitable divisions (Ramazanoglu, 1989).

Gender/Feminist Issues in the 'New South Africa'

There have been powerful constraints against the use of the term feminist in SA. The term seems to have been most comfortably used by tiny groups of white, middle-class women who grouped themselves in the 1970s but was ridiculed in the media and regarded with suspicion by most. In recent discussion with feminist *psychologists*, it seems that at times we compartmentalize these aspects of our identities. Reflecting on the past decade, one said she thought of herself as a psychologist at work, where she was paid, and a feminist in other contexts.

Although known and described as feminists locally, we ourselves are cautious about where and when we describe ourselves as feminist: here, as elsewhere, the term has multiple and eliding meanings. What is and what is not regarded as feminist differs for us and for others. For example, a paper concerning women's treatment in a local hospital by a woman colleague was described by another as not being feminist; we feel it was. A local psychotherapist declared that she would not be prepared to work with a man who had sexually abused children on the basis that she was a feminist psychologist; as psychotherapists and as feminists, we feel such work to be significant. In recent workshops involving some 180 to 200 magistrates, black and white, it emerged that the description feminist is strongly associated with being disreputable and unreliable (Budlender, 1995, personal communication). For large numbers of university students, a declaration that the teacher holds feminist views may undermine the value of what is taught. On the other hand, an increasing number of black women who have been educated in other parts of the world and have recently returned to SA, readily declare themselves feminist and are playing a significant role in contemporary political life (de la Rey, 1995, personal communication).

Setting the Scene

In 1985 few women (2.8 per cent) served as members of parliament. The 1993 interim Constitution (which incorporates the principles of non-sexism and equality for women and prohibits discrimination on the basis of sexual orientation) established a two-house parliament: the National Assembly, elected in terms of proportional representation, and the Senate comprising regional delegates nominated in terms of proportional representation. In the May 1994 elections, 117 of the 490 seats in the National Assembly and Senate of the transitional government of national unity were taken up by women (33.3 per cent was declared the aim). This placed SA seventh in the world in the nominal representation of women in legislatures. Although the particular views of many of these women on sexism and gender oppression is largely unknown, 'New legislation in all spheres is presently being enacted and women are often specifically mentioned as a sector which needs attention' (Bonnin, 1995: 1). This dramatic change came about through a number of feminist processes, in spite of the absence of a unified and coherent feminist lobby.

The deliberations of CODESA[1] (a large scale collaborative effort involving all stakeholders in discussions to plan the first democratic election in 1994, and the preliminary drafts of the new constitution) in its last phase (March to June 1992), through pressure from many organizations including the ANC Women's League, brought about the establishment of a Gender Advisory Committee; its task was to assess all decisions for their implications for gender relations (Meintjes, 1993). In 1993 the Multiparty Negotiation Process met to conclude the 1993 Constitution (Act 200 of 1993); women from the Inkatha Freedom Party led a caucus of women to protest against the initial absence of women in most party delegations (Govender et al., 1994). This resulted in a decision to incorporate women representatives in each party's negotiating team. Earlier the Women's National Coalition was established in 1992 by a wide range of political and non-aligned women's groups. The aim was 'to influence the constitutional process by mobilizing women in the country around a campaign to draw up a charter that would ensure women's equality through the new constitution' (Meintjes, 1993: 38). Important gains were made in the negotiation process although some significant issues were lost or not addressed, for example abortion, the issue of 'horizontal application of the Charter of Fundamental Rights – the extent to which the charter is applicable against private actors or institutions of private power, such as the family and the workplace' (Govender et al., 1994: 6).

The Women's National Coalition represents diversity across race, class, culture and ideology in 70 national organizations and 13 regional alliances and coalitions. Its current work is to implement the Women's Charter for Effective Equality which, launched in 1994, was drawn up after widespread consultation and research carried out through the period 1991 to 1994. The plans in progress at present to ratify and modify the new constitution specifically include details aimed not only at eradicating racism, but also gender/power transformation. In general, those involved in the negotiations and discussions around the constitution know that it is now politically correct never to talk only of racism but always also to include sexism – it remains to be seen how this transfers into practice.

Where Were Feminist Ideas Fostered?

Recently, Brigitte Mabandla, Deputy Minister of Arts and Culture, Science and Technology, commented on the gap which has appeared between women inside parliament and women in civil society; she said 'parliament is now open, but you see very few women coming to make representations in portfolio committees' (*Weekly Mail & Guardian*, 1995: 7). According to Frene Ginwala, speaker of the National Assembly, the absorption of highly politicized and ener-getic women into government and the various associated working groups has resulted in some disarray at grass roots levels (*Weekly Mail & Guardian*, 1995: 8). In spite of monumental changes in SA much remains that is problematic or paradoxical and, given the diversity of women's interests and emotional investments, this picture is unlikely to change (Ramazanoglu, 1989).

The changes which have come about have not come through longstanding work of a national women's movement with clearly defined feminist objectives and a readily accessible public forum. There are pockets of women throughout the country whose ideas have been shaped or influenced by education on modernity feminisms. There are also pockets of women whose commitments arise from either their experience around specific feminist concerns (for example personal reactions to male abuse) or in local com-munity or trade union-based workshops. Scattered through these diverse sites, and in the educational, health and other sectors of the educated population, are women whose names are recognizable to us as feminist in some sense of the term. Some have been educated in psychology but most come from community organizations or have other disciplinary studies as their backgrounds.

Feminist Psychology in South Africa

While it might be apparent in the UK and North America that feminism is starting to have some impact in psychology, this is not so in SA. Remarkably few South African papers related to feminism or feminist issues have been published in psychological journals or were evident at local conferences before 1995. No psychological texts related to women's issues have emerged over the last 10 years, nor is there evidence of the kind of proliferation witnessed elsewhere of 'psychology of women' courses on psychology degrees. At our own university (which prides itself on its progressive leadership) there are no gender or women's studies courses leading to a degree although a number of courses, seminars and discussions around feminist issues take place in various disciplines. According to Bonnin (1995), since 1984 a Women's Studies Centre has existed at the University of South Africa; this does not offer a women's studies teaching pro-gramme. In 1989 the first courses offering multidisciplinary studies for postgraduates were offered at the University of Natal, Durban, and later at the Pietermaritzburg campus, but courses have been suspended at the University of Natal since the retirement of a significant pioneering woman academic. At the University of the Western Cape courses leading to honours and master's degrees in Women's Studies began in 1995. Few psychologists are involved with these courses. On the other hand, at many SA universities women staff have fought for improved conditions of service and for recognition of issues such as maternity leave, creche facilities and sexual harassment; women in trade unions have also taken up similar issues (Bonnin, 1995).

On cursory examination the main local psychological journal, the *South African Journal of Psychology* (*SAJP*), launched in 1970, published 15 papers concerning gender in the period 1983 to 1994. Since four issues appear each year, each containing six to eight articles, in this period there were some 280 articles. Of the 15 papers concerning gender (5 per cent), the first or sole author is a man in six instances. These articles mostly report studies of 'sex differences', study only women (e.g. examining experience of mastectomy) or report studies of sex role stereotypes. Only one uses the term feminist in the abstract (Prinsloo, 1992: 76). Prinsloo argues among other things that 'the Feminist Movement has led to sex role confusion' (1992: 76). Four of the 15 papers concern sexual violence (Collings, 1987; Flisher and Isaacs, 1987; Levett, 1989; Levett and Kuhn, 1991). Incorporating feminist understandings and interpretations to differing degrees, none makes explicit mention of feminism or feminist psychology, although the works of North American and British feminists are cited. What factors led to this absence?

The Subordination of Gender to Anti-apartheid Politics

In the 1980s the journal *SAJP* was informally boycotted by many progressive South African psychologists because of its link to the Psychological Association of SA (PASA) and the association between many of its members and apartheid-dominated state institutions. The perception, confirmed by an acknowledgement and an apology at its formal demise in early 1994, was that PASA never challenged the operations and goals of the white nationalist State. It was necessary to mark clear differences between ourselves (progressive psychologists) and the others (PASA members). In 1983 at the University of the Witwatersrand and in 1985–86 in Cape Town, an alternative (largely service oriented) organization was instituted: Organization for Appropriate Social Services in South Africa. OASSSA became the home for progressive psychologists, social workers and others who identified with the anti-apartheid struggle.

Mostly white and middle class but committed to remain in SA (others emigrated, to mark their difference) a strong sense of purpose grew in this group. Ways were developed to enhance the relevance of psychology as a service to political activists who lived and worked in constant anxiety and pressure. Much of this psychological work related to violence (torture and detention of activists) (Foster et al., 1987), the consequences of violence (Straker et al., 1992), legal work in the defence of activists and people charged with public violence in the context of demonstrations and societal disruption. While there was no evidence of discussion concerning gender or feminist theory in PASA, in OASSSA[2] there was a lobby of psychologists who raised such issues on occasion. This tended to be infrequent and amounted to token verbalizations although the concerns were real (e.g. women activists who were detained were sometimes sexually abused and harassed).

Traces of 'Feminist' Psychology

Within psychological circles in SA, such notions can be discovered in the journal *Psychology in Society* (*PinS*). *PinS* was established in 1983 by a loosely associated group of progressive and/or leftist psychologists at the historically liberal white SA universities to provide a 'forum for the publication of papers, especially of an exploratory nature, for polemic, discussion and debate'. The editorial of the first volume (1983: 16) pointed to 'the major problem areas which constitute a crisis for South African psychology'. The crisis referred to the perceived irrelevance of psychology to the social problems and political concerns of the country. An aim was to move away from 'a tendency to glibly equate research with doing experiments and . . . the positivist image [which] haunts South African psychology' (Editorial, 1983: 16). The oppression of women is mentioned twice in the 20-page launching editorial. 'The effects of exploitative interpersonal relations and other forms of social oppression (including that of women) need to be examined with regard to the production and prevalence of pathology' (Editorial, 1983: 4). Seven issues are listed as typifying the proposed focus of the journal; the last one is 'Ideological practices in society, especially with regard to race, class and the position of women, and their relationship to psychology' (1983: 18).

An analysis of the 19 issues of *PinS* published between 1983 and 1994 reveals that of 140 articles, nine (6 per cent) focus on feminist issues – five are book reviews. Only four are articles (Gould, 1985; Jackson and van Vlaenderen, 1994; Levett, 1987; Perkel, 1994). Women author three. The vast majority of papers in *PinS* focused on issues related to apartheid and oppression. This is not surprising given that up to the late 1980s the national liberation movements regarded sexism as a potentially divisive issue (this point will recur, below).

In 1981 one of us completed a Masters dissertation on rape (Levett, 1981). At the time there was little interest in gender violence; rape was a topic for jokes. Research on apartheid-related violence, and later on violence against *children*, increasingly became a politically legitimate arena for psychologists. Violence against children (like torture) evokes feelings of horror and outrage. In the past three to four years there is a wider acknowledgement of, and reaction against, violence against women. This may well be part of the public discourse which now tags sexism on to racism and is mainly concerned with discourses of equality. The point that issues concerning women's legal status, pay and employment are implicated in issues of violence against women is obscured even though violence itself may be a readily identifiable mobilizing issue for women (Papanek, 1993).

The scanty published feminist psychological research has directly concerned sexual violence. Around 1989 this became the one arena where there was some support from the national liberation movements and also a focus that all women seemed able to identify with. Where violence against women and children is discussed in public fora it is more often regarded as a moral issue than political; concern is couched in discourse decrying disruption of 'the community' or 'the family'; thus violence against women is serving the interests of a new conservatism among women in SA (de la Rey, 1995, personal communication).

The Betrayal of Women?

In the 1980s and early 1990s progressive SA social scientists were firmly positioned in an anti-apartheid discourse. For example, Kottler (1990), without touching on issues of gender, addressed South African psychologists' dilemma of multiple discourses of difference. It is also evident in the work of others: Dawes has published widely on violence and is well known internationally for his work. For these reasons we examine his work here.

Drawing on the work of sociologists Meer and Mlaba (1982), Dawes (1985) discusses the indisputable ill effects of the Migrant Labour system in which rural men would be contracted into services (e.g. on the mines) and would have to leave their families for months and years at a time. Interestingly, and this is our point, the women left to fend for themselves, the old and the children, are not mentioned. First, concern is expressed about the children who may, according to some dubious psychological notion, become 'personality disordered people'. However, large numbers of SA black children grow up in single parent and multiple caretaker circumstances and are not 'personality disordered'. Secondly, concern is expressed regarding the conditions of the men's lives, their small living space, the levels of tension this promotes and the fact that their 'sexual needs cannot be met through the channel of marriage' (Dawes, 1985: 60). There is an implicit comment about homosexuality here.

In using this paper as an example of the omission of women in psychological work on the effects of capitalist apartheid, we are not suggesting that Dawes felt no concern for the women involved. However, omissions like this are dangerously misleading in a paper which addresses the importance of power. Dawes argues that if

> we operate with lack of awareness of the ideological influences in our work, we can believe passionately that we are dealing with the truth. This lack of awareness can lead us to play a role (*unwittingly*) in exploiting our discoveries of what is natural about a social or psychological phenomenon to support a particular socio-political order. (Dawes, 1985: 56, our emphasis)

The omission throws light on how women's oppression and pain in this and other arenas remained invisible.

Dawes was writing at a time when Ramphele and Boonzaier noted 'race relations form the core of the political debate and concern about gender relationships is either irrelevant or overshadowed by the more pressing problems associated with relationships between different races, ethnic groups, cultures, tribes and so on' (Boonzaier and Sharp, 1988: 153). No one in psychological circles saw fit to challenge this view in a public arena: the significance of apartheid marginalized women's oppression. Curiously, in spite of shifts in policy and 'public speak', consciousness has not altered in published work. Burman (1994b: 68) reviewed Dawes and Donald (1994) and commented that 'gender issues received little sustained attention'. The only paper in the collection which concerns feminist issues is one by Levett (1994). In a recent article 'Violence in South Africa: a psychosocial perspective', Dawes (1994: 31) does include current statistics on rape but omits any discussion of violence against women.

A Forum for Women: Scribbling in the Margins

In 1987 the journal *Agenda* was launched by a group which included feminist psychologists in Durban, Natal. Unlike the *SAJP* and *PinS*, this journal was multidisciplinary and explicitly committed to giving women a forum, a voice, and skills to articulate their needs and interest towards transforming unequal gender relations in SA. As is true for *PinS*, *Agenda* was not initially recognized by university authorities as an acceptable academic journal (earning 'points' for an academic CV). Since 1992 *Agenda* is formally accredited. In 23 issues (1987–94), even though the majority of papers in *Agenda* come from a wide range of disciplines, 21 articles were published by *psychologists* who would probably refer to themselves as feminist.

In *Agenda* SA feminist psychologists found a receptive audience. Support is provided by women in other disciplines for our work. The reviewers are known to appreciate feminist theories and methods. There have been passionate debates between feminist academics (and non-academics) in this forum, including some where one feminist accuses another indirectly of not being feminist. However, because this is a multidisciplinary journal with a very small readership, this is a bit like scribbling in the margins of the 'real texts'. Papers published in *Agenda* are unlikely to have any serious impact on the discipline or practice of psychology in SA.

So, what of the 'real texts'? Mainly because of economic factors and the small literate market, very few psychological texts have been published at all in SA. These have mostly been undergraduate introductions (e.g. Louw and Edwards, 1993). On the other hand, a growing number of South African women who are sociologists, historians, educators and from other disciplines have published important feminist studies and collections (Bazilli, 1991; Bozzoli, 1983; Cock, 1980, 1991; Walker, 1990). There is, however, no text on feminist psychology or the psychology of women or even challenges to accepted androcentric psychological models. One book (Vogelman, 1990), reporting a study of men who are rapists, appeared. Vogelman, a man, is now involved in providing psychological services for trauma survivors in Gauteng.

An acclaimedly progressive 500-page text on social psychology (Foster and Louw-Potgieter, 1991) contains no chapter on sexism, women, or feminism. There is a three-page subsection on patriarchy in Chapter 11 on 'Ideology'. In a book review Campbell comments 'Foster's reference to patriarchy is a welcome one in a volume that tends to be conspicuously gender blind and class blind' (1993: 61). There are three references each in the subject index to feminism and sexism. Given that two of the contributing authors are well-known feminist psychologists in SA, and each has written a chapter for this text (de la Rey, 1991; Finchilescu, 1991), how is this to be understood? In part this concerns the ready compartmentalization of psychology and the overwhelming omission of gender in the basic body of conventional psychological theory which one feels obliged to teach.

Over the last 10 years the only site where there is any substantial lasting evidence of feminist thinking in South African psychology is at the level of honours, masters and doctoral research dissertations. These are rarely available through publication and are available to academics only through library services. So, there are psychology students who are concerned and inspired by the encouragement of certain teachers to study and write about issues which are of central concern to women, but there have been powerful constraints on feminist debate in the public arena in psychology.

Pedagogical Struggles

In the late 1970s and 1980s in the department of psychology at our university, long associated with activism against violence and the struggle for democracy in our country (Dawes, 1994: 27; Foster et al., 1987), discussions among staff were frequently characterized by strong disagreement around the teaching of 'pure' psychological theory as opposed to progressive politically-motivated applied critiques illuminating racism and class oppression and the practices related to these forces, and their consequences. It felt politically important as progressive, middle-class, white South Africans in apartheid times (when no pain other than that experienced by our black countrymen and women felt legitimate) to be aligned with the progressive group. One of us (AL) used the most common avenue available to introduce feminist ideas and literature, through conventional developmental psychology in the period 1976 to 1985. In teaching psychological assessment, psychodiagnostics, psycholinguistics and psychotherapy in the period 1981 to 1995, the same strategy was used by both of us and others. So, although feminist ideas were not explicit in curricula or discussed in departmental fora, they were present. Issues concerning racism and class oppression were introduced via the same routes and in social psychology.

Courses entitled 'psychology of women' or 'feminism and psychology' have not proliferated in South Africa. At our university, for example, it took one of us years to legitimate the introduction of a postgraduate honours course on gender studies in 1989, where feminist research methods, issues of concern to feminists, and homosexuality could be formally introduced as part of the academic curriculum. This had been opposed in previous years because of its 'peripheral importance' to psychology. Methodology courses, which are given great prominence in our department at every level of study,

until recently have not taken account of feminist and other contemporary critiques of positivist approaches.

Self-censorship

The paucity of published literature on feminist psychology – whether
on issues of concern to women and our oppression, feminist debates,
or shifts in research methods advocated by feminists – cannot simply
be attributed to the overriding importance of the issues of race and
class oppression, although these clearly play a role in the phenomena
of white guilt. As white middle-class women academics tend to, we
willingly took on huge teaching and administration responsibilities
and undervalued our time and research (or feared they would be
undervalued by others). We often marginalized ourselves in public
contexts; our energies often went to fostering and mentoring women
students. Among these were black women (few in senior classes until
the late 1980s; blacks now represent about 50 per cent of the
University of Cape Town's psychology undergraduate classes). We
ourselves lacked strong, successful women models and mentors in the
realm of departmental politics, writing and publishing. We worked
to please and placate our colleagues and students. These are signs of
the internalization of the law of the father. This contributed to the
conspicuous absence of our work in the public arena. An example is
Levett's (1988) unpublished doctorate on discourses of child sexual
abuse, centrally concerned with gendered subjectivity and issues
around the control of women. Little of this has been published, but it
is widely used by students nationally because it challenges
conventional ideas and is fundamentally concerned with women's
oppression. Being women, we blame ourselves for this and continue
to do so; it is difficult to recognize the structural constraints.

From 1995 a Gender Institute has been established at our university; this aims to provide black women from elsewhere in Africa
the support they need to write and publish. Doubtless this will be an
important and valuable resource and a link between women in
Africa. Interestingly, however, women academics at our university
are not organizing for this kind of support for ourselves.

Where progressive psychologists had felt psychology to be
irrelevant to the needs of the political struggle in earlier years, we
felt isolated, parochial and somewhat ashamed of our perceived links
with 'middle-class white western feminist' concerns. In fact such
theoretical links were practically tenuous during the years of the
boycott of South Africa. As distinct from the successful economic
boycott (1985–93) the cultural and academic boycott was incoherent
and fragmented. Foreign progressive academics did not visit South

African universities; many refused to send us their papers. Ironically, the boycott really affected progressive and feminist psychologists. Our conservative colleagues, although limited in choice of conferences to attend, were generally able to maintain links with colleagues overseas. Curiously, the editorial group of *Feminism & Psychology* continued this boycott of SA feminist psychologists to the end of 1994, even though the ANC ended the cultural boycott in 1991, and formally ended the economic boycott early in 1993. Although we provided evidential documentation from prominent ANC sources, in 1993, at the request of the *Feminism & Psychology* editorial group their boycott continued. We had no idea why this was so. Apparently the issue was hotly debated in the editorial group which it seems received conflicting information about the boycott from other sources at the time.

Students' Perspectives

In the psychology student body (increasingly cohorts of women, as courses at more senior levels have tended to draw fewer and fewer men) feminist psychology is not only unpopular but often is viewed with suspicion. Feminist women – particularly those who are not publicly heterosexual – are frequently regarded as lesbians, often incorrectly. Issues concerning women tend to be understood as being potentially disruptive to the 'social order' whether this order be that of conservative Christianity, conservative Islam, liberal anti-socialism, or black concerns around the disruption of traditional customs and family life. There is a small handful of women and men (often among the best students) who embrace, read and write about feminist ideas. However, there is still a potent risk in SA gender studies of ignoring sexuality and homosexuality – this is similar to the privileging of racism over sexism.

Public Presences

So, what has happened in the public arena recently? At the momentous and historical occasion of the Psychology and Societal Transformation conference launching the new all-inclusive national Psychological Society of SA (PsySSA, replacing PASA) (Burman, 1994a) in Cape Town in January 1994, papers concerning feminist psychology were fragmentary and barely visible.

   At the election of a new executive, a last-minute lobby of feminist psychologists (black and white) ensured that three women were elected to the executive of the new body; this also aided the election of a black woman (Rachel Prinsloo) as the first President of the new organization. This result led to great consternation because progressive votes were split; the 'old guard' of PASA had strategically pre-arranged numerous proxy votes which further complicated the results. This, of course, supports the long-held view that promoting feminist issues leads to downfall because of divisions in progressive lobbies. Several prominent black (male) psychologists withdrew as nominees and some well-known, previously centrally involved progressive men were not elected as expected through this democratic process. This has led to some disarray in the new national organization and the effects have been serious. Turnouts at local meetings have been poor and at the 1995 conference, where a largely new executive was elected, similar problems continued. How PsySSA will manage to draw the various factions together and especially the apparently alienated majority of black psychologists is a major challenge and some suggest that there is no need for a single organization.

The first issue of the *SAJP* devoted to gender issues (edited by Gillian Finchilescu) was published in September 1995. Also in 1995 there had been a marked change in the inclusion of feminist content in courses on research methodology in psychology at our university, mainly because of the appointment of a black feminist to the staff (Cheryl de la Rey). Both these women were and are part of the editorial team of *Agenda*. There is now a strong contingent of women on the staff in our department and a black woman has just been appointed as the Vice Chancellor, Dr Mamphele Ramphele. It appears that, despite the relative absence of feminism, things are changing, but this remains to be seen.

Confronting Simplistic Dualisms

In South African political strategizing the temptation is to depict all social problems (including apartheid) in terms of dualistic categorizations: black/white, women/men, etc. In studies of racism, many progressive South Africans tended to de-emphasize difference (identified with apartheid policies) and to adopt argumentation which focused on similarities (Kottler, 1990, 1996) except, for example, when discussing class and the differences of ethnic groups in access to education and other resources. However, neither dualistic comparisons nor a simple focus on similarities is useful. Contemporary research requires that when we take gender as a starting point in an analysis of power we must re-examine all aspects of social life and take account of not only race and class but also language group and cultural identity, the historical past, and the current material conditions of everyday life of different groups. In South Africa, for much research we need also to incorporate education, sexual orientation, religious and political affiliation, and whether or not participating women concerned have children – different experience, status and position are likely to be accorded in these terms. The category of gender is too simple, hence feminism is too simple: everyday conditions of life are different in terms of affluence, access to education, living in rural or urban contexts and, within the latter, whether as 'squatters' or more stably housed in rented or owned homes. These multiple varied conditions contribute to differences in women's experience of violence, political affiliation, access to resources and work, and very different perspectives on other psychological issues relevant to the lives of women. The notion of 'a feminism' which will bind diverse groups of women into a political force seems naive and inappropriate.

The legacies of apartheid and other forms of oppression show in the power differences which exist between black and white women as well as *among* black and white women respectively. Oppression is multiple, shifting and paradoxical, and the meanings which each woman imputes to her own situation are bound to be accordingly unique.

Marks, in her review of Walker's (1990) collection of historical papers on women and gender in Southern Africa up to 1945, draws attention to Walker's point about the oversimplification of comparing the interaction and conflict of indigenous and settler sex-gender systems as a duality which conceals what Bozzoli termed the 'patchwork quilt of patriarchies in South Africa' (1983: 139). There are numerous differences within sex-gender systems – 'both of class and of ethnicity within and between, for example, the Afrikaner, English and Jewish sex-gender systems on the one hand, and between these European-derived models and the Indian, Khoisan and African models on the other' (Marks, 1991: 87). To varying degrees (and taking account also of the range of factors mentioned above, for example education, class, language group, etc.) this still applies today. The need for such analyses has hardly been acknowledged by psychologists in South Africa, mostly middle-class and/or white women at this time. Little work has been done on sex-gender systems in SA and, as Marks notes, 'It is . . . a reflection of the failure of an almost entirely white female South African scholarship to take the history [and experience] of white South African women sufficiently seriously' (1991: 87). Thus it is not only psychologists who have been preoccupied with political struggles around racism and the needs of the national liberation movement, to the neglect of women's oppressions.

The powerful belief in the political legitimacy of channelling all available progressive energy into the struggle for national liberation has of course paid off for SA. This may have resulted in the polarization and fragmentation of 'women's issues' and issues concerning sexuality and class. The tensions have contributed to ideological and organizational disunity and also to some acrimony among women in South Africa. Some of this was evident at the first feminist conference organized in this country – Women and Gender in Southern Africa, at the University of Natal in Durban in 1991 – however a diffuse and fragmented range of feminisms may be most useful.

Turning Points: Malibongwe and the 1991 Women and Gender Conference

As Shefer and Mathis (1991) comment, 1990 marked a turning point for gender issues in South Africa. The Malibongwe Conference in Amsterdam, organized by the African National Congress, drew in women from many walks of life and varied organizations and institutions in SA to discuss issues of concern around women's oppression. The Lawyers for Human Rights also hosted a conference on women and the law the same year and the ANC Constitutional Committee organized a workshop called 'Gender Today, Gender Tomorrow'. In spite of these good signs, at the Durban conference 'The legacy of apartheid in South Africa was brutally evident throughout the proceedings. The inequalities and differences between women was an undercurrent of tension. Deep-rooted emotions were ever-present and could not be contained. Conflict had to, and did, emerge' (Shefer and Mathis, 1991: 14).

The conference organizers drew in not only academics and researchers, but also women from a wide range of community, labour and women's organizations and activists. The majority of the women present were white and English-speaking and most speakers were academics or researchers rather than grassroots activists or trade unionists (who were black and white). 'Through its process, the conference exposed the voices that speak and the voices that were silent or absent' and, at times 'the hall crackled with heated emotions' (Shefer and Mathis, 1991: 14). Issues of activists versus academics obscured racist issues. An 'activists' meeting' made several suggestions which were adopted. Two were that speakers avoid academic terminology and shorten their inputs to facilitate discussion; this meant that many speakers found themselves with five minutes to present their work. Everyone in their own way felt marginalized in the context of this conference: black women academics, white women, white women academics, activists involved in grassroots organizations, men, etc.

Those who identified closely with political activism had difficulty with the academic language of many research papers, others were unable to see the relevance of a number of the studies to their own lives (or for shaping policy). There was a wish to hold academics accountable to a particular political base. On the other hand, there were women (mainly academics) who pointed out that important ideas and criticism arise in the contexts of academic research. Naila Kabeer (cited in Shefer and Mathis, 1991: 15) reinforced this view noting that 'research throws up unpopular findings and academics should be free to pursue those and disseminate them'. Another discourse drew attention to the ways in which academic women struggle against the patriarchal elitism of academia and frequently also participate in activist research and community-based organizations (Klugman, cited by Shefer and Mathis, 1991: 15).

A psychologist, Kedibone Letlaka-Rennert (cited by Shefer and Mathis, 1991: 16), remarked that 'the effect of [white women's] work is important in terms of documentation but it's limited in terms of advancing the struggle, and more specifically advancing the emancipation of the oppressed [black women]'. Both she and Mavivi Manzini pointed out too that in researching black women's lives, white women are neglecting research on white women in SA. The way that gender oppression crosses the boundaries of race and class is obscured (Shefer and Mathis, 1991: 16). The energy produced by the feelings reflecting the diversity of the conference lasted. This fed the 18-month process of consultation and planning that went into the Women's Health Policy Conference in Johannesburg, 1994, which was very successful.

We do not imagine, while setting out some of the diversities of women's positioning in South Africa, that there are not equally complex matrices of power in other parts of the world. Detailed analyses are required because it is surely through diverse understandings of these and other kinds of differences in history and positioning that the shared interests of humanity and, in this instance, of women, can come to be addressed more effectively.

Since the Gender Conference, and in South African women's studies, the debates on who can speak and for whom has continued. Both competence and rights are implicated in 'representation', involving moral/political issues as well as methodological ones (Hassim and Walker, 1993).

SA Women's Needs

There are few women-centred services in the country and, although from time to time psychologists have been involved, there has always been a tension between professional and lay volunteers. Few psychologists have managed to deal appropriately with these tensions and personal challenges to their knowledge base, particularly where the diverse lives of women are concerned. Although not systematically documented anywhere to our knowledge, there is a widespread mistrust of professionals, not only among working-class and other underprivileged groups but also among middle-class women. This mistrust is probably well founded in substantial ways since professionalism is perceived to create a wealthy elite who are anxious to protect their terrain (from the untutored, charlatans, etc).

Concerning sexual violence, Ngcobo comments:

> It is . . . true that few of us are feminists in the sense understood by white middle class women. Ours is an ambivalent position where we may be strongly critical of our men's assertive sexism . . . yet we are protective of them, not wanting them attacked . . . or even grouped with other men for their sexism. (In Tang Nain, 1991: 2)

This is understood to be a widespread attitude, especially among rural and impoverished black women. It is implicated in the problems encountered in attempts to reduce the spread of HIV infection (Strebel, 1995). Feelings have slowly begun to change in relation to rape. Rape Crisis was launched in Cape Town in 1976 by middle-class white women, including one of us (AL). Over the years, 'coloured' and 'Indian' women became involved and, in the past three to four years, black African women have begun to take up the issue. There are now Rape Crisis groups in Guguletu (Ilitha Labantu) and in Khayelitsha, historically black townships near Cape Town. However, there is some mistrust of the Cape Town group, perceived as white, middle-class and ignorant of the family perspective (i.e. feminist). 'Our culture is different.' The issue of wife battery has also served gradually as a focus of growing concern across the boundaries of race, class, education, cultural and political affiliations. Detailed histories of these contexts and perspectives need to be documented as there are lessons to be learned.

There is a great deal of research to be done in SA. It is well known that the modernity discourses around feminism which arose mainly in North American and western European contexts gave rise to challenges issued by minority groups of women (e.g. black and Hispanic Americans) who claimed their own, obscured histories of resistance. More recently, questioning of new forms of oppression experienced has begun. The imposition of feminist ideas and practices by modernity educated women on women living in conditions and circumstances which are markedly different in various respects is experienced as a form of imperialism. Levett (1994) draws attention to different ways women have in understanding the meaning and place of experience which many feminists would term child sexual abuse.

In parallel, notions of what it is to be feminist and the concerns likely to bind women who call themselves feminist in joint lobbies and enterprises, have been conceived largely among middle-class women. In more recent years, as the grassroots activists and women in labour organizations have begun to expect, demand and insist on the review and re-visioning of the situation of SA women's place in power structures, challenges have been issued to women perceived to hold power.

Hassim and Walker (1992) discussing the debates around representation in women's studies point out that there are many levels and shades of political assumptions and positions. They suggest three important aspects to the debate which must be taken into account in SA. The first is the relative lack of black women in academic positions. We regard this as a major problem at our and other historically white liberal universities. Despite affirmative action policies (which are a topic of controversy, because policies are poorly formulated and applied and because of different understandings of the term black), there is an acknowledged major shortage of qualified black psychologists in contemporary SA, particularly in academic and research positions. Secondly, studies concerning black women have been done by white women who claim they are providing an understanding of black women's lives. This is often regarded as patronizing misrepresentation. Third is the thorny question of rights and the accountability of researchers, including feminists. Who has the right to speak on behalf of whom is an issue often aired in grassroots contexts. While sometimes the challenge is appropriate, it can be problematic when careful academic work is dismissed for other reasons, for example, because it is unpopular or simply because it is academic and not easily accessible.

None of these issues is likely to lead to a simple resolution. Such debates are part of the health and vigour of the situation, provided all perspectives are permitted to present a case and provided no one withdraws from the discussion.

We strongly assert the need for the recognition of difference. In each research instance, we need to clarify the limits and point of the analysis in order to decide the extent to which the varied possibilities of women's lives can be included in the understandings which are offered. The shifting ways in which anyone is likely to position themselves, depending on context and perceived aims for identifying with any one group rather than another at a particular point in time, including the moment of participation, will affect the analysis. Psychologists who are largely trained in contemporary derivatives of the Galtonian experimental model (Danziger, 1990), as they tend to be in South Africa (Louw et al., 1993), do not easily accommodate their methods to the requirements of such textured understandings. Many may feel uncomfortable to do so.

Some Final Reflections

We offer here a particular set of experiences which have shaped both our sense of identity and our ideas about what is important for psychologists and others to recognize in SA today. We would hope that in spite of this great diversity of positions and re-positioning that we are all capable of, the practical concerns that do affect the majority of women (e.g. sexual violence and the legal status of women), or very large numbers of women (e.g. abortion and childcare) could constitute particular platforms of consensual policy development.

What gets lost in the development of organizations, and in organizing women and lobbying, is that within each lobby there are inevitably individuals and groups struggling for dominant or better positions, or for particular slices of the cake. We have tried to facilitate insight into some of our own struggles. For all that psychology is based in modernity claims to knowledge, there are things that psychologists can contribute to a better understanding of what happens in these situations and how power plays can be understood and averted or otherwise dealt with, provided there is a forum and space in which to study these factors.

Finally, missed in the debates around representation and misrepresentation is the understanding that all writing, and all research, is refracted through interpretation. When we speak of our own lives, we offer an interpretation of our experience and the way we interpret one event or situation can vary from one context to another. Talk, in verbal or in written form, is an interpretive text. In any approach which adopts a deconstructionist perspective, it has to be understood that all people are talking from their own positions within existing and perceived power structures and draw on discourses of power to jockey their positions. Sometimes these discourses are progressive and transformative and sometimes they are conservative and de-energizing, or simply not what we think they are.

While some are saying you cannot speak for others, they still are talking for others in a number of ways. We are talking here about the problems which beset all political work (and all social research is political) – these arise in the tensions between individualist ideology, which is increasingly a global phenomenon, and the notions of group and ethnic identities which also cannot be divorced from a global tendency to demarcate boundaries and emphasize differences. Against this background, it is difficult to identify clearly what a 'feminist psychology' could be.

Notes

We wish to acknowledge and thank Debbie Budlender, Cheryl de la Rey and Gillian Finchilescu for their helpful discussion and commentary on an earlier draft of this chapter. We also want to acknowledge all the Masters and Honours students who have helped sustain us as we have worked with them.

1 Convention for a Democratic South Africa.
2 Organization of Appropriate Social Services of South Africa.

References

Bazilli, S. (ed.) (1991) *Putting Women on the Agenda*. Johannesburg: Ravan Press.
Bonnin, D. (1995) 'National report on women's studies in South Africa'. Unpublished paper.
Boonzaier, E. and Sharp, J. (eds) (1988) *South African Keywords*. Cape Town: David Philip.
Bozzoli, B. (1983) 'Marxism, feminism and South African studies', *Journal of Southern African Studies*, 9: 139–71.
Burman, E. (1994a) 'Changing psychology for a new South Africa', *Changes*, 12(2): 136–40.
Burman, E. (1994b) 'Children and adversity: psychological perspectives on South African research'. Book review, *Psychology in Society*, 19: 66–70.
Campbell, C. (1993) 'Social psychology in South Africa, edited by Don Foster and Joha Louw-Potgieter'. Book review, *Psychology in Society*, 17: 59–64.
Cock, J. (1980) *Maids and Madams*. Johannesburg: Ravan Press.
Cock, J. (1991) *Colonels and Cadres: War and Gender in South Africa*. Oxford: Oxford University Press.
Collings, S. (1987) 'Barriers to rape reporting among white South African women', *South African Journal of Psychology*, 17(1): 20–4.
Danziger, K. (1990) *Constructing the Subject: Historical Origins of Psychological Research*. Cambridge: Cambridge University Press.
Dawes, A. (1985) 'Politics and mental health: the position of clinical psychology in South Africa', *South African Journal of Psychology*, 15: 55–61.
Dawes, A. (1994) 'Violence in South Africa: a psychosocial perspective', in J. Martin Ramirez (ed.), *Violence – Some Alternatives: Can Experiences of Other Countries Help South Africa?*. Madrid: Centreur. pp. 27–36.
Dawes, A. and Donald, D. (eds) (1994) *Childhood and Adversity in South Africa*. Cape Town: David Philip.
de la Rey, C. (1991) 'Intergroup relations: theories and positions' in D. Foster and J. Louw-Potgieter (eds), *Social Psychology in South Africa*. Johannesburg: Lexicon. pp. 27–56.

Editorial (1983) 'The production of knowledge', *Psychology in Society*, 1: 1–20.

Editorial (1987) *Agenda*, 1: 1–2.

Finchilescu, G. (1991) 'Social cognition and attributions', in D. Foster and J. Louw-Potgieter (eds), *Social Psychology in South Africa*. Johannesburg: Lexicon. pp. 207–36.

Flisher, A. and Isaacs, G. (1987) 'The evaluation of a training programme in rape crisis intervention for lay therapists', *South African Journal of Psychology*, 17(2): 40–6.

Foster, D. and Louw-Potgieter, J. (eds) (1991)   *Social Psychology in South Africa*. Johannesburg: Lexicon.

Foster, D., Davis, D. and Sandler, D. (eds) (1987) *Detention and Torture in South Africa*. Cape Town: David Philip.

Gould, D. (1985) 'Gender-based alienation: a feminist/materialist theory of rape', *Psychology in Society*, 4: 72–8.

Govender, P., Budlender, D. and Madlala, N. (1994) *Beijing Conference Report: 1994 Country Report on the Status of South African Women*. Cape Town: Ministry without Portfolio in the Office of the President.

Hassim, S. and Walker, C. (1992) 'Women's studies and the women's movement', *Transformation*, 18: 78–87.

Hassim, S. and Walker, C. (1993) 'Women's studies and the women's movement in South Africa: defining a relationship', *Women's Studies International Forum*, 16(5): 524–34.

Jackson, C.A. and van Vlaenderen, H. (1994) 'Participatory research: a feminist critique', *Psychology in Society*, 18: 3–20.

Kottler, A. (1990) 'South Africa: psychology's dilemma of multiple discourses', *Psychology in Society*, 13: 27–36.

Kottler, A. (1996) 'Voices in the winds of change', *Feminism & Psychology*, 6(1): 61–8.

Levett, A. (1981) 'Considerations for the provision of adequate psychological care for the sexually assaulted woman'. Masters dissertation, University of Cape Town, Cape Town.

Levett, A. (1987) 'Childhood sexual abuse: event, fact or structure', *Psychology in Society*, 8: 79–100.

Levett, A. (1988) 'Psychological trauma: discourses of childhood sexual abuse'. PhD dissertation, University of Cape Town, Cape Town.

Levett, A. (1989) 'A study of childhood sexual abuse among South African university women students', *South African Journal of Psychology*, 19(3): 122–9.

Levett, A. (1994) 'Problems of cultural imperialism in the study of child sexual abuse', in A. Dawes and D. Donald (eds), *Childhood and Adversity in South Africa*. Cape Town: David Philip. pp. 240–60.

Levett, A. and Kuhn, L. (1991) 'Attitudes towards rape and rapists: a white, English-speaking South African student sample', *South African Journal of Psychology*, 21(1): 32–7.

Louw, D.A. and Edwards, D. (1993) *Psychology: An Introduction for Students in Southern Africa*. Johannesburg: Lexicon.

Louw, J., Binedell, J., Brimmer, W., Mabena, P., Meyer, A., Robins, E., Roper, K. and van Rooyen, D. (1993) 'Constructing the subject: South African psychological research before World War II', *South African Journal of Psychology*, 23(2): 59–63.

Marks, S. (1991) 'Review of Cheryl Walker (ed.) Women and Gender in Southern

Africa to 1945, David Philip Publisher, Cape Town/James Currey, London, 1990', *Agenda*, 9: 82–90.

Meer, Y.S. and Mlaba, M.D. (1982) *Apartheid – Our Picture*. Durban: Institute for Black Research.

Meintjes, S. (1993) 'Dilemmas of difference', *Agenda*, 19: 37–42.

Papanek, H. (1993) 'Theorizing about women's movements globally', *Gender and Society*, 7(4): 594–604.

Perkel, A. (1994) 'Deconstructing the patriarchal myth', *Psychology in Society*, 19: 3–17.

Prinsloo, C. (1992) 'The tenacity of sex-role stereotypes', *South African Journal of Psychology*, 22(2): 76–86.

Ramphele, M. and Boonzaier, E. (1988) 'The position of African women: race and gender in South Africa', in E. Boonzaier and J. Sharp (eds), *South African Keywords*. Cape Town: David Philip. pp. 153–66.

Ramazanoglu, C. (1989) *Feminism and the Contradictions of Oppression*. London: Routledge.

Richards, M.P.M. (ed.) (1974) *The Integration of a Child into a Social World*. Cambridge: Cambridge University Press.

Shefer, T. and Mathis, S. (1991) 'The search for sisterhood', *Work in Progress*, 73: 14–16.

Straker, G., Moosa, F., Becker, R. and Nkwale, M. (1992) *Faces in the Revolution: The Psychological Effects of Violence on Township Youth in South Africa*. Cape Town: David Philip.

Strebel, A. (1995) 'Whose epidemic is it? Reviewing the literature on women and AIDS', *South African Journal of Psychology*, 25(1): 12–20.

Tang Nain, G. (1991) 'Black women, sexism and racism: black or antiracist feminism?', *Feminist Review*, 37: 1–21.

Vogelman, L. (1990) *The Sexual Face of Violence*. Johannesburg: Ravan Press.

Walker, C. (ed.) (1990) *Women and Gender in Southern Africa to 1945*. Cape Town: David Philip.

Weekly Mail & Guardian (1995) 5–11 May: 7–8.

Index